The Struggle for the World

The Struggle for the World

LIBERATION MOVEMENTS FOR THE 21ST CENTURY

Charles Lindholm and José Pedro Zúquete

Stanford University Press
Stanford, California

Stanford University Press
Stanford, California

Printed in the United States of America on acid-free, archival-quality paper

Library of Congress Cataloging-in-Publication Data
Lindholm, Charles, 1946–
  The struggle for the world : liberation movements for the 21st century / Charles Lindholm and José Pedro Zúquete.
    p. cm.
  Includes bibliographical references and index.
  ISBN 978-0-8047-5937-3 (cloth : alk. paper) — ISBN 978-0-8047-5938-0 (pbk. : alk. paper)
  1. Anti-globalization movement. 2. Social movements. 3. Millennialism—Political aspects.
4. World politics—21st century. I. Zúquete, José Pedro. II. Title.
  JZ1318.L56 2010
  322.4—dc22

                                                                    2009038250

Typeset by Thompson Type in 10/14 Minion Pro

To My Mother,
Maria de Lourdes Zúquete.

To the Memory of Nate Raymond

CONTENTS

PREFACE

THIS BOOK IS A COLLABORATION between a European political scientist and an American anthropologist. Despite our different disciplinary backgrounds, each of us has a strong interest in the culture, history, psychology, and structure of social movements and political organizations. Zúquete has written about the "missionary politics" of populist movements and issues of identity and culture in contemporary times; Lindholm has written about charisma and authenticity and has made cross-national studies of power and compliance. In conversations about our own work, we realized that although the world-saving groups we were studying often present themselves as totally opposed to one another, they seem to share a great deal, structurally, ideologically, and experientially. These similarities were ignored by most studies, so we decided to explore them. The resulting text is a truly cooperative endeavor. Each of the authors has substantially contributed to every chapter, and we have shared the burdens and pleasures of reading, commenting, and editing through many drafts. At times the labor did feel of worldwide proportions due to the abundance and enormous variety of material and sources at hand. "Yours in struggle!" soon became a common way of ending our many e-mail exchanges. Maybe the reader will appreciate the irony. We certainly do.

While the book was written, the world, at least according to the media, seemed to be on the verge of an abyss. Dark predictions about the future loomed everywhere. It looked as though the lonely bearded man standing on the corner of the street holding a sign proclaiming the imminent end of the world was right after all. Prophecies of disaster, of course, are as old as humankind.

But the beginning of the twenty-first century seemed especially prone to dismal predictions about the environment, the global economy, or the explosion of religious and ethnic conflicts. It was as if the "struggle for the world" was the struggle to redeem a world that was already ruined. The book is our reflection on and analysis of these fears and anxieties, which, although specific to the era, are universal in their implications. Our aim is to shed light on the ways in which people imagine salvation from the ills of today and pursue a better world in the future.

In order to give credit to the actors' own understandings and experiences, we have used the methodology of "archival anthropology." Most of our data come directly from the ways the groups portray themselves in their internal communiqués, their propaganda, their statements of purpose, and other public presentations and performances. We have also used member's personal accounts, and we have referred as well to commentaries from writers who have had firsthand experience of the particular movement. Whenever possible, we have read these texts and accounts in their original languages (English, French, Italian, Portuguese, and Spanish).

From our analysis of a wide variety of concrete cases, we reveal the fundamental similarities existing among movements that look very different on the surface. Our intent is to take an initial, but essential, step to a comprehensive and realistic understanding of the political and spiritual climate of our times. At the end of our project, after identifying the shared features, dynamics, and goals of utopian resistance to globalization, we summarize our findings, consider why these commonalities exist, and interpret their implications.

Our task in this book is not to judge the validity or morality of any of the antiglobalization movements that we discuss. Although we do not see ourselves as detached observers standing on Olympian heights, for the most part we have foresworn enthusiastic endorsements as well as expressions of skepticism or scorn. Our goal has simply been to illustrate, contextualize, compare, and make some sense of some of the most powerful alternatives to globalization. Whether readers like the destination, we hope they will still enjoy the ride.

· · ·

We very much appreciate the support and wise advice of our editor at Stanford University Press, Kate Wahl. We are also glad to have had the pleasure of working with Jennifer Helé. Joa Suorez was always very helpful in getting the manuscript ready for publication, as was our expert copyeditor, Margaret Pinette.

We are grateful as well to the two anonymous reviewers who commented on the manuscript and suggested ways of improving it. We thank those who, at one point or another, took their time to comment on drafts or generously provided us with original material: John Barnes, Nigel Copsey, Carlos de la Torre, Sarah Garton, Jenny Huberman, Courtney Jung, Pierre Krebs, Siv Lie, Richard Loren, Nancy Postero, Matt Stefon, Marco Tarchi, Michael Walker, Rob Weller, Lew Wurgaft, and Bernard Yack. A great deal of the research for the book was done at Harvard University, and we are much indebted to the staff at Widener Library as well to the Center for European Studies and its executive director, Trisha Craig. We are also obliged to Deirdre Habershaw at Boston University for her diligent work in preparing the manuscript.

Finally, we would like to express our gratitude to our families for sustaining us throughout this journey: António Zúquete, the Silveira Zúquete family, and Cherry Lindholm. To all of them, as always, our thanks.

1   THE STRUGGLE FOR THE WORLD

If way to the Better there be, it exacts a full look at the Worst.[1]
—Thomas Hardy

These days of universal death must be days of universal newbirth, if the ruin is not to be total and final![2]
—Thomas Carlyle

BRINGING A NEW DAWN

According to an ancient Chinese proverb "It's better to be a dog in times of peace than to be a human being wandering in times of chaos."[3] Today we cannot live as peaceful dogs. For modern human beings, the only choice is to persevere through the tumult of what has increasingly been defined as the "global century." In fact, if one word could encapsulate the zeitgeist of our time, the strongest contender would surely be *globalization.*[4] Although the present-day flow of commodities and consequent interconnectedness between peoples and cultures has many historical antecedents,[5] globalization in its twenty-first century form is unique in its intensity, range, speed, and transformative technology.[6] The shelves of bookstores groan under the weight of texts that seek to refine, expand, or reinterpret the meaning and significance of this new phenomenon. Some have argued that because of globalization the world has become flat, while others say it is still a very rugged place.[7] We do not intend to add to this already too copious literature.

Instead we set our sights on analysis of some of the many political organizations and social movements that fervently oppose capitalist globalization. We call them aurora movements because they promise a new liberating dawn that will banish the dark injustices of the previous era. As a Zapatista manifesto puts it: "If this world does not have a place for us, then another world must be made . . . What is missing is yet to come."[8] This is only one example of popular protest against the insecurity and rootlessness associated with the "explosion" of the free market ideology.[9] It began in the 1990s as violent street protests and increased support for antisystem populist-nationalists spread from Latin America to Europe. The collapse of the financial systems in Asia led to widespread panic and riots culminating at the end of the old millennium in the "Battle of Seattle," where thousands of demonstrators, ranging from traditional trade unionists to militant ecological activists, took over the streets in protest against the meeting of the World Trade Organization. Although the protest was quelled, it engendered a new unity (however fleeting) among a wide variety of opponents to the globalization process.

The 9/11 jihadist attacks on the World Trade Center and the Pentagon brought a new phase to the struggle, demonstrating that some zealots were quite willing to destroy this world to bring another. The military conflicts that ensued were felt by those on both the antiglobal left and antiglobal right as a confirmation that imperialism and war were the touchstones of an inhuman globalization based on suffering and misery. And so the twenty-first century was born in fire, fury, and blood. Subsequently, a global financial meltdown raised fresh doubts about the sustainability of the path taken by neoliberal globalization and added increased urgency to the search for radical alternatives to save a world apparently plunging into chaos.

Oppositional movements can be purely instrumental, but the ones we will discuss have much higher ambitions. They span the political spectrum from right-wing groups and activist intellectuals in Europe to left-wing political parties in Latin America, along with the "movement of movements"—the World Social Forum. We included as well groups with no apparent "wings" at all, such as Muslim "holy warriors," nomadic ravers, and the international "slow" movement. These groups gain inspiration from multiple contexts, cultures, and traditions. Some seek to recapture lost indigenous truths; some preach universalism; others worship the nation; while jihadists hope to return Islam to its primal roots. The more leftist of this varied lot have generally defined themselves as *alter*-globalizing or as "global justice" movements, to distinguish themselves from *anti*globalist groups on the right, which are portrayed by their opponents as nationalistic, restrictive, and politically conservative.[10] We shall show that the mind-set of the aurora movements blurs the old right/ left distinction. As will become evident, whether they come from the right or left or from someplace completely different, they all wish to redirect the course of history and inaugurate a new world where human potentials are realized, justice reigns, and happiness is universal. All are more active than contemplative, polarizing rather than pragmatic. Their shared goal is to defy and transform, not adjust and reform.

These groups are also alike in that they are at one and the same time reflections and shadows of globalization. As active opponents to global processes, they must propose solutions that are global in their ramifications, while also reversing the order of the present. So, the affirmation of difference implies the construction of an alternative belief system with many of the same universalizing characteristics found in global capitalism. Just as global capitalism is accused of affecting *all* areas of life, the changes pursued by these oppositional groups are *total*. All these activists tend to see themselves as soldiers in an existential battle[11] for redemption of the world from the evils of globalization. They are, they believe, engaged in a life-or-death conflict between two expansionist models of the human future—one rational, bureaucratic, commercial, and immoral; the other spiritual, humane, heartfelt, and righteous. This battle, in its various permutations, is the subject of our book.

THE PAST OF THE STRUGGLE FOR THE FUTURE

In many ways the search for a new world is nothing new. Throughout Western history, there has been no shortage of movements that strive to abolish the injustice, indignity, and inhumanity of the present. Popular rebellions in the form of peasant uprisings and urban revolts were a significant force all throughout premodern times. Though many were driven by specific complaints (against taxation, for instance), others aimed to completely transform society. Millenarian movements built on a Christian narrative of sin, purification, and redemption were devoted to ushering in a promised land of eternal peace, prosperity, and happiness.[12] For example, in the early sixteenth century, the Anabaptist messiah Jan Bockelson declared the death of the old world and the advent of a new age of free love and equality. In the German city of Münster (heralded as the "New Zion"), 10,000 of his followers held off the army for a year before their final defeat and annihilation.[13] And in seventeenth-century England, "it seemed as though the world might be turned upside down" by the radical passions of the Levellers and the Diggers.[14]

The French Revolution of 1789 was undoubtedly the most influential, ambitious, and successful effort to transform the world; it was fueled by the philosophers of the Enlightenment, who, in the name of reason, questioned the existing traditions, superstitions, and institutions of the age. By eroding the foundations of the taken-for-granted universe, these thinkers opened the way for the revolutionary deluge. Gracchus Babeuf, swept along by the flood of history, prophesied that "all should return to chaos, in order that out of the chaos a new and rejuvenated world emerges."[15] As the romantic French historian Jules Michelet described the Revolution: "The world is waiting for a faith, to march forward again, to breathe and to live . . . Everything has gravitated towards one point, and that point now speaks forth; it is a unanimous prayer from the heart of France."[16] Inspired by the unifying "prayer from the heart of France," a surge of movements aimed at the regeneration of humankind swept through nineteenth-century Europe and beyond. "No period before or after has experienced so luxurious a flowering of Utopian schemes purporting to offer a coherent, complete, and final solution to the problem of social evil."[17] Dostoevsky described the prevalent revolutionary attitude in his novel *The Possessed* as a "fire in the minds of men."[18] The revolutionary flame burned bright in Karl Marx's impassioned declaration of communism as the liberating last stage of history. The 20th century would turn many of these utopian impulses into actual projects to liberate man from the evils of history, starting with the soviet attempt to make the communist ideal a reality. The sense of a "new beginning" and the belief that "history itself was at a turning point" also nurtured the fascist quest "to purge civilization of decadence, and foster the emergence of a new breed of human beings which it defined in terms not of universal categories but essentially mythic national and racial ones."[19] The hope for radical transformation carried over into the Third World as well, where many anticolonial liberation movements promised not only the pragmatic advantages of an autonomous nation-state but also the launching of an entirely new epoch in human history. This millenarian intention was clear in the writings of Frantz Fanon, the intellectual prophet of the Third World anticolonial struggle, for whom "decolonization is not merely the establishment of a New State or the achievement of Sovereignty but the replacement of one species of man by another species of man. The world is turned upside down, the last become the first."[20]

According to Fanon, the struggle against colonialism "infuses a new rhythm [into existence], specific to a new generation of men, with a new language and a new humanity. Decolonization is truly the creation of new men."[21] Symbolic performances such as the so-called cargo cults[22] that flourished among indigenous peoples in the Pacific islands and elsewhere during the mid-twentieth century also aimed at overturning colonial authority in preparation for the imminent arrival of a new golden age. So did the "Grounded Utopian Movements" such as the Rastafarians in Jamaica, the American Indian Ghost Dance religion of the late nineteenth and early twentieth centuries, and the Guatemalan Maya movement of the 1980s (among others).[23]

Sadly, Marx's utopian program of liberation provided the ideological justification for totalitarianism, the fascist project descended into the horrors of the Holocaust, the regimes of decolonized states often proved to be as exploitative and brutal as their colonial predecessors, and the bounty promised by the cargo cults did not materialize. In the era of "the God that failed," it seemed that dreams of a blissful new age had become nightmares instead. As a result of these catastrophes, postwar antiutopian intellectuals from both the left and right repudiated any possibility of collective emancipation. On the right, Karl Popper portrayed utopian blueprints as inevitably dangerous, pernicious, and self-defeating. Ideal societies are known "only from our dreams and from the dreams of our poets and prophets. They cannot be discussed, only proclaimed from the housetops. They do not call for the rational attitude of the impartial judge, but for the emotional attitude of the impassioned preacher."[24] From the left, Hannah Arendt asked: "And what else, finally, is this ideal of modern society but the age-old dream of the poor and destitute, which can have a charm of its own so long as it is a dream, but turns into a fool's paradise as soon as it is realized?"[25] Aleksandr Solzhenitsyn, who had intimate experience of one such "fool's paradise," knew where the blame lay: "Thanks to *ideology*, the twentieth century was fated to experience evildoing on a scale calculated in the millions. This cannot be denied, nor passed over, nor suppressed."[26]

Others concurred. For Raymond Aron the time had come to "challenge all the prophets of redemption" and to celebrate the "advent of the skeptics."[27] Judith Shklar agreed that "the urge to construct grand designs for the political future of mankind is gone. The last vestiges of utopian faith required for such an enterprise have vanished,"[28] while Daniel Bell proclaimed that chiliastic hopes, millenarianism, apocalyptic thinking, and ideology itself had come to "a dead end."[29] In this same period Otto Kirchheimer described the transformation of the ideological mass parties of old into political machines, centrist and practical, constructed with the sole purpose of winning elections. Instead of organizations devoted to provide "spiritual shelter" and a "vision of things to come," the new type of parties would be committed to efficient, narrow, short-term goals suited to a time of "deideologization."[30]

However, the normative end-of-ideology narrative was seriously challenged in the 1960s and 1970s by liberation theologies, hippie and drug subcultures, civil rights crusades, antiwar activism, feminist protests, and a New Left committed to overturning "the system" and to achieving a total transformation of the modern world. The content of the dreamed-of utopia differed in its details but usually included the elimination of sexual and other taboos, the end of violence, the establishment of complete equality, and the rise of all-embracing communities of love and sharing. As the Students for a Democratic Society (SDS) declared in 1962, "If we appear to seek the unattainable, as it has been said, then let it be known that we do so to avoid the unimaginable."[31] Or, as the protestors who took over the streets of Paris in 1968 declared: "In a society that has abolished all adventures, the only adventure left is to abolish society."[32]

Although these utopian visions failed, their reappearance led some to rethink the end-of-ideology paradigm. While remaining a proponent of rational liberalism, Isaiah Berlin took note of the resurgence of the "age-old dream" that "there is, there must be—and it can be found—the final solution to all human ills."[33] The Polish philosopher Leszek Kolakowski resigned himself to the "unavoidable" and "irreconcilable" conflict between skeptical and utopian mentalities. "The victory of utopian dreams would lead us to a totalitarian nightmare and the utter downfall of civilization, whereas the unchallenged domination of the skeptical spirit would condemn us to a hopeless stagnation, to an immobility that a slight accident could easily convert into catastrophic chaos."[34] Anthropologist Victor Turner took a more positive view of utopianism arguing that carnivalesque upsurges of "liminality" and celebratory egalitarian "communitas" are necessary to offset an overly rigid social order.[35]

But the majority of intellectuals remained certain that there were no possible positive alternatives to the status quo. Utopian movements were merely aberrations, soon to be subsumed in the inevitable march toward a rational future. This perspective received powerful confirmation with the disintegration of the Soviet Union. Its collapse was taken as convincing evidence that the predicted "end" of history had indeed arrived, as well as the end of ideology and the end of revolution. Indeed, it seemed the Western world had entered a period of "endism"[36] in which transformative utopias were no longer to be imagined.[37] Bureaucratic rationalism, it seemed, had crushed all rivals; representative democracy had emerged victorious; industrial capitalism was eternally triumphant. The only future imaginable was the "weary utopianism" of the unfettered free market as realized in the pure entrepreneurial spaces of monochromatic export processing zones.[38] Though some waves would continue to ripple across the surface, stormy conflicts over what political and economic (not to mention spiritual) systems should govern human affairs had been permanently settled. Francis Fukuyama, the most eloquent spokesman for this perspective, wistfully remarked in 1989 that "the end of history will be a very sad time." Nonetheless, the "worldwide ideological struggle that called forth daring, courage, imagination, and idealism" was a thing of the past. It had been "replaced by economic calculation, the endless solving of technical problems, environmental concerns, and the satisfaction of sophisticated consumer demands."[39]

Other social scientists and public intellectuals of the late twentieth century agreed that humanity had indeed permanently entered into a postrevolutionary era.[40] The worldwide spread of rationalism and capitalism had decisively eliminated all traces of outmoded radicalism except among the most inconsequential groups. War also had been finally understood to be repulsive, uncivilized, and economically counterproductive; it would soon follow the path of dueling and slavery and simply cease to exist.[41] Even the nation would soon disappear, according to the Marxist historian Eric Hobsbawm. As he wrote: Despite "men's and women's longing for group identity" and notwithstanding ethnic "reactionary upheavals," a "new supranational restructuring of the globe" would "inevitably supersede nation-states."[42]

The appearance of violent apocalyptic sects in the latter part of the twentieth century, such as Jim Jones's Peoples Temple (whose members laid down their lives in what Jones called an "act of revolutionary suicide protesting the conditions of an inhumane world"),[43] the Branch Davidians, Aum Shinrikyo, and the Order of the Solar Temple, among others, were explained as vestiges of a bygone age of zealotry and irrational belief, reminding the majority how far humanity had advanced on the road toward its predestined goal of pragmatic reason. These sects and their destructive trajectories confirmed that it was time to "return millenarianism to the religious realm, where it belongs."[44] From this perspective, expressions of apocalyptic imagination and the radical pursuit of transcendence would perhaps continue to exist, but only among a few religious fanatics and pathetic remnants of the 1960s.

Though there was strong dissent from the majority opinion:[45] With reluctance, nostalgia, and even a sense of tragedy, intellectuals at the turn of the millennium by and large accepted a present that brooked no alternatives. Benjamin Barber's famous essay about the forthcoming battle between the forces of McWorld (liberal globalism) and jihad (the tribal reaction of identity and community) entertained the possibility that "Jihad may be a last deep sigh before the eternal yawn of McWorld."[46] Francois Furet lamented: "Here we are, condemned to live in the world as it is."[47] The active quest for salvation in this world was no longer imaginable; the potential for redemptive political transformation had faded forever into the mist of history. Zygmunt Bauman complained that we were all living in a shameful "postideological" and "postutopian" age, with no grand designs except for the relentless pursuit of individual self-interest and happiness.[48] The struggle for another world was a ghostly remnant of a dead idealism, to be recalled with regret, but impossible to revive in a world "cold and grey" in which "a light has gone out."[49]

THE RETURN OF THE STRUGGLE FOR THE FUTURE

While the end of the twentieth century was marked by a resigned acceptance of the demystification of the world and the predominance of instrumental rationality, the beginning of the millennium brought with it the unexpected "counterhegemonic" irruptions we mentioned earlier in our introduction. As a result, studies on "resistance to globalization" greatly increased. However, the bland term *resistance* does not adequately reflect the fiery hopes of movements that wish to totally overturn what they see as an illegitimate neoliberal order. For them, the defining struggle of our era is between liberal-capitalist "globalism" and its "ideological challengers."[50] The fate of the twenty-first century—and of humanity—will be sealed by the "clash between a singular market civilization . . . versus the possibility of a diversity of civilizations."[51] The world itself has become both the stage and frame of reference for groups challenging the status quo, as a "global imaginary"[52] becomes predominant, linking oppositional forces everywhere.

Within this new global consciousness, the old paradigm of social class has increasingly been replaced by categories such as "humanity" and "future generations," while class warfare has been subsumed by demands for identity and respect.[53] Furthermore, the ultimate goal of many of these movements is not restricted to achieving the emancipation of a territory, a people or a particular group—though such objectives often serve as the starting points for action. Instead, "the extent of the hoped for community-of-the-liberated" has been expanded to include all of humanity.[54] As we shall see, this also holds for "right-wing," "left-wing" and "no-wing" antiglobalists. Consequently, there has been an increased focus on achieving solidarity among movements and transnational actors around the globe, all seeking the linked goals of liberty and respect. The current internationalization of resistance is not a wholly new phenomenon. Abolitionism and female suffrage had already developed international moral networks in the nineteenth century.[55] However, as noted by Charles Tilly, "the international construction of 'We' became an increasingly familiar feature of twenty-first century social movements."[56]

A variety of theories have emerged to explain the rise of worldwide resistance to the capitalist global order and its future implications. Many authors have resurrected Karl Polanyi's thesis that an unregulated market economy necessarily creates instability, the erosion of safety nets and communal bonds, which in turn inspires countermovements to reestablish community, belonging, and a sense of security.[57] World-systems theorists, focusing on the long term, understand the present antagonism to globalization as an example of a recurring pattern of resistance that is typical of periods of imperial collapse.[58] In a more heterodox fashion, Michael Hardt and Antonio Negri have argued for the existence of a new global revolutionary force—the "living thing" they call the "Multitude"—that transcends nation-states, ethnicities, and races. To them, this radical and shapeless force has created a counterempire engaged in a war of liberation that will end in "authentic social peace" and the arrival of a radically transformed world.[59]

Much of this new literature, though accepting the multifaceted nature of resistance to globalization,[60] stresses fundamental underlying commonalities between rebellious groups who believe "another world is possible."[61] We will return to some of these perspectives in our conclusion. However, in our view, this research, useful as it is, has not yet achieved a comprehensive understanding of the *nature* of the present-day opposition to globalization. This is because the spiritually grounded and emotionally compelling redemptive aspect of resistance has been understudied and underestimated. Instead, the focus has overwhelmingly been on abstract and often mechanistic models that stress strategies of contention, mobilization, and activism or on the differences between leftist "global justice" alter-globalism and "rightist" nationalist antiglobalism, while ignoring other "no-wing" transformative movements. Utopian impulses, conceptions of society and humankind, theories of emancipation and salvation, and the values, feelings, and experiences that motivate activists to struggle and suffer for their beliefs have tended to pass unnoticed.[62] As a result, one study concludes: "There can be no new grand strategy or grand narrative across such a diversity of struggles."[63] While we acknowledge that strategies differ, we argue that there is indeed a *grand narrative* based on a "common ethical core and a common mental map"[64] that has arisen in response to globalization. Theodor Adorno, in one of his final aphorisms, stated that in the face of despair the only available option "is the attempt to contemplate all things as they would present themselves from the standpoint of redemption."[65] This redemptive narrative is clearly voiced from within the varied movements we consider in the following pages.

A disinclination to address parallels in the way these movements understand and pursue their millennial goals is related to another significant absence in mainstream analysis of global resistance to the global order. With a few exceptions,[66] there has been a noticeable reluctance to include jihadis, nationalist groups, violent groups, "new new religions," or ecstatic movements under the umbrella of resistance to globalization. Rather, there has been a tendency, as noted by Ronaldo Munck, to distinguish between "good and bad social movements" or "serious" and "less serious" groups and to exclude discussion of the "bad" ones for fear of tainting the others.[67] As we will show throughout this book, despite many apparent differences, there are nonetheless striking similarities in the discourses, beliefs, and motives of groups, whether "good" or "bad," "global" or "nationalist," "alter" or "anti," "serious" or "frivolous," "left" or "right," which see themselves engaged in an all-out struggle to liberate humanity from its chains and bring about the dawning of a new era.

2 THE LATIN AMERICAN QUEST FOR INDEPENDENCE

> *The looking-glass school teaches us to suffer reality, not change it; to forget the past, not learn from it; to accept the future, not invent it . . . Yet perhaps—who can say—there can be no disgrace without grace, no sign without countersign, and no school that does not beget its counterschool.*[1]
>
> **—Eduardo Galeano**

> *The messianic millennium will never come. Man is born only to depart. Nevertheless, man cannot live without the creed that the new journey is the final journey.*[2]
>
> **—José Carlos Mariátegui**

ZAPATISTAS!

The War against Globalization

The story has by now become famous. In the mountains of the Mexican southeast, in the state of Chiapas, at the dawn of the first day of 1994, on the very same day as the North American Free Trade Agreement (NAFTA) was implemented, a movement calling itself the Ejército Zapatista de Liberación Nacional (Zapatista Army of National Liberation; EZLN),[3] emerged from obscurity to demand political and economic democracy for marginalized, impoverished, and disenfranchised local people, mostly of Indian descent.[4] The spokesman for the Zapatista movement was "Subcomandante Marcos," who hid his former identity as a university professor of philosophy behind his pseudonym and his black mask. While the Mexican government at first dismissed the Zapatistas as one more attempt by a leftist guerrilla group to seize power by force, it soon became clear that the rhetoric of the movement was not aimed merely at a local or even a national audience. In one of the group's first communiqués, addressed to "the people and governments of the world," the EZLN declared that it sought "liberty, justice, and democracy" because "in our dreams we have seen another world, an honest world, a world decidedly more fair than the one in which we live now."[5]

Subcomandante Marcos garnered global support for the Zapatistas by portraying their struggle for economic and political justice as the forerunner of a titanic battle for the soul of humanity against implacable and overwhelming global forces of repression. Thus, Marcos greeted the thousands of people who came to Chiapas from all over the world to attend "Encounters for Humanity and against Neoliberalism" with the words: "Welcome to this territory in struggle for humanity."[6]

The Zapatistas frame rebellion in the context of an ongoing "Fourth World War," which began after the end of the Cold War.[7] Marcos paints a powerful picture of this apocalyptic struggle:

> We Zapatistas say that neoliberal globalization is a war of conquest of the entire world, a world war, a war being waged by capitalism for global domination. Sometimes that conquest is by armies who invade a country and conquer it by force. But sometimes it is the economy. In other words, the big capitalists put their money into another country or they lend it money, but on the condition that they do what they are told to do. And they also insert their ideas in tandem with the capitalist culture, which is the culture of merchandise, of profits, of the market . . . Then neoliberal globalization, capitalism, destroys what exists in these countries; it destroys their culture, their language, their economic system, and it also destroys the ways in which those who live in that country relate to each other. So everything that makes a country a country is left destroyed.[8]

Therefore, when the Mexican government accused the Zapatistas of seeking to annihilate the Mexican state, the Zapatistas responded that the state had already totally compromised itself by succumbing to the blandishments of capitalism. Only the Zapatista movement could provide the last line of defense against the neoliberal attack against the Mexican nation and its authentic indigenous culture.

For the Zapatistas, the "international war, of Money versus Humanity, [is] carried out by a handful of financial centers, without homeland and without shame."[9] But even though the global conspiracy is rootless and shameless, it is not without character. The villain responsible for the international expansion of money and market is the United States. As Marcos writes, "The dignity of indigenous history of the countries of the American continent, the brilliance of European civilization, the historic wisdom of Asian nations, and the powerful and rich antiquity of Africa and Oceania, are attacked by the North American way of life." According to his argument, the ultimate aim of the "total war" waged by the neoliberal world state is to bring all nations into conformity with the "North American capitalist model."[10] Mexico's cosmopolitan and deracinated elite classes have capitulated to the neoliberal agenda of radical homogenization; they have become members of the new global class of "nonpoliticians . . . produced in the centers of 'high' technocratic education (Oxford, Harvard, Yale, Coca Cola?)" and then "exported" to all countries.[11] Revolutionary action must necessarily begin by "recovering the concept of nation and homeland."[12]

Recovery requires wresting control over language away from the neoliberal elites and their minions, who have instituted a new mode of speech that gives legitimacy to their conquest of the world.[13] According to the Zapatistas, these elites call the destruction of local culture "modernity" while the thievery of local resources is "civilization"; the imposition of homogenizing and inhuman foreign values is called "democracy" and alienation is "progress."[14] The delusory neoliberal discourse obscuring human suffering is likened by Marcos to his own mask, which he has promised to remove when his country is freed from the oppression "imposed upon it by 'modernity.'"[15] All those who, like the Zapatistas, have "failed modernity"[16] are brothers and sisters in the struggle. They must unite to save a world cut adrift from its spiritual moorings by the inhuman project of neoliberalism. The ultimate goal is not a return to an idyllic past but to "build an alternative modernity" devoted to "reason, justice, equality, liberty, and, above all, fraternity."[17]

As is the case with the other antiglobalization discourses we shall investigate, the Zapatista narrative combines high spiritual content with a strongly polarizing intent. Capitalism, Marcos proclaims, "turns everything into merchandise" by commodifying and devaluing human life, emptying it of all content.[18] "In the financial market millions of human beings of all races and colors are always worth less and less, as the devalued currency of their blood turns a profit."[19] "Instead of humanity . . . [neoliberalism] offers us stock market value indexes. . . . instead of dignity . . . [it] offers us globalization of misery, [and] instead of hope . . . offers us emptiness."[20] Globalization, Marcos laments, "destroys nation-states. . . . and not just that. It destroys the human beings in them. The only thing that matters is the law of the market."[21] As a result of the expansion of the instrumentality of the global marketplace, real people, with all their hopes and dreams, will cease to exist. In their place, "there are only buyers and sellers."[22] The pretensions of the developed world are a fraud, and a favorite Zapatista chant is, "First World? Ha Ha Ha!"[23] The Zapatistas call on all the oppressed of the world to resist the spiritual erosion caused by globalized materialism or risk losing not only their identities but also their very humanity.

Paradoxically, just as globalization erases national and local distinctions, so does resistance to globalization disintegrate differences; but it does so in a positive and empowering manner. Though different in surface aspects, under the skin all rebels against globalism are fundamentally the same as the Mexicans of Chiapas. As Marcos wrote: "Here and there, neoliberalism destroys nations in order to own them . . . There and here, neoliberalism offers us only dejection." As a consequence, "We'll no longer speak of 'here' and 'there.'" . . . "For this reason, this ocean no longer separates us or makes us different . . . Because the war they impose on us makes us compañeros and compañeras."[24] The brotherhood of resistance transcends nations, languages, cultures, races, or genders. The new global collective is "united by dissatisfaction, rebellion, the desire to do something, by nonconformity."[25] The Zapatista movement is a "spark in the Mexican mountains, in which all rebels of the world recognize themselves, even without being indigenous." It is "like a mirror that helps us to know ourselves and say: We exist."[26] As a Zapatista National Liberation Front member asserts: "If the system does not allow you to live as a human being, there is nothing left but to struggle, to rebel, and to show that you have alternatives to its world. Otherwise you rot, you become a zero, a zero in history."[27]

This encompassing but ambivalent attitude—simultaneously supporting and occluding local distinction—is the ideological root of the Zapatistas' commitment to the establishment of a global network of resistance supporting all linked causes in what has been called a "new internationalism . . . based on a sense of interconnectivity, mutual dependence, and identification among struggles against neoliberalism and for other possible worlds that nonetheless maintain their autonomous character."[28] As members of the "globalization of resistance" movement proclaim, the Zapatistas "rebel yell: 'Ya Basta!' (Enough!) announced the end of the end of history. . . . The Zapatistas translated struggle into a language that the world can feel, and invited us all to read ourselves into the story, not as supporters but as participants."[29]

From its inception, the instantaneous international medium of the Internet served as an appropriate vehicle as well as a metaphor for the horizontal, homogenizing, and encompassing Zapatista message, strengthening its global base of support while at the same diffusing its particular local content. In this sense the Zapatistas are pioneer cyberspace guerrillas,[30] creating a "new electronic fabric of struggle to carry their revolution throughout Mexico and around the world."[31] The Internet also allowed the movement to circumvent the global commercial media system, which they saw as "determined to present a virtual world, created in the image of what the globalization process requires."[32]

To spread the liberating word, the Zapatistas not only made use of the Internet, they also created their own media outlets, including the magazine *Rebeldia* and a Zapatista radio network called Radio Insurgente, which advertizes itself as "the voice of the voiceless." Their alternative media focuses on the underreported or *hidden* news, on *forgotten* history. They proclaim "a life work, a political project and purpose: to let the truth be known."[33] Independent videographers have been crucial as well in disseminating the Zapatistas' struggle worldwide.[34] Marcos insists that the power of *true* words will break the taboos imposed by the powerful and will shatter the hegemonic discourse of the ruling elites. As he states, "Our word is our weapon."[35] A communiqué from the Zapatista Army for National Liberation reinforces this point: "Silence is what the powerful offer our pain in order to make us small . . . the powerful use the word to impose an empire of silence. We use the word to renew ourselves . . . We raise the word and with it break the silence of our people."[36]

The Red Star of Humanity

According to the Zapatista ideology, the powerful forces of neoliberal globalization are inexorably and implacably arrayed against the "globalization of rebellion" that is arising among the indigenous people and all of the oppressed everywhere.[37] The recurring theme of the Zapatista leader is the struggle of the "powerful versus the people." As Marcos says, in the "the world of money" and among "those who live in power and live for power . . . there is no space for hope, no place for tomorrow."[38] The Zapatistas are the revolutionary vanguard inspiring mass resistance against the evil global capitalists who unjustly rule the world:

> This is who we are . . . The red star calling out to humanity and the world to be heard, to be seen, to be named . . . behind our black masks . . . Behind us, we are you. Behind we are the same simple and ordinary men and women, who are found in all races, painted in all colors, speak in all languages, and live in all places. The same forgotten men and women. The same excluded, the same discriminated against, the same persecuted. We are you.[39]

Or, as the Zapatista Army of National Liberation announced: "On one side is neoliberalism with all its repressive power and all its machinery of death. On the other side is the human being."[40]

As we have seen, the Zapatistas' discourse defines the resistance in Mexico and everywhere else as an apocalyptic battle that must soon end in a final showdown between the forces of good and evil. As Marcos declared during the protests against the World Trade Organization (WTO) meeting in Cancún, Mexico, "This is not the first time that those of money have hidden behind high walls . . . the high command of money has come to Cancún to dominate the world in the only way it knows how—destroy it! The hotel zone is a symbol of the world they would construct—the only way we ever get in there is as servants and maids. Behind those walls, they are plotting out how to change death into money."[41] It is no surprise then that the Zapatistas define the resistance in Mexico and everywhere else as "the search for life and the struggle against death."[42]

This "search for life" in opposition to the artificial and soulless forces unleashed by capitalist globalization has many dimensions. Above all, the truly human being is profoundly connected to inner spiritual resources and genuinely rooted within a local cultural tradition. Authenticity is the most common value referred to and sought within the movement and is starkly contrasted to the homogenous and reduced humanity produced by neoliberal globalization. Peoples and cultures must not be faceless pawns at the mercy of the global market. Rather, all persons and all ways of being have their own intrinsic worth and identity and therefore deserve respect and recognition. As an inscription in a Zapatista community announced: "We have no gold, silver, diamonds, but we are millionaires, we have dignity."[43] In Marcos's words:

> For Power, money carries weight; for the rebel, dignity carries weight . . . in its story Power constructs a virtual reality where dignity is unintelligible and not measurable. . . . (For them) dignity exists because money will buy it and convert it into merchandise that circulates according to the laws of the market . . . of Power. But, it turns out that the tale as told by Power is just that, a tale that disdains reality and, therefore, is a badly told tale. Dignity continues escaping from the laws of the market and begins to have weight and value in the place that matters, that is to say, in the heart.[44]

The quest for dignity extends beyond Mexico. "Dignity is that nation without nationality . . . that rebel irreverence that mocks borders, customs, and wars."[45]

The twenty-fifth anniversary of the appearance of the Zapatistas was entitled a "Worldwide Festival of Dignified Rage."[46]

An important dimension of the quest for dignity is the Zapatista demand to replace representative democracy with a new "true" direct democracy in which the people *actually* govern themselves. The "purported democracy" in place now, Marcos says, is a technique to disguise the enslavement of the people. The Zapatista concept of democracy, in Marcos's mind, is "much more radical" than the "Western" one.[47] As in other antiglobalizing, anticapitalist movements, the equalizing call is for the political elite "to govern by obeying [the people]."[48] Consequently, the Zapatistas defend mechanisms of direct popular consultation; for example, they held a nationwide referendum in 1999 for the "Meeting for the Recognition of the Rights of the Indian People and for the End of the War of Extermination."[49] Moreover, they have established new forms of direct democracy in their own communities and villages in the state of Chiapas, including the creation of Autonomous Municipalities and Good Government Juntas. To "resist neoliberal homogenization"[50] these communities have inaugurated autonomous schools in which locally chosen young Zapatistas (the average age is twenty) replace the government-appointed teachers.[51] The successful self-governance of these Zapatista communities, in Marcos's view, is a "model for a new world"[52] that is waiting to be born: "We understand that we must construct a society in which those who rule do so through the will of the people." Marcos adds, "There is no other path."[53]

Obviously, the idealized bottom-up political system requires high levels of participation by local communities, who are obliged to originate plans, programs and initiatives for themselves—a time-consuming public process that must inevitably draw them away from their own households and personal interests. How this commitment will actually take place is still not clear, and some critics have warned against taking a romantic view of the self-governing potential of the Zapatista communities.[54] Another difficult issue is the tension between Marcos's own larger-than-life persona and his vigorous opposition to the imposition of the authority of "self-enlightened vanguards" on the people. Marcos himself has vehemently "renounced the role of vanguards; to obligate anyone to accept our way of thinking over any other argument wouldn't be reasonable." He concluded by saying, "I shit on all the revolutionary vanguards of this planet."[55] Yet, Marcos has been unable or unwilling to halt the spread of myths around his person and the development of charismatic dynamics within the Zapatista movement, where his writings are studied as gospel.[56] As a result, some former supporters have attacked him for his narcissism and theatrics, which are seen as detrimental to the movement's left-wing legitimacy.[57]

Restoring Memory and Joy

Like other aurora movements seeking to inspire voluntary participation, the Zapatistas strive to recapture, preserve, and appropriate collective memory and revitalize forgotten collective practices. They argue that the identity of Mexican indigenous communities has been under siege since the first European colonizers arrived. "In 515 years they have not managed to destroy us, and now it's even less likely, when we are joined together against a common enemy."[58] Mexican Indians are "united by our shared misery, by the collective oblivion into which we were cast 501 years ago."[59] In this way the Zapatistas stress the historical continuity between their current struggle and the struggles of their ancestors, who are imagined as belonging to loving utopian collectives where people fought as one against oppression. At a rally with indigenous supporters Marcos declared,

> Yesterday they "civilized" us, and today they want to "modernize" us. . . . They tell us that their world is better, that we need to leave our land, our home, our history; that we need to go to their lands and live there; that we need to live in their houses and serve them; that we must be part of their history and die in their history.[60]

According to one of the EZLN communiqués: "We continue to resist because our grandparents resisted more than 500 years of contempt, humiliation and exploitation."[61] Resisting a "capitalist modernity" devoted to progress and contemptuous of history, the Zapatistas put great emphasis on respecting the sacred authority of the elderly and the wise "ancestors" who, as one Zapatista rebel declared, "taught us that a people with pride is a people that does not surrender, that resists, that has dignity."[62] To achieve the desired communion with the past, the Zapatistas frequently invoke the *Popol Vuh*, the Mayan sacred book that depicts the deeds and glories of the Mayan Gods since the dawn of creation.[63] As Marcos puts it: "We, the indigenous, are the guardians of history. In our memory we guard all colors, all routes, all words, and all silences. We live so that memory might live and, living, not be lost."[64]

To strengthen their identity as the descendents of the first peoples of the continent, the Zapatistas have adopted Mayan symbols such as the *caracol*, a conch shell, recalling the horn that the ancient Mayans used to rally the community. The term *caracol* also designates each autonomous region in rebel Zapatista territory. Images of the Zapatista's caracol of resistance, as well as such icons as pyramids (alluding to the pyramids of the ancient Mayas), have become prominent in murals and textiles in Zapatista villages.[65]

The Zapatistas also draw strength from the story of their namesake, Emiliano Zapata. "From the first hour in this long night of our death," Marcos said, "our most distant grandfathers say there was someone who gathered up our pain and our oblivion."[66] Marcos has continually stressed need to "rescue Zapata" from the museums and put his living example back in the streets and fields of Mexico.[67] Zapata is also conflated with the indigenous (Tzeltal) mythical figure of Votán, creating a new redeeming myth for the Mexican Indians:

> In us, in our arms, in our covered faces, in our true words, Zapata united the wisdom and the struggle of our most ancient ancestors. Joined with Votán, the Guardian and Heart of the People, Zapata rose up again to struggle for democracy, liberty, and justice for all Mexicans. Although he has Indian blood, Votán-Zapata does not struggle only for the indigenous, he also struggles for those who are not indigenous but who live in the same misery.[68]

The Zapatistas thus become the medium through which the sacred mission of Votán-Zapata will be accomplished.

The symbolism was maintained when the Zapatistas named the site of their first national convention the Aguascalientes, after the location of the constitutional convention convened by Zapata and other revolutionary leaders in 1914. The autonomous communities in Zapatista territory were also initially named Aguascalientes. In 1994 the Zapatistas held a rally that included a large parade and dancing to commemorate the anniversary of the assassination of Zapata, and Marcos announced that "Our heart is happy because Emiliano Zapata has returned."[69] The key role that Zapata plays in the EZLN symbolic world was further emphasized in 2001 by the three-week "march of indigenous dignity, the march of the color of Earth," which paralleled the march of the peasant army of Zapata and Villa into Mexico City during the Revolution.[70] During the march, the rebels met members of Zapata's family in his hometown of Anenecuilco, reaffirming their connection with his memory.[71]

Marches and rallies are also part of a general effort to celebrate important dates, announcements, and declarations.[72] As is the case with other movements we will consider, when the community feels itself threatened by the destructive and dehumanizing forces of global capitalism, these effervescent communal festivals provide participants with a felt sense of spiritual richness and the sensual experience of fulfilling their destiny as "true" human beings. "Seen from above, the world is very small, because it disregards people; and, in their place, there is a bank account number," said Marcos. But "seen from below, the world is so spacious that there is room for joy, music, song, dance, dignified work.[73] Through the organization of dances, folk and rock concerts, poetry sessions, and sports tournaments, the Zapatistas ritualize joy and make it part of their movement. For example, the announcement by Marcos of the creation of Good Government Councils was part of a three-day collective party in which the Zapatistas celebrated "the joy of staying alive and being a rebel."[74] These moments of *alegria* give the movement an exciting carnival-like atmosphere[75] and provide vivid, embodied expressions of an alternative to the cold, inhuman, and technocratic global order. As much as anything, such celebrations are crucial in inspiring commitment and participation among the followers.

On the day of the eleventh anniversary of the EZLN, amid a public celebration in the highlands of Chiapas, the Zapatistas released a communiqué that reaffirmed the fundamental goals of the group: "The Zapatista plan has been always the same: to change the world, make it more just, more free, more democratic, that is, more human."[76] The plan is based on a holistic conception of politics as a tool for universal human renewal. In the opening ceremony of the Encounter for Humanity and against Neoliberalism, Marcos proclaimed the "beginning here in the mountains of the Mexican southeast of the construction of a new and good world."[77] "We'll build another world," Marcos pledged on another occasion, "a better one, bigger, better, one in which all worlds can fit."[78] Of course, the arrival of the new era will require sacrifice and martyrdom: "We, Zapatistas, put a high price on our lives. They are worth a better world, nothing less."[79] In support of this great global transformation, the Zapatistas firmly reject any notion of the *inevitability* of global domination by capitalism as disseminated by powerful elites who convert "today" into a new religious creed, which fosters submission, apathy, and hopelessness among the masses. From the Zapatista standpoint, the notion that the current world is "the only one possible" and the inevitable "culmination of the ages"[80] is the biggest lie of our times. Rather, on top of the ruins of a world "withered by the powerful" another world is rising.[81] And even though global capitalism might seem momentarily triumphant, its decay is already evident. "If something new is born," observed Marcos, "it is because something old is dying."[82]

Following these premises, the anticipation of *tomorrow* has become the driving force of the Zapatistas' critique of the current (neoliberal) state of the world. Marcos frequently defines the role of the Zapatistas as pioneers, the first ones, those who "plant the tree of tomorrow." As Marcos says: "The tree of tomorrow is a space where everyone is, where the other knows and respects all others, and where the false light loses its last battle. If you press me to be precise, I would tell you it is a place with democracy, liberty, and justice: that is the tree of tomorrow."[83]

The utopian alternative world envisioned by the Zapatistas[84] is hailed as a pure and potent creation of the human imagination, built on the premise "that the monuments that neoliberalism erects for itself are nothing but future ruins."[85] The certainty that "tomorrow" will come and that good must inevitably prevail over bad runs throughout the Zapatista narrative. "If today we are on the defensive it is because evil still rules during the daylight," Marcos declared in a speech, "but a time will come in which we will find evil and will expel it."[86]

It should be clear by now that, though profoundly invested in the defense of their homeland (both their own native soil of Chiapas and Mexico in general), the Zapatistas have from the outset characterized their struggle as part of a wider struggle "for humanity" against global capitalism; a struggle of marginalized, deracinated, and colonized peoples, cultures, and nations worldwide.[87] In the Zapatista worldview, Chiapas is first and foremost a living symbol of rebellion that will demolish the "new religion"[88] of neoliberalism; it is the harbinger of a humane global revolution that will inevitably overthrow today's globalization of greed. For them, the words of the Mayan *Popol Vuh* ring profoundly true: "We have no names . . . We're just orphans, we have nothing to call our own, young man. We're just making our way among the mountains, small and great . . . And there's one great mountain we saw that's just growing right along. It's rising really high! It's just swelling up, rising above all the other mountains."[89] The Zapatistas' dream is to inspire all those who have nothing, who are oppressed, who are marginalized, to dare to climb that distant mountain.

THE BOLIVARIAN REVOLUTION

The Resurgence of the Heroic Masses

On February 4, 1992, officers of the Venezuelan army led a failed military coup against the unpopular government of President Carlos André Pérez. Called on by officials to put an end to the rebellion and prevent further bloodshed,

Lieutenant Colonel Hugo Chávez Frías, one of the leaders of the unsuccessful attempt to overthrow the government, made a live television appearance in which he asked his comrades to surrender their arms. The thirty-eight-year-old Chávez said that "unfortunately, *por ahora* [for now]" the mission could not be accomplished. Further, he took "full responsibility for this Bolivarian military movement."[90] This media event familiarized millions of Venezuelans with the young military officer who, in the popular mind, became instantly associated with an image of resistance, heroism, and dignity.

Although the insurrectionary path to power did not yield immediate results, the electoral path did. In December 1998, after spending most of the postcoup years crisscrossing the nation garnering local support, the former rebel was elected president of Venezuela and was later reelected twice, in 2000 and 2006, both times under the aegis of the new Fifth Republic of the country. Gradually, throughout his presidency, Hugo Chávez emerged as the founder and guide of what came to be known as the "Bolivarian Revolution," aimed both at prying the country from the claws of U.S.-driven imperialism and at offering Latin America and the world a new model of democracy and society for the twenty-first century. This model, as we shall see, has much in common with those provided by other antiglobalization or alter-globalization movements elsewhere.

The image of rebirth has been a symbolic centerpiece of the Chávez presidency from its early stages, as Chávez has proclaimed himself the new leader of a revolution originally initiated by the "liberator" Simón Bolívar. In Chávez's view, the grand enterprise of the Bolivarian Revolution can be carried forward only by the poor and oppressed who have been subjugated for decades by the corrupt and greedy elites beholden to capitalist-imperialist foreign interests. These elites are the enemies of the authentic nation constituted by the impoverished and downtrodden masses. They are the "heroic people of Simón Bolívar"[91] who now, under the inspiring leadership of Chávez, have been "resuscitated from the ashes and are driving a revolutionary process"[92] that will fulfill their historical mission of liberating Venezuela, then Latin America, and ultimately the world. The verbal and symbolic discourse of the Bolivarian leader is based on a narrative of suffering and redemption similar to that of the Zapatistas. As he says, during the oligarchy that lasted throughout the Fourth Republic (1958 to 1999), "Venezuela fell into a sort of collective tomb" because "[there was] a collective surrender" by the people. With the rise of the Bolivarian Revolution, this sorrowful past has been redeemed. At that moment, "the people recaptured a dream, a pathway that had been lost for decades, long and gloomy decades."[93]

The rhetoric of a long-delayed "people's liberation" weighed heavily in the discussion and subsequent approval by referendum of a new constitution for the country in 1999. That year, the charter favored by Chávez superseded the "oligarchic" Fourth Republic with a "popular" Fifth Republic that aimed to recapture the original fervor of Bolívar's movement. At this time, the country was renamed the "Bolivarian Republic of Venezuela." The new populist national liberation project was portrayed in stark opposition to the "neoliberal dogma" promulgated by the West, which, Chávez said, erases everything that "gives strength to a nation." The Bolivarian state must be autochthonous and authentically Venezuelan and must strenuously resist the corrupt "foreign models" inspired by neoliberalism. As he argued, "the market cannot create republics because it is grounded on the dogma of individualism that led to a worldwide state of affairs in which we are savages, fighting against each other."[94]

In Chávez's view, the liberation of the oppressed masses demands a constitution based on authenticity. This will provide the people with a strong sense of community and belonging, while also offering them a genuine means to express themselves within the national collective. Chávez declared that the new constitution was an expression of a "Bolivarian ideology" that embodied the specific characteristics and yearnings of the Venezuelan people. It was, he said, in radical contrast to the postmodern American proclamation of the "end of ideologies," which imagined humanity on the pathway to a "technocratic and robotic era, where ideas cease to exist."[95]

According to Chávez, the Fifth Republic marks the transformative rejuvenation of Venezuela. But this rebirth was announced and prepared for by specific historical events that are constantly on Chávez's lips. The first occurred in the late 1980s and took the form of popular riots (known as *Caracazo*) that exploded into a full-blown rebellion. More than a thousand people were killed in this uprising, most of them from the shantytowns on the hills surrounding Caracas. "The Caracazo," Chávez stated, "was the bell that started this revolution."[96] The second episode was the failed coup of February 4, 1992, that initiated his rise to power. Chávez calls this event "lightning that cleared a way."[97] As he has proclaimed: "The twenty-first century in Venezuela began on February 4, 1992—we advanced history."[98] Chávez locates both the *Caracazo* and the 1992 coup as the beginning of a *sacred narrative* that inexorably leads to the Bolivarian Revolution of the turn of the millennium. Both moments are interpreted not only as signs that anticipated the future but also as *essential aspects* of an inevitable cataclysmic struggle to achieve the millennial goals of the revolution. Addressing his supporters in the Venezuelan capital, Chávez triumphantly proclaimed that "the neoliberal paradigm (has been) . . . smashed in a thousand pieces by the people" who "began to break it in 1989, in the Caracazo, and in 1992, on February 4."[99]

For Chávez and his followers, the revolt of the people of Venezuela occurred under the symbolic guidance of a pantheon of historical figures. As already mentioned, paramount among these icons is Simón Bolívar, who led the liberation struggle of several Latin America countries against colonial domination. Within this mythical narrative, Bolivar is portrayed not only as the ancestral patron saint of the movement but also as a living spirit and active guide for revolutionary activism. This has led to the criticism that under Chávez the cult of Bolívar is truly "out of control."[100] To mark the tenth anniversary of his presidency, Chávez returned to the tomb of the "liberator" and announced: "Ten years ago, Bolívar—embodied in the will of the people—came back to life."[101] Chávez identifies himself very closely with the potent Bolivarian presence, filling his speeches with verbatim passages from the great leader's writings and speeches while also comparing his own actions with episodes from Bolivar's life or legends about him. For example, he often quotes the "Chant to Bolívar" written by the Chilean writer Pablo Neruda, which announced that the Liberator returns "every 100 years, when the people awaken."[102] The implication, obviously, is that Chávez is the modern reincarnation of Bolivar, inspiring the dormant people to achieve their destiny. Within this richly evocative symbolic framework, every meaningful new episode of the Bolivarian Revolution is portrayed as a continuation of incidents from the revolutionary past. No wonder then that Chávez and his followers often chant: "Look out, look out, Bolívar's sword is passing through Latin America."[103]

Chávez and his disciples also often invoke the writings and teachings of a friend and mentor of Bolívar: Simón Rodríguez, who is hailed as the "Socrates of America."[104] Rodríguez—who also used the pseudonym Samuel Robinson— insisted on the importance of *originality* in Latin American politics and argued that Latin America should construct institutions and a framework of government based on principles uniquely intrinsic to the region. A standard trope in Chávez's speeches is taken from Rodríguez, who wrote in 1828 that "either we shall innovate, or we shall wander aimlessly and in error."[105] Chávez interprets this to mean that all deference to alien ideas from the "developed" West must end. As he told Colombia's Congress, "One of our tragedies has been the urge to import and copy models wholesale."[106] As Chávez's remarks, Venezuelans must create

> our own thought, adapting it to our own roots . . . as inspired by Simón Rodríguez, who called upon us to invent our own models, not to copy them . . . "Either we invent, or we fail." Consequently, in order not to make mistakes we are forced to invent our own paths, our own models. We are [in the middle of] a process of invention that knows no limits.[107]

The Venezuelan president sees the *invencionismo Robinsoniano* (the inventiveness of Robinson) as an essential weapon in the struggle to defeat the pervasive "neoliberal dogma" that "wants to erase us from the map."[108]

To bolster his claims as a liberator of the people, Chávez resurrects other figures whose historic deeds are said to reveal the spiritual link between past struggles for social justice and today's battles against neoliberalism and American domination. Outstanding among these is the general Ezequiel Zamora, the popular leader of peasant forces against oppressive landowners in the civil war of 1840s and 1850s. In rallies, Chávez has often joined his supporters in singing the hymn *"Oligarcas temblad, viva la libertad!"* (Oligarchs tremble, long live liberty!") made famous by Zamora and his troops. In the narrative of the Bolivarian Revolution, old battles are continually fought anew. For this reason, the new 2001 land-reform law came into force on the anniversary of the 1859 battle of Santa Inés, where the peasant army of Zamora defeated the landowners' army. Chávez traveled to the battlefield to officially enact the law against what he called the "reactionary oligarchy." He concluded by shouting, "Long live Zamora!"[109] Chávez's references to the "Bolivarian, Robinsonian, and Zamoranian spirit"[110] provide a mythical and historical local basis to his movement, setting it apart as a specifically Venezuelan redemption of the promises made by their revolutionary ancestors.

Though these three figures occupy center stage in the movement's sacred narrative, many others are celebrated in what has become a cult of nationalism.[111] Chávez regularly pays homage to all the heroes and martyrs of Bolivarian history at the National Pantheon, and the anniversaries of their births and deaths are commemorated. Above all, the focus on these figures provides a *redemptive narrative* of the origin and spirit of Venezuela, which is comprised of popular rebellions and tales of resistance and liberation.[112] To reinforce the symbolic and spiritual connection between the glorious past and the present republic, a broad range of subsidized social welfare and education programs targeting the poor bear the names of revered historical figures. For example, exactly ten years after the Caracazo, the government launched its first social program, Plan Bolívar 2000, which was a military-led program focusing on infrastructure projects, food distribution, and health care in poor neighborhoods. Subsequently, the government implemented a series of programs, entitled "missions." One land reform program was named after Zamora, while education reform missions were named after Robinson and other heroes (Ribas and Sucre). One state program aimed at eliminating homelessness and drug addiction, the Mission Negra Hipólita, was even named after Bolívar's nanny.

Following from his invocation of the populist champions of the past, Chávez believes that for the people to be freed from oppression and domination, they must recapture their long-repressed history. He often denounces the way that the "official" and "elitist" histories written by the minions of powerful ignore or dismiss the contributions of the heroes of the original Bolivarian struggle.[113] But his new revolution will right this wrong. By reawakening the people, it has "brought back" the exemplary figures unjustly "buried" under the cultural domination of the despised (and now defeated) oligarchs. To accomplish this act of resurrection, one of the new government's first measures was to inaugurate a "National Center of History" with the aim of "democratizing the national memory."[114]

Another significant effort to return to national roots—which contain the "true" and "authentic" character of a people—is the regime's celebration of the ancient struggles of the indigenous populations. For Chávez, the subversion and corruption of the indigenes of Latin America by European conquerors was the first instance of "imposition, of domination" by the forces of oppression.[115] The Bolivarian Revolution is heir to those Native Americans who fought against "what was not a discovery but the beginning of an invasion."[116] To break with a legacy of colonialism, in 2002 Chávez signed a decree that officially changed October 12 from "Columbus Day" to the "National Day of Indigenous Resistance." Though the number of present-day indigenous peoples in Venezuela is relatively small,[117] the Chávez government made the protection of these communities a central tenet of the revolution. For the first time, indigenous representatives were present at a Constituent Assembly, and the new constitution recognized and defended indigenous rights by guaranteeing the right to collective ownership of land. To symbolize the commitment of the revolution to its imagined indigenous roots, the remains of the sixteenth-century tribal leader Guaicaipuro, who was killed by the Spanish forces, were moved to the National Pantheon in a ceremony led by Chávez.[118] Further, the government launched Mission Guaicaipuro, a social program aimed at ensuring the development of indigenous rights and infrastructures in the country.

The message is that, to transform Venezuela and spread the revolution across the Latin American continent and to the world, the "heroic people" of Venezuela must realize that their true origins stretch back to the pre-Columbian inhabitants of South America. From this source spring their authenticity and uniqueness as a people. The destruction of these aboriginal communities marked the beginning of a long history of oppression and domination that, with the exception of episodic periods of liberation and greatness, has continued until the end of the twentieth century, only to be finally overturned by the Bolivarian Revolution. "Until we recognize ourselves in the faces of the indigenous peoples who have battled for 500 years we will not find our true direction,"[119] Chávez declared.

Building Our Own Train

Chávez has persistently placed his struggle within a global framework. The evils that continue to plague Venezuela and Latin America are blamed on a tragic "illusion" that leads governments to blindly ape foreign (mostly American) "discourses of modernity and postmodernity" and neglect their own civilizations.[120] Very early in his career, Chávez violently repudiated the United States of America as a destructive world power. When he first took office, he expressed a more moderate vision of a *multipolar* world vision. "God save us from a unipolar world," he said at the end of a world tour. "The world of the twenty-first century," he added, "cannot be bipolar or unipolar, it must be pluripolar," free of the hegemonies of any power.[121] However, Chavez's rejection of a unipolar world has steadily evolved into a comprehensive and teleological narrative that casts the "United States neoliberal world system" as the archenemy of the peoples of Venezuela, Latin America, and the world. The Bolivarian Revolution bravely stands up against this destructive and repressive force. Chávez often explains to his supporters how the New World Order came about and its ultimate goals:

When the Berlin wall fell in 1989 and the Soviet Union collapsed in 1991, the triumphant flag of neoliberalism was erected and the "end of history" theory emerged. History was over, capitalism won, that was what they said in the early nineties. . . . It was a conformist, stereotyped mindset; there was no alternative.[122]

As we have seen, in contrast to the neoliberal narrative, Chávez claimed credit for initiating a liberating movement based on ancestral roots and ways. In an address calling for South American and Caribbean integration, Chávez stated that "according to the neoliberal thesis, we, the black, Indian, mestizo peoples, have missed the train of history. But they are wrong because we are on our own train, we are building our own train."[123] The international system of globalization and Americanization is a disastrous expression of the wider hegemonic designs of the powerful; a continuation, *in practice*, of colonialism: "What globalization? A globalization to hide neoimperialism? Let's speak clearly."[124] Chávez portrays his own Bolivarian Revolution as the vanguard of a wide-ranging general movement of resistance against the neoliberal, neocolonialist, and imperialist end-of-history narrative.[125]

According to Chávez's logic, because the Bolivarian Revolution guides the Venezuelan people in its new battle for liberation, it is a natural enemy of the oppressive and monstrous "New World Order."[126] Chávez frames his blistering criticism of America historically, tracing the origins of its imperialism to the time of Bolívar, and regularly refers to the "prophecy of Bolívar" written in 1829 in a letter to a British diplomat: "The United States appears to be destined by Providence to plague America with misery in the name of liberty."[127] At a rally held in Caracas against "Yankee intervention" in Venezuela, Chávez repeated Bolívar's words and declared: "We are here today facing the same threat, the same historical reality . . . two hundred years have passed since the warning of the great leader, the great visionary."[128]

Chávez sees America's imperialism as "a hegemonic system that, through different eras, embodies itself in names, figures and individuals."[129] Within this ideological framework, the all-powerful empire of the North has always suborned the Venezuelan elite, turning them into its willing minions "who knelt down to the American empire and did not have the dignity to defend the dignity of the homeland."[130] The failed 2002 coup attempt by members of the old Venezuelan elite is only the final proof of the existence of a counter-revolutionary alliance between the "fascist" "reactionary" oligarchy and the

"American empire."[131] To the Venezuelan leader, this was the historical moment in which the Bolivarian Revolution declared "its anti-imperial character for the first time."[132] The events of April 11–13, 2002, were soon transformed into another sacred date in the chronology of the revolution, to be celebrated annually with the glorification of its martyrs.

From this point onward, in Bolivarian rhetoric, the United States has been unequivocally portrayed as the ultimate source of all the hostile initiatives undertaken by the Venezuelan opposition. Furthermore, in the leader's discourse, the failures and successes of the Bolivarian Revolution are now taken as episodes in a relentless international battle with the "most cruel, cynical, and savage" empire that the world has ever known.[133] Increasing polarization was clear in the fall and winter of 2002–2003, when the opposition organized a general strike that led to a halt the oil industry and business sectors. Chávez denounced this "economic sabotage" as part of a wider "imperialist" strategy to bring the Bolivarian Revolution to its knees.[134] In his victory speech after his reelection in December 2006 (he won more than 60 percent of the vote), Chávez announced: "This is one more defeat for . . . the devil that wants to control the world . . . Venezuela will never again be a North American colony."[135] Similarly, after losing a referendum intended to deepen constitutional reforms, Chávez chillingly reminded his followers that this loss was, above all, a victory for the evil forces supporting the United States: "We are not confronting the petit-Yankees from here, but the empire of the United States, the most powerful empire on Earth."[136]

In his speeches, Chávez often refers to American-led plots to topple his government, to assassinate him, to invade Venezuela, to inflict electoral fraud, or to foment separatism.[137] These accusations are especially common in electoral campaigns, where they serve to mobilize supporters. "If anything happens to me," he warned gravely a few days before the December 2007 referendum, "[I want] everyone to know that [the responsible] was the president of the United States. I am announcing it to the whole world."[138]

One of the major weapons the "enemies of the revolution" have at their disposal is their powerful media apparatus. From the early stages of his presidency, Chávez has tied the success of the revolution to victory in a "communications battle."[139] Chávez often accuses the privately owned Venezuelan media of manipulating public opinion and promoting a value system at odds with the ethos of the revolution. During the strike that paralyzed the country, the Venezuelan leader called the private TV channels "the four horsemen of the apocalypse."[140]

Chávez argues that the private media have "demolished the authentic values" of Venezuela and promoted "horrible ideas," such as individualism and materialism.[141] But the battle with local media is just one dimension of a multifaceted war against what Chávez (paraphrasing the editor of Le Monde Diplomatique, Ignacio Ramonet) calls the global "media dictatorship." His favorite target is CNN, which he calls an "agent of imperialism" bent on promoting a falsified view of the Bolivarian process across the world.[142] The notion that the Bolivarian revolution is the target of "media terrorism" is widespread.[143]

To fully engage in a "communications battle," the Bolivarian Revolution quickly created its own media network, including many community-based radio and television channels (such as Catia TV in Caracas) as well as Venezuela's state television. It has also launched a new channel, Vive, which focuses on "genuine" Venezuelan values and on "education for liberation."[144] As part of the struggle for control over the media, the government refused to renew the license for an opposition-aligned TV station and put a new channel in its place, which vows to contribute to Venezuela's "cultural transformation and emancipation."[145] The government has also created a "Bolivarian" News Agency and launched Hello President, a call-in radio and TV show where Chávez speaks directly to the people for hours. The Bolivarian Revolution is also supported by myriad websites both in Venezuela and abroad. Moreover, in the summer of 2005, on the date of Bolívar's birth, Venezuela inaugurated a pan-American satellite channel, teleSUR, the "television of the South," to "rescue our traditions, our cultures." On this new channel Latin American people will "see our faces and hear our voices and not what CNN and the other big networks of the North want."[146] During his speech at the Seventh Conference of Ministers of Information of the Non Aligned Movement (COMINAC), Chávez proposed the creation of a world communications network, extending from the Caribbean region to Africa and Asia, which would "voice the words of our people" against the hegemony of the global capitalist media.[147]

Coincident with his indictment of the media's cultural imperialism, Chávez has implemented policies aimed at strengthening "popular conscience" through support of "authentic" Venezuelan arts. This mobilizes the "heroic people" to work toward an aesthetic vision of the "beautiful homeland." In 2004, the government passed the "Law of Social Responsibility in Radio and Television" requiring radio stations to broadcast a specific quota of Venezuelan music. In 2005 the National Assembly declared the revolutionary music of Venezuelan singer Alí Primera (which Chávez frequently sings) to be part of the "national patrimony."[148] In honor of the event, the government distributed free CDs of Primera's songs. The government also founded a publishing house, El Perro y la Rana ("The Dog and the Frog," a title inspired by indigenous folklore) under the slogan "a revolution of the conscience." To fulfill its mission, it publishes Venezuelan literature, poetry collections, indigenous history, and books that promote an alternative to capitalism and a unipolar world system. In 2006, to circumvent what he called "Hollywood's dictatorship," which "inculcates messages that are alien to our traditions and destroy our culture [and] morality," the Venezuelan president inaugurated Villa del Cine (Cinema City), a state-financed movie studio.[149] The head of the studio announced that the main goal was to achieve "Venezuela's audiovisual sovereignty."[150]

Alongside his concerted effort to revive local aesthetic traditions, preserve alternative histories of the people, and renew authentic customs, Chávez also strongly supports Venezuela's cultural and political struggle against American hegemony and globalization within a broader Latin American and Caribbean framework. Regional unity, Chávez argues, is the only way to free the people from America's historic "divide and rule" imperial strategy. To this end, he has promoted the creation of regional alliances and companies such as PetroSur, PetroAndina, and PetroCaribe. These provide discounted or free oil from Venezuela's oil company (Pdvsa) to Central American and Caribbean countries. He has also championed the idea of a Banco del Sur (Bank of the South) to finance development projects and infrastructures in the entire region. In 2003 Chávez gave a new form to one of his old projects[151] and inaugurated the Bolivarian Congress of Peoples as a pan–Latin American forum with the mission of "furthering the path of integration and unity." "The people, not economists, academics, legislators, or technicians" will drive this mission.[152]

At the same time, Chávez has become the major opponent of the U.S.–backed project of a Free Trade of the Americas (FTAA), which he has called the "most blatant and purest" example of the neoliberal New World Order.[153] In its place, he has proposed a Bolivarian Alternative for Latin America and the Caribbean (ALBA, a Spanish acronym for "Dawn"). Once again, Chávez framed this alternative project within a historical lens, presenting the choice between the two projects as a reenactment of the nineteenth-century struggle between U.S. President James Monroe's "America for Americans" and Bolívar's "South America for South Americans."[154] He argued as well that Latin American integration must not be based on a neoliberal model addressing only the needs of the market but should be built instead on the authentic cultural roots of the region.[155] The creation of ALBA will not be sufficient unless, in the words of a supporter, "we build a new noncapitalist world order that achieves harmony between the nations."[156] As an agent in the global struggle, ALBA "is not exclusively directed at Latin America, it's a unitary liberating alternative; a union for the poor of the world, for the exploited of the Earth."[157]

Toward Twenty-first Century Socialism

According to Chávez, Latin America "is at the vanguard of a new world."[158] For him, both Soviet-style state socialism and neoliberal capitalism are totally exhausted models that must be replaced. On the one hand, neoliberalism is roundly condemned as the "path to hell, to death, to the destruction of the poor, of the little ones dominated by the powerful."[159] On the other hand, the "dogma of the state" is equated with the "Leviathan of [the Book of] Job."[160] After the collapse of these corrupt ideologies, Venezuela is poised on the verge of a millennial moment in history, in which the Bolivarian Revolution will "serve as inspiration for the people whose historical consciousness of what it is, and of what it can be, is very low."[161] Once in power Chávez reaffirmed his Third Way philosophy and vowed to adopt an intrinsically Venezuelan and Latin America model in opposition to both the "dogma of the market and individualism." According to his vision, Venezuela and humanity in general are now living in an axial era of creation and transformation. "We are living through a time of birth. Our America is giving birth, nothing can stop it. A new time is being born."[162]

The deepening of Venezuela's revolutionary process—and the increased role given to an anti-imperialism ethos—led Chávez to label this new creation a "Bolivarian socialism" with a twenty-first century message. He announced his socialist agenda for the first time at a World Social Forum meeting in January 2005: "To deny the rights of the peoples is the path to barbarism, [and] capitalism is barbarism. Everyday I become more convinced that [the choice is between] capitalism and socialism . . . capitalism can't be transcended from within capitalism, but only through socialism, true socialism, based on equality and justice."[163] For Chávez and his supporters "twenty-first century socialism" is the ultimate goal of the Bolivarian Revolution. But in line with Simón Rodríguez's call for innovation within the cultural framework of Latin America, Bolivarian socialism is promoted as a unique and original Venezuelan creation—not an imitation of outdated European socialist ideals and policies. In typical fashion, Chávez legitimized the "socialist" mission of the Bolivarian Revolution by harking back to the past. As he told a meeting in Jamaica: "If Bolívar had lived a few more decades, I am absolutely convinced that he would have become a socialist." Socialism "was the [natural] direction and evolution of his thoughts and actions and that is why he was crucified by the oligarchies."[164] Similarly, Simón Rodríguez was now reconfigured as "a great revolutionary and socialist."[165] The Brazilian General Abreu e Lima, initially praised only as a revolutionary and loyal friend of Bolívar, was now hailed for his socialist writings.[166]

Certainly, Chávez's embrace of socialism with a Venezuelan face was influenced by his close relationship with Cuba, which began in 1994 and has continued ever since. For example, Chavez established the Mission Barrio Adentro, which brought thousands of Cuban doctors to provide health care in poor neighborhoods. Although the Cuban Revolution and the examples of Fidel Castro and Che Guevara served as a general inspiration in Chávez's early years, in the new socialist phase his references to the Cuban experience have grown in number and intensity. He increasingly sprinkles his speeches to supporters with such battle cries of the Cuban Revolution as "Until Victory Always!" and "Fatherland, Socialism, or Death!"[167] Other sources of Venezuela's original and unique socialism are found in its indigenous traditions. Chávez has described the new Venezuelan socialism as "Indo-American"[168] and asserts that the revolutionary new order is based on "Bolívar, Simón Rodríguez, Jesus Christ, and our aborigines."[169]

As the above quote indicates, Bolivar, Castro, and the American Indians are not the only models Chávez draws on to justify his political stance. Even more often, he affirms Christianity as the eternal source of Venezuelan socialism. In truth, from the moment he was elected, he immediately established an analogy between the life and teachings of Jesus Christ and the spirit of the Bolivarian Revolution. Chávez frequently introduces Jesus as "my commander in chief" and as "the Lord of Venezuela."[170] At a 2002 march in Caracas to commemorate the six-month anniversary of the April coup, Chávez announced that the revolution "is the path indicated by Jesus of Nazareth, the kingdom of Heaven, but on Earth, the path of life."[171] He portrayed the rescue of Venezuela from neoliberalism as the fulfillment of Jesus' pursuit of justice and equality for all humanity. If Jesus returned to Earth "he would be antineoliberal."[172] During the 2004 campaign to remain president, Chávez told a rally in Caracas that the rejection of his recall was "the NO of Christ to imperialism . . . the NO of Christ when he said 'Leave the dead to bury their own dead; but as for you, follow me for life [and] for the liberation of the human being.'"[173] He also often remarks that the foundation of each political policy must be the human being, because "as Jesus said, 'man is the Alpha and Omega, the Beginning and End.'"[174]

Christian rhetoric permeates the millennialism that is at the heart of the Bolivarian revolution.[175] As Chávez says, "Christ was one of the greatest socialists of our history. Who crucified Christ? The kings, the powerful, the rich."[176] The Bolivarian Revolution will continue until "the kingdom that Christ announced becomes reality, the kingdom of Equality, the kingdom of Justice. That is our fight."[177] After Chávez declared this earthly kingdom of God to be "socialism," Jesus was transformed into an even more openly ideological and militant actor. In a monologue during a "Hello President" program, the Venezuelan president made this point clear to his audience:

> Christ was a rebel. Christ lived, he was a human being, an antiimperialist rebel who fought the Roman Empire, the powerful, the economic, political, military, and ecclesiastical elites of his time; and, as we know, he ended up crucified. In my view, the Christian philosophy—and I ask everyone to study authentic Christianity—is one of the most powerful sources of the socialism of the twenty-first century; Christ is the man, the one who needs to be in front of this revolution; Christ, the real Christ, redeemer and martyr.[178]

Chavez frequently attacks conservative sectors of the Venezuelan church for promoting a "false" image of Christ. "Christ was a true communist . . . but the Catholic Church often manipulates Christ's message in order to convert religion, as Marx said, into the opium of the people."[179] The relationship between Christ and the Bolivarian Revolution was symbolized when state-funded efforts to achieve "zero misery [and] zero poverty [while inaugurating] equality and liberty in the land of Venezuela"[180] were collectively named "Christ's Mission." Chávez's religious invocations become especially pointed when he feels persecuted. For example, when he returned to Venezuela after the Spanish King D. Juan Carlos told him to "shut up" during an Iberian-American summit, Chávez paraphrased Jesus' warning to the Pharisees, telling the waiting crowd that "the stones of the peoples of Latin America would cry out if I were silenced."[181]

The millennial aspect of this polymorphous revolutionary project is exemplified in the timeline Chávez set for the implementation of Bolivarian socialism, which is scheduled to occur between 2007 and 2021. The Venezuelan leader named this new socialist era the "National Project Simón Bolívar." Continued commitment over time is crucial for completing such a towering project, hence Chávez's insistence on ending presidential term limits, which he finally managed to achieve in 2009 through a popular referendum.[182] Significantly, the final transformation of the country will be completed on the bicentenary of the famous 1821 battle of Carabobo, in which Bolívar's army defeated the colonial forces. A central pillar of this transformational enterprise is a new mass party, announced by Chávez during the 2006 presidential campaign.[183] After his victory Chávez dubbed this new "revolutionary party" the Partido Socialista Unido de Venezuela (PSUV—United Socialist Party of Venezuela). The mission of the party is not restricted to electoral campaigns. Rather, the aim is to engage in what Chávez called a "war of ideas," changing and shaping popular mentalities to prepare the ground for the success of an endogenous socialism allegedly emerging from below and not imposed from above.

To achieve this ultimate goal, the government must educate the populace so they are able to make appropriate decisions and not act out of ignorance. "We all have to study, read, discuss" as well as "distribute information and printed material."[184] A focus on education has been present throughout Chávez's presidency. He publicly declared Venezuela a "territory free of illiteracy"[185] and has backed up his words with vast government financed literacy programs in low-income neighborhoods. Literacy is understood to be crucial for raising popular consciousness, enabling self-empowerment, and furthering the construction of a new value system that will overturn and replace capitalism's repressive ethics. Taking inspiration again from Bolívar,[186] Chávez named a new education reform initiative Moral y Luces (Morals and Enlightenment). The rationale for this reform was couched in terms of *purity* and *cleansing* and the "need to demolish the old values of individualism, capitalism, and egotism [while] creating new values [which] can be reached only through education."[187] In pursuit of this goal, Chávez has pushed for the installation of a new school curriculum that promotes "human values" and a "Bolivarian education."[188] Clearly influenced by the educational ideas of Che Guevara,[189] Chávez advocates teaching a Bolivarian and socialist ethical system that will purge the "poison of capitalism" from the society.

A Moral Revolution

Implementation of the socialist project will transform humanity: "A revolution has to produce not only food, goods, and services. Before that, it must produce new human beings: the new man, the new woman. And our missions and our struggles for 'morals and enlightenment' are aimed at this necessity, [the creation of] new men and women."[190] These new men and women will be products of a "moral revolution, giving an example of a socialist ethic, of unselfishness, of solidarity and love between us."[191]

Accordingly, the new party is described as a "school of transformation" based on the revolutionary need to "create conscience, which is the sum of science and knowledge."[192] To promote this revolutionary goal, the government has created "Socialist Centers" of popular education in communities across Venezuela. These have been designated as locations where "we mold the new woman and the new man." The same rhetoric is used by the leading Bolivarian youth organization Frente Francisco de Miranda, which promotes itself as a "territory of formation of the new man."[193] In the same vein, Chávez asserts that the government-funded project to develop and expand a "new homeland" of socialist communes all over the country will "transform values" so that the "humanism, equality, and solidarity that Bolivar always proclaimed" will become a reality.[194]

In a speech to the Sixth World Social Forum, Chávez asserted that the Venezuelan construction of a "new society of equals" is built on a "revolutionary, participatory, and activist democracy" that rejects and transcends the "old" representative democracy, the "democracy of the elites."[195] Hence, the new socialism is anchored in what the Venezuelan president calls "popular power," in which the people spontaneously organize and transform society from below. This idealistic attempt to "reinvent democracy" by dispensing with institutional frameworks while stimulating popular involvement has been a cornerstone of the Bolivarian Revolution. The new constitution consecrated a "moral power" (made up of a people's defender or ombudsman) and an electoral power based on the ideal of a "participatory democracy" and on such mechanisms of direct democracy as plebiscites. The government has also sponsored multiple voluntary social movements and popular organizations, including "Bolivarian circles," which address community needs while also transmitting the revolutionary ideology. There is no formal affiliation required for participation in these circles; the only necessity is loyalty to Chávez.[196] The creation of these organized groups in 2001 was viewed (by supporters and opponents alike) as one of the first steps toward the realization of the "Bolivarian" mobilization through the arousal and ideological indoctrination of the masses.[197]

The goal of forming an authentically participatory society was also the driving force for the institution of a "Special Law on Communal Councils," which the government passed in the spring of 2006. These communal councils are defined as "the means through which the newly enlightened and organized masses can take over the administration of the policies and projects created to address the needs of the community in the construction of a fair and just society."[198] These communal councils have access to public funds in developing their projects, with the final decision belonging to a citizen's assembly. The citizen's assembly also elects the executive body of the "communal banks" created by the government.[199] The self-professed aim is to build a radically democratic and anticapitalist model of the economy[200] and "create a communal state" while simultaneously "dismantling the bourgeois state."[201] These experiments in direct democracy are aimed at bridging the gap between revolutionary rhetoric and practice by providing the *experience* of "true democracy" for people who have felt excluded from the political process. The slogan of the Bolivarian government is "Venezuela now belongs to everyone." However, Chávez's opponents fear that these policies promote the obliteration of the boundaries between the private and public domains and may initiate a descent into mass-based totalitarianism, with Chávez as ultimate authority.[202]

As we have seen, the narrative of the Bolivarian revolution portrays the world of today teetering on the verge of destruction, as the "dark and evil path" of neoliberalism leads humanity on the "way to Hell."[203] Yet this era of fear and trembling is also a time of great hope because the Venezuelan experience of revolution will contribute to the "creation of a new world."[204] As with the Zapatistas, the Bolivarian Revolution benefits from the solidarity of a global network of left-wing intellectuals and the activism of many groups.[205] Chávez's policies—either the government-funded programs aimed at educating, empowering, and organizing the poor or the anti-imperial project of a unified Latin America—are hailed as world changing, offering suffering humanity a future of universal meaning and infinite potential.[206] "We are fighting not only for our people but for all the peoples of the world who deserve justice, life and dignity, and that is our struggle."[207] The battle with vicious neoliberal forces is necessarily apocalyptic: "Either [our] society builds socialism, or society and humanity will cease to be."[208] The Bolivarian Revolution must destroy the unnatural corruption of capitalism and American oppression to provide what Chávez often calls a "utopia" in the modern world, a terrestrial kingdom of God.[209]

In the eyes of the Bolivarian leader, Venezuela is at the very center of this final struggle for the soul of humanity, as the nation discovers its own pathway to salvation and then offers it to all of humanity. During a Christmas Eve address Chávez made this point vividly: "The world cannot end, we cannot let it happen. We cannot let the world end, as stated in the biblical story of Christ, in degradation, where man devours man, where we kill each other . . . If we sacrifice ourselves for the many, for the homeland, for the collective, only then we will save the homeland and contribute, from here, in saving the world."[210]

INDIGENOUS POWER

The Pachakuti Era

From the greatness and prosperity of the past they turned to the present, mourning their dead kings, their lost empire, and their fallen state, etc. These and similar topics were broached by the Incas and Pallas (female royalty) on their visits, and when recalling their departed happiness, they always ended these conversations with tears and mourning, saying: "Our rule is turned to Bondage."[211]

Thus, in the early seventeenth century, the "Inca" Garcilaso de la Vega described the sorrowful fate of his mother's people, once free and proud but reduced to servitude by their brutal colonizers.[212] The memories of past greatness continue to shape the politics in the Andean region. In December 2005 Evo Morales Ayma, a former llama herder, *cocalero* (coca leaf grower), head of Movimiento al Socialismo (Movement to Socialism, or MAS), and member of the Aymara Indian tribe was elected president of Bolivia by an overwhelming majority. Morales was supported by peasants and left-wing activists, but most importantly he was elected with the massive support of Bolivia's Indian population.[213] He did much less well among the more affluent voters of European descent, particularly those from the eastern lowlands areas. His victory made him the first indigenous president in the history of the country.[214] It is no surprise that this breakthrough occurred in Bolivia because 71 percent of the population identify themselves as members of the thirty-six designated "first nation" groups, the most numerous being the Aymara and the Quechua.[215] All of these peoples had been de facto barred from voting until 1952 (if not by law, in practice).

From the late 1980s into the 1990s, Evo Morales led farmers from the Cochabamba tropics in their struggles against the U.S.-backed policy of eradication of coca crops. In his presidential campaign, he promised to deliver Bolivia, one of the poorest and least developed countries in the continent, from foreign control over its vast resources of natural gas reserves and oil. The economic power of transnational companies had long been adamantly opposed by the majority of Bolivians, whose protests had already ousted one president and led to another's resignation by the turn of the millennium.

The source of Morales's authority was symbolically expressed on January 21, 2006, the day before he was sworn in. On that day, he journeyed to Tiwanaku, a pre-Incan site in the Bolivian Andes, a place of genesis, creation, and cosmic order that indigenes regard as the center of the ancient Andean world.[216] Amidst the sound of Inca *pututus* (ceremonial horns) and against the colorful backdrop of thousands of Bolivian flags and *wiphalas* (emblems of the Andean first nations), Aymaran spiritual leaders (*yatiris*) invested Morales with traditional signs of cosmic power. Dressed in a red tunic, his head covered with a four-cornered hat symbolizing the cardinal points, he was given the traditional baton of authority (*báculo*) and consecrated as the supreme leader of the aboriginal peoples of the American continent.[217] After a ritual offering of incense, liquor, and coca leaves to "Mother Earth" (*Pachamama*), representatives of the different indigenous ethnic groups offered ritual gifts to their new leader, including a woven bag to carry the sacred book of the *Popol Vuh*.[218] From this sacred space the newly elected president addressed the crowd:

> Today, from *Tiwanaku*, from Bolivia, a new year starts for the original peoples, a new life in which we search for equality and justice; a new era, a new millennium for all the peoples. I am convinced that with the strength and unity of the people we will end the colonial state and the neoliberal model. I pledge, from this sacred place of Tiwanaku, to defend the first peoples not only of Bolivia but also of the entire America, which used to be called *Abya Ayala*.... We need the strength of the people to twist the empire's arm.[219]

Morales added that after "500 years of indigenous and popular resistance" a new era of liberation of the Latin American peoples had begun, starting with the "refoundation" of Bolivia.[220] This was not the first time that Morales had gone on pilgrimage to the spiritual center of the Andean peoples. His campaign as the MAS party candidate for president had concluded at the same holy site.[221] And in October 2007 he returned to Tiwanaku to celebrate the adoption by the U.N. General Assembly of the "Declaration of the Rights of Indigenous Peoples."[222]

Morales also drew a parallel between the struggles of indigenes in the past and rebellion against neoliberalism in the present in his evocation of the Andean cosmological notion of the *Pachakuti*—the founding event or break in historical time in which an unjust world is destroyed and a new one is born, renovated, and redeemed.[223] While campaigning for the presidency, Morales often summoned up this cataclysmic image: "Let us walk together to create a new country—a Pachakuti!"[224] The theme of the "coming of the Pachakuti" is clearly present in the minds of many of the indigenous ministers appointed by Morales.[225] As one of his supporters proclaimed: "Morales Ayma is the new Pachakuti, who announces a profound change in Bolivian society, its institutions and habits, customs and behavior of men."[226]

To an even greater extent than the movements led by Hugo Chávez and Subcomandante Marcos, Morales and his supporters idealize pre-Hispanic times as an era of order, justice, and communal ownership over ancestral lands and goods. They portray the present-day struggle in Bolivia as a restoration of the *Tawantinsuyu*—the Quechua term for the great precolonial Inca Empire.[227] Morales and his supporters regularly recall the widespread Indian and peasant insurrections against colonial authority that swept through the southern Andes in the 1780s. These are invoked as precursors to the "new independence" that rejects the present "colonial state" forcibly imposed by American neoliberal authority. The depredations of capitalism can be fought, Morales says, only by returning to ancient native cosmologies and attitudes. In particular, to resist Western-style consumerism and greed, humans must retrieve the ancestral symbiosis between humanity and nature:

> We, the indigenous peoples, the humble and honest peoples of this planet, believe that the time has come to stop, [and] to rediscover our roots and the respect for Mother Earth, [respect for the] *pachamama* as we call it in the Andes. Today the aboriginal peoples of Latin America and the world are being called on by history to become the vanguard of defense of nature and life.[228]

The historical parallel was evident in the address Morales made to the National Congress on the day of his official inauguration. He began by asking for a minute of silence to remember Túpac Amaru, Túpac Katari, and Katari's wife, Bartolina Sisa, leaders of the pan-Andean rebellion, which occurred over 200 years ago.[229] Nor was this ritual of remembrance a novelty. In 2005, Morales and the MAS successfully pushed the National Congress to recognize Túpac Katari and Bartolina Sisa as "national heroes."[230] Although their rebellions failed and they were publicly executed and dismembered by the Spanish,[231] they have become symbols of Indian resistance in the rhetoric and imagination of the MAS. In times of contention and popular mobilization, the popular leader Bolivian indigenous people recall most is the great Aymara chief Túpac Katari. In the 1970s the most powerful indigenous and peasant labor union was named after Katari.[232] Álvaro García Linera, Morales's vice president, was imprisoned for five years in the 1990s for being a member of a small guerrilla group called Túpac Katari Guerrilla Army.[233] Morales often professes his belief that the transformation of the present world is a continuation of the eighteenth-century rebel leader's mission:

> This is not the first time that the aboriginal indigenous peoples fight for their natural resources; This is not the first time that the aboriginal indigenous peoples, peasants, workers, miners, have battled to recover our territory. This fight began five hundred years ago. It is not a coincidence that we had a leader such as Túpac Katari and a sister such as Bartolina Sisa. . . . This fight goes on and it is up to us now to fight for these principles [of independence, sovereignty] of our brothers and sisters, our grandparents, our ancestors.[234]

Morales lauds the MAS movement "as the struggle of our ancestors, of Túpac Katari" and "the struggle of Túpac Amaru, (the struggle) of many political movements of liberation in all of Latin America."[235] When first nation peoples living on the outskirts of La Paz blockaded roads in protest against a government plan to outsource Bolivia's natural gas, MAS party officials characterized the event as a resumption of the 1781 siege of La Paz by the Aymara Indians led by Túpac Katari.[236] Before becoming vice president, García Linera, who is of Creole ancestry, wrote that, though separated in time, these actions stemmed from the common "history, suffering, and destiny" of the Aymara nation.[237]

The link between Katari's example and the Morales revolution was further cemented in popular consciousness when Morales was ejected from Congress in 2002 for inciting riots against the government. At that fateful moment, Morales repeated Katari's famous prophecy, which he had uttered before his execution: "You can kill me, but I will return, and I will be millions."[238] Later, MAS campaign posters showed images of Morales with those potent words inscribed above his head.[239] The link is made even more apparent in a propagandistic biographical movie entitled *Evo Pueblo* (Evo People). The film opens with the image of the execution of Katari, followed by a retelling of Morales's impoverished childhood.[240] This hagiography is one aspect of what Morales's enemies call "Evolatria" (the worship of Evo).[241]

Though recognizing the emancipatory importance of previous struggles, such as the 1825 battle for independence from the Spanish and the 1952 revolution that turned Indians into citizens, for Morales these are "mutilated" victories. The new Bolivian Revolution will not only fulfill the promises contained in previous liberating events, it will also go beyond them and reverse 500 years of Indian humiliation. In a speech to mark "514 years of colonialism" Morales celebrated October 12 (Columbus Day) not as a "day of disgrace" but as a new "day of liberation, sisters and brothers, it is the day of dignity of our Americas, of our *Abya Ayala*, beginning from Bolivia."[242] To distinguish his transformative rule from the lesser actions of previous governments Morales has vowed to govern according to the "law of the original indigenous peoples. . . . Do not steal, do not lie, do not be lazy, and do not be servile. . . . This is the cosmic law of our ancestors that brought us, and we have the obligation to carry it forward to change our country."[243] From the beginning, Morales planned to rewrite Bolivia's constitution to bring it closer to the aboriginal moral code, so it can express the "second independence" of the indigenous peoples.[244] As he says:

> In 181 years of republican life, the moment has come to reclaim our beloved homeland and its peoples who have been victims of discrimination, abuse, and pillage of our natural resources . . . I feel that the new history of Bolivia starts today, [an era] of equality, where there is no discrimination . . . I am convinced that we will change this dark colonial history . . . We are not talking about a simple constitutional reform, we are talking about founding Bolivia once again.[245]

The Constituent Assembly "is the way to make a cultural, peaceful, and democratic revolution."[246]

Decolonization as Emancipation

Morales's political agenda goes far beyond mere reforms; it promises a new world based on an alternative Andean vision of utopia. The aim is to overturn global capitalism in favor of a "democratic and cultural" revolution. To put an end to 500 years of plunder of the country's riches (intensified in the modern neoliberal era), the new constitution demands "state ownership of natural resources."[247] This has been a major position of the MAS party and of Morales.

It began as part of an effort to keep "sacred coca" from being eradicated from the country. Whenever he can, Morales chews coca leaves at international meetings to prove this point. This policy is then expanded to include other local riches. In an interview Morales declared: "After more than 500 years, the Quechuas and Aymaras are still the rightful owners of this land." Therefore, "retaking of power [by indigenes] is a step toward the recovery of our natural resources, such as hydrocarbons."[248] One of Morales's first measures as president was the nationalization of the country's reserves of natural gas, oil, and coal. The revenues from taxes and royalties on hydrocarbons were then used to fund education initiatives, road construction, and a pension program for the elderly, which was significantly entitled the Renta Dignidad (Dignity Pension), echoing a favorite Zapatista slogan.

Of course, the nationalization of resources is not unusual in populist political movements, but in Bolivia it has been framed in a millenarian manner, as the natural outcome of an ancestral Indian struggle for land and territory. Following the same ideology, the government launched a land reform that distributed state-owned land to peasants and challenged large landowners in the eastern lowlands of the country.[249] This further antagonized opponents to Morales's government, who conducted referendums calling for regional autonomy and de facto independence.[250] This confrontation between pro- and antigovernment forces was marked by episodes of violence and bloodshed.[251]

The decolonization project of MAS has been buoyed by nostalgic images of a "true democracy" built on pure, egalitarian indigenous ancestral ways. Particularly since the 1990s, there has been an upsurge across the Andes of indigenous parties and movements, advancing the cause of alternative and deeper experiments in democracy at a local level.[252] According to their rhetoric, representative democracy—dismissed as the "democracy of the few" at the expense of the many—has run its historical course. Bolivia will inaugurate an era of *authentic democracy* that Morales often describes as based on communal ideals: "I would like to remind [everyone] that to live in the [indigenous] communities is to live in equality, in a collective, in community. I keep saying that where I was born there was no private property."[253] As he declared during a speech in the National Congress to celebrate Bolivia's democratic era: "I lived in the *Ayllu* [a self-governing Indian community in Bolivia's highlands], and [in these communities] there are no majorities or minorities, things are approved by consensus. . . . The democracy of majorities and minorities is imported; it is Western."[254] Like Subcomandante Marcos and Hugo Chávez, Morales promises to inaugurate an emancipatory and "consensual democracy" that will replace a "subjugated and colonial democracy."[255]

The push toward participatory, immediate, and consensual processes is nowhere more evident than in the role given to mechanisms of direct democracy, such as referendums, and, in the new constitution, the recall of electoral mandates.[256] At the same time, the draft constitution legitimized indigenous customary practices, particularly in the realm of law, proclaiming that indigenous and peasant leaders "will apply their own principles, cultural values, norms, and procedures" to the meting out of justice.[257] Customary law has therefore become as valid as the laws of the civil court. The nationalization of the energy sectors, land reform, the inauguration of a participatory and consensual democracy, and the validation of communal local justice are all understood by Morales as crucial steps for the creation of a distinctly Andean economic and societal model. Tellingly, Bolivia's vice president promotes this "Bolivian creation" as "Andean and Amazonic capitalism," which is a temporary stage toward the long-term goal of a "socialist utopia."[258]

As in Venezuela, many of the new middle-class and old elite fear that this utopian project will lead to curtailment of freedom of expression and the concentration of powers in the hands of Morales.[259] Morales's project is also opposed by the leadership of the Bolivian Catholic Church, which fears the transfer of its cultural and spiritual influence to the state and pre-Christian traditions. In response, Morales told a meeting of the World Social Form, "another faith, another religion, another church is also possible, brothers and sisters."[260] But the real obstacles on the path to emancipation, as Morales repeatedly insists, are those national oligarchs who oppose his policies and who are hand-in-hand with the neoliberal agenda of American imperialism. Following the rhetorical path favored by Marcos and Chávez, Morales views all actions by the U.S. government through the prism of America's "inherent" imperialism: "The empire is always present to conspire, to confuse the population, not only in Bolivia but all over the world."[261] Morales sustained attack on America has its roots in his history as a labor leader who battled against the U.S. war on drugs. At that time, he ended many of his speeches to his fellow cocaleros by uttering, in Quechua, "Death to the Yankees."[262] In an interview before becoming president, Morales observed: "The United States has always tried to impose a global hegemony and, as a consequence, it needs to control all of Latin America. The fight against narcotraffic is a pretext; [it is] an excuse for the United States to control our economies."[263] In the same vein, a biographical booklet distributed during the 2005 presidential campaign depicts the evolution of Evo Morales from a "humble herd-boy" to "a nightmare for the empire, for neoliberalism and the transnational [corporations]."[264]

After his election, Morales continued to favor imagery of a polarized world. Ten days after becoming president, he traveled to the coca-growing region of Chapare and, addressing peasants and cocaleros, described a "battle of two green colors." The coca leaf, "which represents in Andean culture: the culture of life, of humanity," is battling the dollar, "also green, which represents in the Western culture, the culture of death."[265] During Morales's presidency, the United States has been accused of waging a war against his government through subversive activities undertaken by USAID (United States Agency for International Development), the Peace Corps, and CNN.[266] Like Chávez and Marcos, Morales argues that CNN, along with powerful media networks owned by his wealthy opponents, promotes a biased, neoliberal view of reality. And, like his fellow revolutionaries, Morales too has sought to create "alternative communications" by funding community-based radio stations and other media.[267]

The groups that oppose his government are often depicted by Morales as racist and treacherous tyrannies, corrupted by their permanent alliance with the United States, particularly through its diplomatic service in Bolivia (Morales famously expelled the U.S. ambassador). This perception precedes his ascension to the presidency. When the candidates of the traditional parties refused to debate him during the presidential election of 2002, Morales commented that he actually would rather debate the U.S. ambassador, because "I prefer to talk to the circus owner rather then talk to the clowns."[268] Under attack by civic committees resisting his project of "decolonization," Morales declared that the choice was between two paths: "[either] we are with the empire, with the U.S. ambassador, with these committees, or we are with the people."[269] In a speech to his supporters during the campaign for the recall referendum of August 2008,[270] Morales, dressed in traditional Indian attire, denounced the opposition as heirs to the colonizers and invaders "who are now called 'neoliberals.'"[271] Therefore, it was not simply Morales's presidency that was at stake during the referendum but the very survival of the "homeland."[272] Morales's electoral successes are much more than a personal victory: His triumph in the recall referendum was dedicated to "all revolutionaries in Latin America and the world."[273]

Redeeming Humanity

Like Marcos and Chávez, for Morales the "struggle against the empire" is waged across the entire hemisphere. Morales strongly supports the "great Latin American unity" that will break free from the evil clutches of the United States. Latin American union is viewed as the result of millenarian aspirations across the region. In a speech honoring Che Guevara, Morales framed the need for unity historically:

> In the same way that some presidents pointed out that Latin America cannot be the backyard of North American imperialism, [we say that] Latin America must not continue to be the victim of pillage of its natural resources . . . The best tribute to Che Guevara is to [carry forward], with honesty and transparency, an anti-imperialist, antineoliberal and anticolonialist project . . . I want you to know that our indigenous leader Túpac Katari always talked about the restoration of *Tahuantinsuyo*, just as Bolívar always talked about the construction of the great homeland. These goals are rooted in our people, and they must continue.[274]

Naturally, Morales opposes the American-led project combining the economies of the continent (FTAA), dismissing it as "an agreement to legalize the colonization of the Americas,"[275] and backs instead the alternative ALBA favored by Hugo Chávez. This alternative will consolidate the "economic, cultural, ethical and ideological struggle" against the destructiveness of U.S. capitalism.[276]

Underlying Morales's rejection of the present is his belief that a non-Western cosmology and knowledge system is humanity's last and best hope to save itself from extinction. Repeatedly, Morales and MAS party officials depict their governmental policies and ideals as rejections of destructive Euro-American systems of knowledge in favor of a deeper local wisdom, long suppressed but now returning to the light. As we have seen, the ideological platform of the MAS party traces the origin of all the failures of the Bolivian state to "500 years of domination by a Western culture cosmology."[277] According to this view, the Western logic of "eternal growth"—and its value system of individualism, rational instrumentality, and commoditization—has inexorably led to exploitation and a dangerous imbalance between man and nature:

> To create infinite growth, the industrial revolution, as a sign of modernity, gave us the *Homo Faber*, man as the fabricator, the representative of the ma-

chine era, of the primacy of man over nature. This mechanical paradigm of the Western culture led man to be the master and lord of creation, whose mission is to subjugate. Because nature is viewed as a lifeless being . . . man breaks with nature in order to assert control.[278]

Morales believes that the indigenous Bolivian animistic and polycentric view rejects a dominant Western logic that exploits the weak while simultaneously conquering and homogenizing all natural and social space.[279] In an open letter to the WTO, Morales attacked the orthodoxy spread by capitalism, which "wants to make us all uniform so that we turn into mere consumers." In a line of argument echoing other antiglobalization rhetoric, Morales deplored development models that are accompanied by "processes of generalized acculturation [that] impose on us one single culture, one single fashion, one single way of thinking and of seeing things." He added that the "harmonic complementarity of the various cultures and economies is essential to save the planet, humanity and life."[280]

From this perspective, neoliberalism and globalization are simply the most recent manifestations of a Western epistemology of rapaciousness and profit, reducing the world to transferrable commodities. Morales continually argues that there is an ontological association between modernity and globalization and the ravages of "savage and inhuman capitalism."[281] To MAS, "globalization is an effective way to take our riches and to increase our poverty for the sake of the hegemony and growth of the industrialized countries."[282] Morales repeatedly describes his personal ethic of public service as the direct reversal of corrupt Western practices. "I am not after money. In Andean culture to be a [political] authority is to fulfill a vocation of service to the people . . . It is not like the Western culture, where to be in a position of authority means to transform politics into a science of gain from illicit enrichment."[283] True to his word, when he became president, Morales cut his salary and those of his ministers by more than half. His devotion explains his bachelor status. As he says, "I am married to Bolivia."[284]

The Bolivian struggle against neoliberal capitalism is therefore not merely regional but global in its implications, gaining the support of many other activist groups worldwide.[285] As Morales says: "We want Bolivia ... with its political, economic, programmatic, cultural and ecological proposals, to be a hope for the entire world."[286] The basic ideological principle of the MAS party declares: "We have a sacred duty to humanity, which is to resume the paradigm of a symbiotic society and of total balance with nature."[287] However, "if we want to save humanity there is no alternative but to change economic models and the capitalist system."[288] The "defense of humanity"—defined as a struggle between "life" (deeply rooted in Andean ways) and "death" (identified with global capitalism)—can be achieved only by returning to the values of the indigenous peoples, who "are the moral reserve of the world." Victory in this struggle is not just a geopolitical reversal or the end of an "imperial order." It is a triumph over the soul destroying commodification of human beings and a defeat of the "selfishness, individualism, and ambition" of capitalism, which, in Morales's view, has torn the world (indigenous and beyond) apart.[289] As in Chiapas and in Venezuela, victory in Bolivia has transcendent significance. It will inaugurate a cosmic renewal of fundamental human values.

3 THE EUROPEAN SEARCH FOR AUTHENTICITY

*One understands absolutely nothing about modern civilization
if one does not first and foremost realize that it is a universal
conspiracy to destroy the inner life.*[1]
—**Georges Bernanos**

Uprootedness uproots everything except the need for roots.[2]
—**Christopher Lasch**

THE EUROPEAN NEW RIGHT

Embattled Intellectuals

The road to a new world is rough and steep. But the difficulty of the climb
has not deterred rebels against the status quo. For the last forty years, self-
proclaimed cultural elitists known as the European New Right (ENR) have
argued that vital local beliefs and practices of Europe have been systematically
undermined and devalued by the universalist, mercantile, hegemonic, and homogenizing values of modernity. This loose school of thought was officially
born in Paris in 1968 with the launching of GRECE (Groupement de Recherche
et d'Études pour la Civilisation Européenne),[3] a cultural association led by the
young journalist, activist, and polemicist Alain de Benoist. The ENR collective
of academics, writers, and journalists is comprised of a variety of personalities, including most notably Marco Tarchi in Italy, José Javier Esparza in Spain,
Michael Walker in England, Pierre Krebs in Germany, and Guillaume Faye in
France (who later helped to develop a rival school within the ENR), as well as a
host of others. The ENR has held many conferences and published any number

of manifestos and books aimed at advancing its program throughout Europe. Over time, some of its ideological positions have evolved substantially, and the movement has experienced several schisms. Nevertheless, despite its diversity, a characteristic set of beliefs animate the movement's critique of globalization, the alternatives envisioned, and the methods to be used to achieve its goals. In sum, the aim is to create a counterhegemonic discourse, to transform European mentalities, and, ultimately, to revitalize a decadent society to overturn the destructive global capitalist world order.[4]

Following the theoretical premises of Italian Marxist Antonio Gramsci, the "manifesto of the New Right for the year 2000" states that "ideas play a fundamental role in collective consciousness and, more generally, in human history."[5] Of course, ideas do not exist in a vacuum. The manifesto recognizes that they are necessarily carried by what Gramsci called an "organic" intellectual vanguard capable of influencing and inflaming the hearts and minds of the people, thus providing the groundwork for future political successes. "One of the tragedies of the right," de Benoist laments, "is its inability to understand the need for [attention to] the *long term* . . . it has not understood the importance of Gramsci."[6] Naturally, the ENR theorists define themselves as that organic intellectual vanguard—though while Gramsci ardently supported a leftist revolution against capitalism, the New Right opposes both liberalism and Marxism, which they call two sides of the same counterfeit coin.[7] The ultimate aim of the ENR, according Pierre Krebs, the founder of the Thule Seminar, a think tank of Germany's New Right, is to achieve an "intellectual coup d'etat" that will destroy both of these false gods.[8]

The ideas promulgated by the ENR are not envisioned as pragmatic programs for change. Rather, they are "metapolitical"; that is, they move "beyond political divisions in order to achieve a new synthesis that renews a 'transversal mode' of thought and links all areas of knowledge together in order to achieve a coherent worldview."[9] Like the ancient philosophical schools of Greece that serve as the ideal for the ENR, "transversal" ideas are said to be the indispensable ammunition for a transformative "spiritual movement"[10] that will transcend the traditional, sterile right–left dichotomy and provide "a global response—at the same time ethnic, political, religious—to the questions posed by every man when facing the world."[11]

Members of the ENR often portray themselves as descendents of a long line of heretics and nonconformists throughout history,[12] defining themselves as the "center of refusal," a "network of resistance," and a gathering of the "free spirits"[13] united to provide a "new sheltering sky and metaphysical home for all humanity."[14] According to the ENR, their inclusive paradigm is a "counter-power" that will inspire a total cultural transformation and a complete political revolution capable of rejuvenating alienated modern consciousness. This millenarian ambition is at the center of the "subversive" hopes of the ENR's rebel intelligentsia and is the source of the proclaimed "originality" of the GRECE cultural association.[15]

The ENR worldview has a familiar ring. It assumes the existence of a widespread crisis precipitated by the disruptive conditions of modernity and the devastating consequences of liberalism, modernity's chief ideology. Symptoms of this crisis include: *individualization* (destruction of communal life), *massification* (standardized behavior and lifestyles), *rationalization* (the primacy of self-interest, utility, and efficiency), *universalization* (a functionalist one-size-fits-all model of society), and, finally, *desacralization*, which subjugates all mythical and religious narratives to instrumental and scientific rationalization.[16] Instead of ushering in freedom, equality, and happiness, the political and philosophical narrative of modernity has exhausted itself, bringing increased anomie and malaise in its wake. The liberal ideology of progress has been revealed as a chimera; instead, the future is unpredictable and terrifying. The signs of imminent collapse are everywhere. As de Benoist and Champetier write:

> The destruction of the lifeworld for the benefit of instrumental reason, (economic) growth, and material development has resulted in an unprecedented impoverishment of the spirit and a generalized anxiety about living in an always uncertain present, in a world deprived both of the past and the future. Thus, modernity has given birth to the most empty civilization mankind has ever known: The language of advertising has become the paradigm of all social discourse; the primacy of money has imposed the omnipresence of commodities; man has been transformed into an object of exchange in a context of callous hedonism; technology has ensnared the lifeworld in a network of rationalism—a world replete with delinquency, violence, and incivility, in which man is at war with himself and against all . . . and where the solitary individual merges into an anonymous and hostile crowd.[17]

This situation is indicative of a deeper human malaise: "Why is it that the offices of psychologists offices are never empty? Why is there massive use of antidepressants? Why this collective anomie?"[18] Parallel sentiments have been voiced throughout the ENR. Krebs writes that the contemporary world is characterized by a "tragedy of disloyalty: the uprooting of every culture, estrangement from our true natures, the atomization of man, the leveling of values, the uniformity of life."[19] In England, ENR ideologist Michael Walker bemoans that "no loyalty is expected to anyone or anything beyond the shore of the little ego. Modern man is deactivated and deracinated . . . Although seldom alone, modern man is deeply lonely."[20] The same disillusionment pervades the manifesto of the Spanish ENR, which rejects the modern world's "passive nihilism of material well-being . . . our souls suffer from the lack of meaning of this civilization." To overcome this depraved condition, "spaces of resistance" must be opened up to inaugurate a "cultural dawn."[21]

The hope for the growth of a new age arising out of the ruins of contemporary society is characteristic of all of the ideologues of the ENR. For them, the imbalances and troubles of modern societies are a sure sign that humanity is passing through a dark interregnum destined to end with the dawn of a radiant future. In their own estimation, ENR writers are not conservatives. They are revolutionaries. As Krebs replied when asked about conservatism: "To conserve what? The values, the laws, the ideas, the institutions of the System? To conserve what we fight against?"[22] For him and his colleagues, the decadence of the modern age requires a total transformation of society.

The revolutionary attitude of the ENR is intellectually and spiritually indebted to the "conservative revolution" against liberal modernity that was espoused by a cluster of German intellectuals in the interwar period.[23] In reaction to the existential anguish triggered by instrumental rationality, secularism, and loss of communal bonds, these young German right-wing intellectuals aspired to a "revolution [that] begins in the souls of men. It is the dawn of a new mentality and a new self-knowledge. It is this; or it is our doom."[24] As with the ENR, the chief enemy of these conservatives was liberalism, and their rejection of the modern world was imminently spiritual. As Moeller van den Bruck proclaimed: "The true revolutionary spirit which bursts asunder the bonds of fate is found not in transitions but in beginnings."[25] The same "cultural despair" and the ensuing urgent search for a "new faith"[26] are visible in many ENR writings. For example, de Benoist writes that "European nihilism is thus in no way the 'rule of *nothing.*' It is the obligatory *transition* to another beginning."[27]

Although words such as *renaissance, rebirth,* and *revival* abound in the ENR's discourses, they admit that the evolutionary process will inevitably be chaotic and painful, for "at the end of every age and during the period of transition, destruction and ugliness rages."[28] As the corrupt modern world collapses, it is the "responsibility" of those who "live in the interregnum" to prepare for a "postcatastrophic conception of the world."[29] Thus, "we are, as long as we know it, understand it and want it, the precursors of the imminent morning of another world."[30] Through undertaking concerted metapolitical action, the ENR intellectual vanguard has the crucial role in smoothing this transition. But their effort will end happily in "the appearance of thousands of auroras, i.e., the birth of *sovereign spaces* liberated from the domination of the modern."[31] In these liberated spaces, where the old gives way to the new, "everything is possible."[32]

The Roots of Evil

Just as we have seen in Latin America, for the ENR the tragedy of the modern world is specifically a product of the West. The major bête noire of the ENR is the West's pretension to universalism—which has assumed the form of an American-led globalization (or *mondialization*). ENR intellectuals trace this pervasive modern faith back to its religious origins. Faye writes that Western civilization is the "monstrous child of . . . the egalitarian ideologies created by Judeo-Christian monotheism."[33] Similarly, de Benoist asserts: "The pathologies of the modern world are the illegitimate but obvious offspring of Christian theology."[34] Here is how he describes the sources of the evils of Western modernity:

> Throughout its history, the West has constantly sought to make the world recognize "universal" values, themes, social, political and organizational methods that, in reality, are intrinsic [to the West]. The way employed to reach this goal has always been by mimetic injunction. First, the West claimed to bring the dogmas of the "true faith" (Christian) to other cultures. Next, [the West] aimed at exporting "civilization" and "progress" through colonization. Today, it advocates "development" and the "rights of man." Successively, the "three M's" (missionaries, the military, and merchants) have tried to *convert* other peoples to a form of religious, political, and economic universalism that today we know very well to be nothing but a veiled form of ethnocentrism.[35]

According to the ENR, the "pathologies of the modern world" are intrinsically connected to the "totalitarian" nature of Judeo-Christian monotheism, which has imposed the absolute primacy of one absolute and uncreated being (God) ruling over an abstract humanity.

Under the hegemonic Judeo-Christian belief system, earlier pluralistic and polytheistic connections to nature and to the divine have been summarily rejected. By devaluing the multiple forms of alterity and worship, the Judeo-Christian model has subjected individual and popular diversity to the worship of one God. From the New Right perspective, totalitarianism, presently embodied in the "project of Westernization" and previously in Soviet communism, emerges every time a "plural, polytheistic and contradictory totality is replaced by a rigid, 'monotheistic' system that is based on an explanatory uniqueness and a fatally reductive unilateralism."[36]

Another disaster resulting from the Judeo-Christian ethos is the disenchantment of the natural world. According to the standard ENR analysis, monotheism introduced a radical distinction between God and nature. "Pushed onto the profane side . . . (nature) finds itself transformed into an object" and is irredeemably devalued.[37] As it loses its place within the realm of the sacred, nature finds itself "appropriated by human reason, in conformance with the injunction of Genesis, which enjoins man to rule the earth." As a result, "what the ancients called the 'soul of the world' suddenly disappears."[38] The degradation of the world as "pure matter lacking Gods and soul" has destroyed the ancient spiritual connection between the human and the natural within a sacralized cosmos.[39] Over time, the regent Judeo-Christian conceptualization of nature as an object to be manipulated became the precursor to modernity's twin creeds of universal reason (utilitarianism) and infinite progress (the secular form of a millenarian and unilinear understanding of history).

As a consequence of this argument and influenced by Nietzsche's portrait of "life-affirming" paganism, many New Right theorists[40] have turned to pre-Christian beliefs and practices as part of their revolutionary "philosophical disposition."[41] Faye's statement is emblematic: "Paganism is essentially the cult of the real and of life in all its dimensions (biological, astronomical, physical) and, contrary to the religions of salvation, it refuses to build a meta-reality, a lie, a phantasm . . . rather, it looks directly at the sweet and hard tragedy of living."[42] Above all, the ENR believe pagan sources offer a potential remedy for the existential-ontological homelessness and uprootedness that characterizes modern life. In this belief they echo other contemporary neopagan movements.[43] Like one of their heroes, the German philosopher Martin Heidegger, ENR thinkers indict the rationalistic and detached Western view of humanity and favor the pursuit of mystical unity instead.

For example, in his book *On Being a Pagan*, de Benoist describes the modern urge for a "spiritual *re-presentation* of society" that would reground it and permit "another beginning" in a world "where everything is collapsing into the sunset of the absolute transatlantic West and a once great history."[44] The image of a modern world bereft by a Heideggarian "darkening of the world" and "flight of the gods"[45] is omnipresent in ENR writings, repeating a theme familiar not only to romantics (such as Friedrich Hölderlin) but also to conservative revolutionaries like Ernst Jünger, who portrayed modern life as the era of the death of Gods (creative and spiritual forces) and the triumph of the Titans (rational and technological forces).[46] To forestall this dire destiny, ENR theorists like Faye regularly say that "new Gods must be invented"[47] while Krebs declares that "the voices of its Gods will be heard again" during the forthcoming rebirth of a spiritually revitalized Europe.[48]

Along with the repudiation of the Judeo-Christian tradition, another one of the most extraordinary claims of the European New Right is its refutation of the taken-for-granted notion that Europe is part of the West.[49] For them, the current shared culture of Europe is an expression and consequence of an imposed foreign *Anglo-American* worldview. "Western civilization" is a "calamitous concept."[50] Anglo-American hegemony is the "number one enemy" of the "self-determination of peoples and vitality of their cultures."[51] The "Europe of Western civilization" is a bastardized version of the "real Europe."[52] The true and authentic roots of Europe, dating back to pre-Christian times, are intrinsically non-Western—that is, non–Anglo-American. Unfortunately, during the course of its history Europe has forgotten its authentic nature and has moved away from its primordial values; seduced and suborned by a false and alien Western liberal ideology, it has fallen from "institutional holism to modern individualism."[53] Faye asks: "How can the peoples of Europe endure the humiliation of being westernized? Those who identify with what is truly European must feel alienated in the modern world." The only solution is to "decolonize" Europe from the Anglo-American "universalist project to convert the world to a 'society' directed by the economy."[54] The task is arduous, but Europe is not alone in the battle against evil: "The Europe of Western Civilization constitutes merely a *place*, albeit the most important, among other zones of the Western occupation of the earth."[55]

But to achieve true decolonization, Europe must free itself from the most vicious dogma of modern existence: individualism.[56] The "original sin that we oppose is not an economic mode of production but a conception of humanity.

... Absolute individualism is the interpretative key of our current historical times."[57] For the ENR, the radical individualism that shapes the modern world originated in the universal egalitarian ethos of the Enlightenment, which in turn is said to be the secularized expression of the Judeo-Christian faith in a universally human moral essence. A second destructive consequence of this value system is the notion of human rights, which is frequently derided by the ENR as a strategic weapon of "Western ethnocentrism." For ENR theorists, the concept of human rights is based on a "contractual and above all individualistic anthropology, on the idea of an abstract man, prepolitical in nature and nonsocial, promoted as self-sufficient, and with the sole aim of perpetually searching his material self-interest."[58] Human rights, then, is really a tool in the "colonizing" project of Western modernity.

Accordingly, universalistic and abstract concepts of human rights and the generic individual reflect and appeal to crass bourgeois aspirations. The bourgeoisie are consistently portrayed as tireless and contemptible seekers after "homogenous and universal needs; well-being, consumption, security."[59] They are the despised "homo universalis."[60] The instrumental mentality spread by the bourgeoisie is anchored in Cartesian rationalism and in theories of humankind as an infinitely malleable tabula rasa. For the ENR thinkers, this false ideology pervades every sphere of contemporary existence—even the human heart and soul. It is the "enemy within."[61] In the bourgeois worldview, "we always seek utility above all. In everything we behave as the trader in the market. We always search for individualism, the primacy of reason, the orientation toward the future, the cult of profit, the attraction for the new."[62] These instrumental values have been deeply internalized within the psyche of modern humanity, marginalizing the humane and ancient cultural values of honor, tradition, and respect that give life its ultimate meaning.[63] The result is what French traditionalist philosopher René Guénon has called a "quantitative civilization."[64]

For the ENR, the passage from industrial capitalism to a postindustrial global financial capitalism has only reinforced the subordination of politics, culture, and faith to the authority of the bourgeois ideal of *homo economicus*. The material imprisonment of humanity is directly linked to never-ending *consumerism*, fueled by the profusion of goods and services available in the globalized market society. As the manifesto of the French New Right proclaims, "liberal economy has translated the ideology of progress into a religion of growth: the 'ever more' of consumption that is supposed to lead humanity to happiness."[65] In this latest and ultimate stage of capitalism, the "colonization of our imagination by mercantile values" has given birth to a new "anthropological type," a "perpetual teenager addicted to nonstop consumption"[66] whose only goal in life "is the constant search for his material interest, which is understood to be the maximum consumption of objects."[67] The contemporary obsession with the body (diets, health foods, botox, jogging!) is really just one more sign of this cult of the self.[68] As one New Right spokesman protests, in a world ruled by appetite, "our desire is everything. Our will is nothing. This is the 'nontotalitarian system.' This is the rule of Narcissus."[69] Yet, despite the irresistible pleasures of consumerism, the New Right ideologues have somehow managed to resist its blandishments and have vowed to wage a moral battle against "humanity created in the exclusive image and likeness of the Western *homo consumans*."[70]

To bolster their case against the corrupting consumerist worldview of the bourgeois, the ENR draws on a wide range of sources, from both the left and right. Often quoted is American social critic Christopher Lasch, who portrayed Western society degenerating into a hedonistic and acquisitive "culture of narcissism."[71] The work of French anthropologist Marcel Mauss serves to bolster the argument that a society based on reciprocal gift exchange would be "more human" because it would cultivate the solidarity and moral bonds sorely lacking in today's repressive capitalist world.[72] The 1960s indictment of modern liberal capitalism by Herbert Marcuse and the Frankfurt School has been appropriated by many ENR writers who believe that these philosophers support their own rejection of dehumanizing self-enslavement of humanity through consumerism. And de Benoist has even rehabilitated Marx's theory of reification and alienation as a crucial issue of today's society: "[Marx] understood that the capitalist system was an anthropological system, even more than a purely economic system."[73]

The bourgeois civilization and the merchant society despised by the ENR are epitomized by America. Enmity toward the "American way of life" has been one of the most significant and most repeated themes of the ENR. In particular, they echo Julius Evola, the twentieth-century paragon of the Italian revolutionary right (and a defender of a "spiritual" and "mystical" fascism), who vehemently decried America as the epicenter of today's materialist and decadent modern civilization. Evola despised the United States because it lacked "any background of transcendence, inner light, and true spirituality."[74] According to de Benoist, "the original defect of America, which confuses its own history [with the history] of modernity, is that it was built from Puritan thought and the philosophy of the Enlightenment."[75] Combining these two ideologies, America has imagined itself to be a "new promised land," a "model of a universal republic" that, with the passing of time, will regenerate and even create a new humanity.[76] Taking his cue from Max Weber's *Protestant Ethic*, de Benoist asserts that, for Americans, worldly success is a sign of divine favor while capitalism is envisaged as the ultimate pathway for the betterment of humanity. The destructive and arrogant American eschatology predicts that a bourgeois lifestyle is "destined" to be imposed everywhere, resulting in world-wide homogenization, deracination, and deculturation. Krebs laments that Europe "has sacrificed all its ideals to Mammon," the idol that "rules America since its origins,"[77] and excoriates the "Americanized human fauna that can be found in all corners of the earth and that constitutes, without a doubt, the greatest enemy of all peoples."[78] America's ultimate aim, argues Faye, is a "social experience of the end of history" in which all humanity universally adapts the American capitalist model as its own.[79]

ENR writings and speeches dealing with the hegemony of the American way of life regularly warn against "cultural genocide" and "ethnocide." At a GRECE conference dedicated to the "danger" posed by the United States, de Benoist cautioned his audience: "Everything comes down to knowing if we want to end up like the (American) Indians."[80] But that fate is hard to avoid because the hegemonic materialist, utilitarian, and antihuman ideology of the United States is disseminated everywhere through the mass media of movies, music, and the entertainment industry in general. Media exposure almost automatically incites imitation among the malleable audience, resulting in a "subtle colonization, held by osmosis, total assimilation, [triggering] a psychological process that activates the subjects' demand for goods."[81] For the ENR theorists, the inexorable spread of the American consumerist ethic is the "biggest enterprise of spiritual colonization that has been ever practiced by any power."[82]

As the American media onslaught permeates the social fabric, it weakens the resistance of those under its sway and convinces them of the inadequacy of their own cultures, in the name of "'universal' guidelines."[83] These deracinated unfortunates then lose their unique cultural identities and are irredeemably merged into the mass of willing consumers. *Homo Americanus*, a "distinct sociobiological species," is everywhere.[84] "Americans for us are not necessarily those who hold an American passport—Americans are all those whatever their nationality who pursue the American dream . . . who would reduce our citizenry to a passive mass, an undifferentiated market potential."[85] This process is symbolized as the "Coca-colonization" or the "McDonaldization of society." It is the insidious "triumph of Mickey."[86] The ultimate hope, as British New Rightist Troy Southgate writes, is to "survive Coca-McDeath."[87]

In sum, America is guilty of promoting a vulgar culture of spectacle that reduces the human condition to the crass pursuit of money and status. The result is the total surrender of the sacred to the profane, the particular to the universal, the individual to the mass. By its nature, America can provide only a "material homeland," and the patriotism of Americans can be only the weak loyalty of the "merchant order," far removed from the profound feelings of Europeans bound to the "long memory" of their histories and cultures.[88]

The Search for Redemption

In the literature and rhetoric of the ENR, *globalization, Westernization,* and *Americanization* are used interchangeably to describe the same worldwide imposition of a *specific* worldview and model of society on humanity's diversity of cultures, traditions, and ways of living.[89] As we have seen, the impulse toward homogenization is understood to be the last stage of a long-term process: "Globalism is simply a new name for the old egalitarianism and universalism of Judeo-Christian liberal capitalism."[90] In its essence, globalization constitutes the expansion worldwide of a capitalistic New World Order. This imperial system relies on the power of the culture industry and the pursuit of "the rights of humankind" to amalgamate lifestyles and mentalities, remaking the entire world in the West's image. Globalization also "spreads a philosophy of life that gives absolute priority to material happiness, to the logic of profit, to the law of money. Its outcome is the transformation of the world into an amusement park, in a supermarket of entertainment. Its motto is: To live is to consume."[91] Capitalism therefore succeeds where communism failed, creating a borderless world inhabited by a faceless new person, the consumer.

The ENR's indictment of the totalizing economism of globalization coincides with despair over the resulting impoverishment of the human spirit. Some characteristic statements include: "The issue is whether a society is capable of organizing itself in the long term without any form of the sacred, without possessing any unity higher than the immediate."[92] "In seeking to find the common factor of humanity which links all members of the species homo sapiens, (globalism) is obliged to reduce us to the common biological

factors and ignore the spiritual side to our nature. . . . In this sense globalization is a kind of anti-evolutionary, even reactionary, trend, which encourages
mankind to return to a biologically unsophisticated, materialistic and superficial fatalistic acceptance of life."[93] The global capitalist system is "incapable
of giving meaning to existence" and is "deaf to the demands of the spirit."[94] It
also dissolves the continuity of past-present-future in favor of slavish worship
of the present, which operates "only in the ledger of immediacy and efficacy."[95]
It is dominated by a "uniform ideology convinced that it can make the present
eternal and that is afraid of any nonprogrammed future."[96]

In a contrast to some of the other antimodernist ideologies we will analyze,
the ENR critique of globalization is generally nonconspiratorial. As stated
in Walker's magazine *The Scorpion*, "the ultimate engine driving the Global
Greed Machine currently devouring the world is not a plot but a process, not
conspiratorial but cybernetic in origin."[97] In fact, many ENR thinkers are
overtly critical of any mentality that posits a hidden hand behind the contemporary evils of globalism.[98] Yet, the end result is the same: Liberal globalization will inevitably end with the universal ascendance of Nietzsche's pathetic
last man. Krebs describes this pitiful condition:

> In the zenith of the era of egalitarianism, when the disintegrated reality of
> the mercantile society has finally managed to dissolve all identities, a doc-
> trine emerges from the twilight of peoples mentioned by Heidegger, a doctrine
> that "extends itself like cold spreads over a dead soul." From this [emerges] a
> type of man empty of any interior, who seems to have suffered a psychological
> lobotomy, a *mechanical man*, whose blind technomorphic look cannot con-
> template the multiform face of a universe that, in order to develop itself in all
> the originality of its differences, must be protected from the homogenizing
> universalisms bent on forcing the natural diversities of a multisided world into
> a single mold.[99]

De Benoist agrees. Today's Westerners "remind me . . . of societies dominated
by the reign of the mediocre, in which atomized individuals are concerned
solely with their own private affairs, each one trying to maximize his best
interest in the here and now."[100] For the ENR, the nineteenth-century German
philosopher's ugly prophecy has finally been realized. But these dark times
can still be reversed and human nature healed.

The ENR has long described its struggle against the menacing homogenization of modern times as an "affirmation of the cause of peoples against a

standardized world society . . . a Cosmopolis of the dead."[101] The choice of imagery reveals the urgency of the problem. "We are at war," wrote de Benoist, "a war in which the history and destiny of peoples is at stake."[102] Accordingly, "the struggle of the future will not be the opposition between the right and the left, socialism and liberalism, but [it will be between] the authentic forces of rootedness that defend the cause of peoples—of *all* the peoples— against the American-centered technomorphic system."[103] This polarizing vision pervades all of the ENR writings. For them, the fault lines of the twenty-first century are "between two conceptions of the world, two ways of seeing the future [and of] conceiving humankind: On one side there are the social masses, state-owned, the planetary egalitarian technocosmos, the cold monster that Nietzsche warned us about; on the other side, the organic communities, the political and cultural identities that reflect the natural polyphony of the world."[104] To win this battle, the notion of organic communities, based on historical and ethnic identities, must enter into the collective consciousness via a "new declaration of the rights of peoples."[105]

The need to protect particularism and differentiation emerges from the ENR's inveterate opposition to all universalisms, which, as we have seen, are regarded as inherently totalitarian. Though initially theorized in terms of essentialist racial and biological distinctions, over time the ENR ideology of difference has been reconceived and promoted in a specifically cultural manner.[106] In de Benoist's words, "Universalism begins by imposing a preconceived or abstract form to the particular. On the contrary, I believe we can only reach universality through particulars, not the other way around."[107] The ENR asserts that individuals belong to humanity *only* through the mediation of a particular culture. Communities and cultures must be defended because they express the spirit of a specific context, a unique way of life, personality, and destiny. To reinforce this perspective, ENR writings refer to romantic anthropological writings, such as eighteenth century theorist Johann Herder's assertion that each culture has its own integrity and metaphysical "creative genius," as well as evoking more recent theories, such as Konrad Lorenz's ethological claim for the *inherited* nature of the biological and cultural conditions that determine human diversity[108] and to Arnold Gehlen's view that every culture provides a distinct, permanent, and vital "second nature to man."[109] For these writers, and their modern ENR interpreters, the diversity of cultures represents an absolute good that must be preserved because, as stated in the ENR manifesto, "all attempts to unify them end up destroying them."[110]

Following this logic, universalist thinking is understood to be intrinsically racist, precisely because it does not value differences. De Benoist decries assimilation as "reducing the Other to the Same."[111] For him, fraudulent neoliberal "humanitarian" racism only recognizes the other "as long as he gets rid of his otherness, his heterogeneity: he is considered a 'human being like me' and is accepted as long as he is not different."[112] An authentic antiracism, in contrast, opposes both exclusion and assimilation and is committed to the "irreducible plurality of the human species."[113] For this reason, those who are part of the ENR criticize other antiglobalization theorists who adhere to universalistic worldviews. Globalization must be contested "in the name of peoples not 'multitudes;'[114] in the name of freedom [and not] in the name of the 'rights of man.' "[115]

Accordingly, members of the ENR defend its strong anti-immigration stand by arguing that policies of open borders are a part of a "deculturalizing Occidentalism," driven by capitalism, which aims at uprooting peoples (starting with the immigrants) and fomenting widespread loss of identity both among the immigrants and in the host society.[116] The argument that each culture has an absolute right to its own specificity[117] has made many ENR members sympathetic to the "identity-driven resurgence of the Arab-Muslim world,"[118] which is praised as "the most well-chosen affront ever inflicted on the civilizational utopia of the American model."[119] For these theorists, the "awakening of Islam" is not "a threat but instead a hope."[120] If Muslims "don't attempt to set up a monotheistic stranglehold in its place, [Islam] is a useful weapon against American globalization."[121] From this point of view, jihadism is a natural identity-based reaction to the hegemony of the West and a normal "symptom of a general crisis of identities."[122] In the wake of the September 11 attacks, de Benoist pointedly equated al-Qaeda's ideology with Western neoliberalism. "The idea that a globalized free trade represents the only possible horizon for all cultures of the world and is thus necessary and desirable is no less 'fundamentalist' than the [idea] that sharia should be imposed everywhere." De Benoist warned that the New Right must refuse any polarizing "jihad vs. McWorld" dichotomy. We "need to reject the jihad without becoming instruments of the McWorld."[123]

This is easier said than done. Some members of the New Right have vehemently rejected de Benoist's policy of awarding émigré communities the "right to difference" within their host nations. For example, Guillaume Faye has argued that the only possible response to the "colonization" of Europe by

Third World countries, and especially by Muslims, is a defensive ethnocentri-cism.[124] To Faye and his followers, combat against the Americanization of Eu-rope is still a worthy and important cause, but the focus of resistance should now be the demographic and cultural threat posed to all of Europe by Islam. Arguing that de Benoist and his followers have lost their sense of priorities, this dissident wing of the ENR has posited that a homogenous, postnational, European ethnicity, categorized as white, is on the verge of being extinguished by Muslim advances.[125]

Authentic Democracy in a Multipolar World

Despite internal arguments, the ENR is united in its belief that American-style capitalism, based on the twin evils of universalism and individualism, has fundamentally debased biodiversity and fragmented all human attach-ments rooted in history, tradition, and memory. Against an abstract, mecha-nistic, and impersonal order, members of the ENR advocate the "return to communities and to a politics of human dimensions."[126] This means the re-discovery of a primordial natural form of existence. "What do we want? [We want] our world to rediscover the humanity [based on] the organic."[127] Be-cause it grows naturally, from its own roots, an organic society exists within its own specific cultural, spiritual, and ethnic context. It is "a personalized expression of a collective way of life, not a 'consumer commodity' marketed to generic individuals situated in anonymous, indifferent social systems."[128] From this holistic standpoint, liberal democracy, heir to Christianity and the Enlightenment and founded on the notion of *individual* rights, is not a true democracy. Rather, an *authentic* democracy must be based on the sovereignty of the people, such as the democracy of ancient Athens.[129]

Unfortunately, under the corrosive regime of Americanized globalization, the feeble authority of liberal democracy has been unable to resist capture by a utilitarian, depersonalized, and technocratic elite (a "New Class"), that places politics under the domination of the economy and treats government as "a market, depoliticized, neutralized, ruled by 'experts.'"[130] The acquisition of democracy by oligarchies,[131] has further widened the gap between the people and the governing elite. As a result, democracy as it is practiced today is a far cry from what democracy *once was* and *should be* again. According to Walker, "The way is long to establish a genuinely democratic community of free men and women."[132] An authentic government, as envisioned by the ENR, would be a "return to a direct democracy, organic and communitarian."[133] Radically decentralized, such a government would foster popular participation from the bottom up and thereby reinvolve "the self-absorbed consumer and the passive spectator citizen"[134] who, by participation, would be able to break free from the shackles of the anonymous, distant, unresponsive, oligarchic, "representative" democracies of today.

This process requires rethinking the nation-state, which is castigated as an outdated construct based on assimilation and the destruction of distinction.[135] Paradoxically, globalization—despite its negative effects—has also had the positive outcome of destabilizing the destructive nation-state system by collapsing the "great national narratives," replacing them with a horizontal network of "regional narratives and local roots" that offers a better chance for the "preservation of identities."[136] Remaining indigenous populations are examples for the future because they still retain a "cosmic and holistic vision of the world in which the notions of tradition, community, and clan have not yet lost their meaning."[137] By giving primacy to local, cultural, historical, and tribal aspects of social life, the ENR aims to reestablish the lost organic solidarities among humanity, community, and the environment.

The ENR's emphasis on establishing an "organic" linkage between the individual, the collective, and the natural world coincides with a denunciation of the destructive ecological consequences of Western materialism that mirrors the fears expressed in many other movements.[138] In the ENR worldview, the conscious individual is primarily an "inhabitant" of Earth, not a mere "producer or consumer."[139] As such, every aware person has the obligation to maintain the ecological balance. In contrast, the Promethean American-style pursuit of unlimited progress, never-ending production, and unbridled consumerism brings about inevitable environmental disaster. The solution, according to de Benoist, is a "postgrowth" society. Unlike proponents of "sustainable development" who think the environmental crisis can be corrected within the current capitalist system, de Benoist proposes a compete overhaul of the "mercantile logic, the economic imagination, the monetary system, and the unlimited expansion of capital."[140] Humankind must reposition itself in relationship with the world, as a *part* of the Earth, not separated or above it. This proposal—a call for a new human modesty—is meant to echo the "pagan" harmony between humanity and the cosmos. It ends anthropocentrism by displacing humankind from the "exclusive position that Christianity and classical humanism had assigned it."[141]

This view coincides with the ENR's consistent call for Europe to distance itself from the "Americanized" Anglo-Saxon West and to affirm a distinctly "European" position in the world. This call was loudest during the bipolar international conflict of the Cold War. Resisting taking sides in the great power rivalry between the United States and the Soviet Union, the ENR theorists argued instead that Europe should pursue an alternative strategy of alliance with Third World nations. This policy was natural because Europe, like the Third World, was "occupied" by both the West and the East and was in need of decolonization. "Military colonization or moral colonization, it is always colonization." As an editorial of the GRECE journal *Éléments* proclaimed: "We certainly don't want to become robots in order to avoid being enslaved."[142] Europe must not fall under the rule of the Gulag nor succumb to the American "air-conditioned Hell" that is "killing souls."[143] Rather, the continent must find a Third Way "between the rule of the party propagandist and the rule of the commercial salesman."[144]

After the demise of the Soviet Union, the ENR feared that United States was now on the verge of achieving "absolute domination of the world."[145] The first Gulf War was viewed by GRECE as the opening salvo of a "Third World War," lasting one hundred years, waged against "the peoples determined to live against the Western-American system of death."[146] The subsequent intervention of NATO in the Balkans and the Afghan and Iraq wars were similarly understood as part of the American plan for world conquest: "War and globalization go hand in hand. Militarization sustains the conquest of new economic frontiers aimed at imposing a market society at a planetary level."[147]

To challenge the destructive designs of the demonic America hyperpower, ENR theorists call for the establishment of an international multipolar order. The model for this coming order is taken from German political philosopher Carl Schmitt's defense of a "new *nomos* of the earth": a united but pluralistic community that guarantees world equilibrium and generates a new, balanced, international law.[148] Following Schmitt's suggestion that the new nomos should be constituted by an equilibrium of several independent geopolitical, cultural, and civilizational blocs (each with its own Monroe Doctrine),[149] the ENR defends a multipolar system (also described as a pluriverse) in which Europe would be a united and autonomous power, committed to its *own* "project of civilization."[150] This European project must not follow the pattern of the nation-state (which is by nature centralized and homogenous) or economism (the "mercantile" and technocratic project of Brussels). Instead a federalized, decentralized Europe will respect local and regional diversities, as did the Austro-Hungarian Empire. A reversion to the imperial model is viewed favorably because "[Empire] always sought to establish an equilibrium between center and periphery, between sameness and diversity, unity and multiplicity."[151] The uniquely European realm of the twenty-first century would be ruled by the imperial principle from above and by direct democracy from below.[152] There is no mention, however, of who would replace the Hapsburgs.

Increasingly relevant for the geopolitics of the ENR is the role played by Russia. As de Benoist states: "Globalization makes it necessary to think of the world in term of continents," which calls for new alliances and the potential benefits of a Paris–Berlin–Moscow axis,[153] while Tarchi sees in Russia "the most logical ally" of Europe in a future multipolar scenario.[154] This trend is manifested in the dissemination across Europe of neo-Eurasianism, promoted by, among others, Russian political geographer Alexander Dugin. Eurasianism is not new. The idea that Russia and the West are incompatible and that the material and spiritual destiny of Russia lies in the steppes of Eurasia was originally spread in Europe by Russian immigrants in the interwar period.[155] But these ideas gained a new impetus in the last decades of the twentieth century. A prominent voice of Russia's New Right, Dugin (who has been close to GRECE and de Benoist since the early 1990s) denounced the post–Soviet Union emulation of the West, announcing that the "rebirth of Russia" would depend on the nation freeing itself from the "American dream" and the "myth of development." As Dugin suggests in an editorial of his journal *Elementy*, Russia then could join the "peoples fighting for their cultural survival against the biggest machine of debasement of souls ever put in place in the [history] of mankind: the American-centered West,"[156] which "takes on the role of both a strategic and cultural model as the . . . hemisphere where the Sun of History sets."[157]

Dugin's geopolitics is built on a bipolar view of history as a duel between distinctive land-based civilizations ("tellurocracies") and homogenizing sea-based powers ("thalassocracies").[158] De Benoist sees today's world in similar terms: "The alternative between a unipolar and a multipolar world is associated with the opposition between the Sea and the Earth, because a multipolar world implies the territorial notion of border."[159] To Dugin, with the onslaught of globalization, which is nothing but an assault of American "Atlanticism" on the rest of the world, the battle between "eternal Rome and eternal Carthage"[160] has entered its apocalyptic final stage. According to the "Manifesto of the Eurasianist Movement," Russia is destined to "play the role of Europe's liberator, this time from American political, economic, and cultural occupation."[161] At the center of Eurasia is Russia's own mission of "transforming Russian distinctiveness into a universal model of culture, into a vision of the world that is alternative to Atlanticist globalization, but also global in its own way."[162] Inspired by Dugin's polarized geopolitics, an "International Eurasianist movement" has been created in Europe and elsewhere.[163] In these circles it is common to find references to the "spiritual unity of Eurasia" as the source of continental resistance to the West.[164] Thus, according to Southgate, Eurasia is "not a uniform bloc in which cultural diversity and regional autonomy are stifled or obliterated" but "a general stream of life, love and liberty which flows in the same direction for the general interest of all."[165]

A related geopolitical project—supported by the racial wing of the ENR—involves the creation of the Eurosiberia federation, stretching from Lisbon to Vladivostok. The "Continent Europa Foundation," a Russophile think tank, has proclaimed that such a geopolitical realignment is a decisive step in the creation of a "new Europe" and is necessary for the survival of aboriginal European peoples. According to its Swedish founder, "The path to European freedom goes through Moscow."[166] The biggest challenges faced by this imagined ethnopolitical entity are competition from the "American mercantile thalassocracy" and, more urgently, the ongoing colonization of Europe by Islam.[167] Though it has been expressed in different ways—from Eurasianism to a European federation—the overall geopolitical orientation of the ENR has been consistently imperial. A cosmopolitan renewal of empire is seen as the best option to preserve diversity in unity and the only way to oppose the unified and homogenous forces of the New World Order of Americanized Western globalism.

As we have shown, the ENR insists that history has not ended in the triumph of the present system. Rather, humanity is moving through a chaotic phase of transition from domination by an inhuman neoliberal global power to a reenchanted and spiritually renewed world of unity in difference. For the new era to arrive, people need to overcome their fatalistic resignation to this world: "In the meantime the most important thing is to fight against the idea that there are no alternatives to the current model of society, to make people understand that they are not living under a horizon of fatalism . . . history remains open." To de Benoist, "People have internalized the idea that, ultimately, there is no other possible society. They feel a profound malaise in living in this society, but they live in an optic of fatality."[168] Despite their stated abhorrence for universalistic thinking, the ENR remedy for the ills of modernity is in fact totalizing and global—even though the sought-for solution is the unanimous embrace of pluralism. This common quest for global emancipation is post-national; it transcends borders. The ENR struggle is often described as the struggle for the liberation of people everywhere. And, despite doctrinal differences, all the ENR theorists agree: "The future needs the return to ancestral values. That applies the whole world over."[169]

To overcome a system that "threatens the humanity of man himself" activists must unify in "working for another world that is not just a transcendent vision or utopia, but a new common world."[170] The end result will be a purified human culture, united in valuing distinction and the environment. As historian Roger Griffin has written: "The groundedness so desperately sought by the ENR must be provided by none other than planet earth itself."[171]

EUROPEAN POPULIST NATIONALISM

The Dark Cloud of Globalism

Like the ENR, other Europeans also perceive a dark, sinister cloud of globalism hanging over the decaying nation. While some watch in passive bewilderment, for European ultranationalists, standing by is not an option. Act they must. Refusing the label of extremism, which they say has been imposed upon them by their enemies,[172] they perceive themselves as the "national opposition" or the "national alternative." In fact, the most widespread ideological feature of these parties is their self-identification as defenders of the nation and its people.[173] This is so even though each movement has different roots and traditions—for example, the Lega Nord (Northern League) emerges from the struggle for regional autonomy, whereas the British National Party (BNP) is heir to indigenous neofascism—and even though some are more electorally successful than others.

According to the vast majority of these right-wing European nationalists, the evils currently plaguing the homeland (whichever homeland it may be), plunging it into decadence and driving it toward extinction, originate in what the BNP has called the "evil spawn of globalism."[174] As Jean-Marie Le Pen, the patriarch of the contemporary European populist-nationalist right, declared in his closing speech to the Thirteenth Congress of the Front National (National Front): "For thirty-five years, since its foundation, the National Front has been engaged in combat for the nation and the French people who are threatened by moral decadence and lax globalist policies."[175]

These parties unanimously believe that the free flow of capital, goods, services, and expertise that defines neoliberal globalization tragically undermines national sovereignty and increases human insecurity. As Umberto Bossi, the long-time leader of the Italian Northern League, stated: "The mystics of the market assure us that we will be all richer in the future, but in the meantime I fear we will be all dead."[176] However, according to British nationalist leader Nick Griffin, the catastrophic crisis that will inevitably destroy the neoliberal one-world economy has one positive potential: The chaos that will inevitably follow the collapse will provide the vanguard national party with an opportunity to seize power and impose the protectionist policies needed to counterbalance the adverse effects of an unregulated free market.[177] The financial collapse of 2008–2009 was "expected" by these parties because the worldwide turmoil was, in the words of Le Pen, "the biological child of globalism, the ideology that worships globalization, instead of controlling it."[178]

Although shielding the nation from a corporate-driven world trading system is vital, the imperative to defend it against the concomitant dangers of cultural and civilizational disintegration is even more important. According to the nationalist right, rampant globalization will inevitably eradicate all natural attachments to the family, to the community, and to the nation, creating an inhuman world, totally integrated and homogenous. The critique of contemporary society by these parties is based in a familiar dichotomy: authentic local identity (national, cultural, ethnic, and in a few cases racial) versus inauthentic global unity. The populist-nationalist discussion of an array of issues (immigration, law and order, social anomie, or loss of sovereignty) is ultimately framed according to this basic opposition. According to Bruno Mégret:[179] "The struggle of the future will not be between Marxism and capitalism, but globalism against nationalism. . . . the party of the foreigners [against] the party of France."[180] As a National Front magazine states, their party is the "only movement" that maintains "identity politics and national ideas in the face of cosmopolitanism and globalism."[181] Similarly, Italy's Bossi states: "Enterprises, peoples, and identity oppose virtual finance and rootlessness. These are the terms of the political dialectic that is progressing. Once in Europe it was atheism against Christianity; now it is materialism against identity."[182] And Pinto-Coelho, the leader of the Portuguese nationalists, proclaims: "Nations are the only alternative to inhuman globalization, the natural hope of salvation against the antinatural monster of globalism."[183]

From the perspective of the nationalists, one way that globalization weakens local identity is by promoting massive immigration to destroy the cultural and ethnic integrity of European nations. Current policies favoring immigration are seen as expressions of the triumph of the American pluralistic melting pot philosophy, which has conquered Europe's ancient culturally distinct communities. As Bossi warned his followers:

> The goal [of globalization] is to transform our country into a multiracial, multiethnic, and multireligious society. The American model is advancing: We will all live in an immense cosmopolitan metropolis where there will be no trace of the tradition and culture of our people.[184]

However, unlike right-wing ideologies of the past, today's populist-nationalist rejection of multiculturalism is not articulated in terms of the racial, ethnic, or cultural *superiority* of Europeans. Rather, these parties have adopted the European New Right's ideology of *differentialism* and argue that their anti-immigration policy preserves the cultural diversity and authenticity of each ethnic community on Earth.[185] In a typical example, Mégret asserted: "We are the champions of the defense of our identity; we must be glad [that different cultures and civilizations survive]."[186] Under the heading "The cause of peoples," his MNR party program states: "We stand for respect for differences and identities."[187] Similarly, the British Nationalist Party has vowed to move away from its traditional philosophy of racial supremacy and toward the position "that human cultural and genetic diversity is as precious as the diversity of the rest of the world, and should be preserved."[188]

The nationalists portray the supposed melting of the "original" peoples of Europe into an indistinguishable mass in absolutely negative terms: "If pure evil ever took form on this earth, it would do so in the plans of the One Worlders."[189] The unadulterated malevolence of globalism is understood as a reflection of the ideology of liberal universalism and egalitarianism. However, unlike the ENR, this ideology is not traced back to Judeo-Christian origins. Rather, as Le Pen states, globalism began with "the ideology of the Enlightenment that ties humanity to 'Man,' an abstract entity that no one has managed to trace, [instead of a world] comprised of men, heirs to different cultures, living in different lands, with different laws, creeds, and customs."[190] Thus, "the truly incorrigible revolutionaries who guillotined the sovereign 200 years

ago today want to guillotine the sovereign people."[191] For Bossi, too, globalization arose in the utopian universalism of the Enlightenment, which ignored
"peoples, that is, history, men of flesh and bone." The West, Bossi says, "is
made of us, made of our work, made in our land."[192] But this truth is ignored,
and difference is obliterated in the globalizing flood.

A Diabolic Conspiracy

For these political actors, globalization is not the logical consequence of a natural evolution in world affairs, nor is it a self-generating system, as the ENR
theorists claim. Instead, they generally adhere to a conspiracy theory of "dia-
bolic causality,"[193] in which globalism is a scheme hatched by specific groups
whose goal is the complete domination over the world. Calamities that befall
local communities are assumed to be the direct result of secret plots hatched
and carried out by nefarious globalists. The following excerpt taken from a
speech by Le Pen perfectly captures this mentality:

> The internationalists want to organize the world according to their own uto-
> pias [which are] fundamentally antinational, antireligion, and inhuman. Men
> and women will be sacrificed to Humanity, and the self-appointed experts will
> define and organize their happiness. This happiness will be the same on all the
> continents . . . We recognize [in this plan], without any doubt, the same totali-
> tarianism responsible in the twentieth century for the death and suffering of
> hundreds of million of men and women. To accomplish this Orwellian proj-
> ect, it is necessary to uproot the people and to dissolve the familiar, religious,
> civic, social, and associational links . . . that is why the family and the Nation
> are their main targets: the family because it is the material link of the trans-
> mission of life and moral values; the Nation because it is a superior principle
> of effective solidarity, dignity, and security.[194]

A variety of agents and groups are imagined to be behind the "barbaric
and anticivilizational" globalism conspiracy.[195] A frequent target is Freemasonry, which the Portuguese Partido Nacional Renovador (National Renewal
Party—or PNR) has portrayed as the secret source of the "diabolical trinity"
of "Liberty, Equality, Fraternity" lurking at the core of globalization's "fero-
cious" world-conquering project.[196] Bossi has asserted that Masonry, acting
in tandem with American capitalism, "is the instrument through which globalization acts at an ideological-cultural level . . . The idea of the traditional
family is in radical contrast to the vision of the American Masonry [and is

an obstacle] to the octopus attempt to control the world through globalization."[197] Jewish organizations commonly share the blame with Freemasonry for undermining the nation and supporting globalism.[198] Le Pen, for instance, has accused the B'nai B'rith of covertly working through the French political establishment to implement "anti-France" policies. The British National Party regards Zionism as one of the main ideologies (together with Marxism and Liberalism) behind the "frantic rush to 'One World.'"[199]And Northern League MP Alberto Lembo has warned that "the goal of the Masonry and the dream of Zionist organizations" is a single, unified world government.[200] Another prominent member of the international globalist conspiracy is the Rockefeller family (and Rockefeller-funded organizations). For example, Bossi believes that favorable Italian immigration policies "started in Geneva with the creation of the Rockefeller Foundation in 1952 [sic]. Its ultimate goal was to make our society as fluid as America."[201] Pinto-Coelho spoke for most of his nationalist cohort when he said: "The real drama of globalization is that it is maintained by shadow governments."[202]

According to populist-nationalist parties, the desired goal of the globalist plotters is the establishment of a one-world government under the inspiration, guidance, and control of America. For them, the end of the Cold War opened the way for the implementation of a long-standing American master plan for totalitarian global control, supported by a globalist "religion" (the Rights of Man), globalist law (the market), globalist elites (international oligarchies), and a global mission (imposing the American multicultural model of society all over the world).[203] A National Front document succinctly outlines the breadth and depth of this supposed American project: "In brief, by shrinking the planet to the dimensions of a 'global village,' the beginning of the twenty-first century would become the antechamber of a new civilization, rendering national sovereignty, rootedness, and ethnic and cultural identity obsolete and unfashionable."[204] According to Bossi, "In the Middle Ages, the Holy Roman Empire dominated; today it is the turn of [another empire] whose royal palace is in Washington." In today's new imperial era, "America wants to impose its vision of the world: mercantilist, consumerist, advocating the disastrous 'melting pot,' the multiracial society that has failed everywhere."[205] The Spanish *Democracia Nacional* (National Democracy, or DN) proclaims that behind the apparently "generous" idea of globalization is the "hegemony and domination of one polarizing actor, the USA, a country that has established a New World Order."[206]

The literature of these parties regularly refers to statements by American politicians and elites that seem to confirm the existence of this hidden project. Much is made of George H. W. Bush's mention of a "New World Order" in the aftermath of the 1990 Gulf War. Also often cited is David Rockefeller's purported statement at a 1991 Bilderberg Group meeting: "The supranational sovereignty of an intellectual elite and world bankers is surely preferable to the national autodetermination practiced in past centuries."[207] So is General Wesley Clark's comment that "There is no place in modern Europe for ethnically pure states [because] that's a nineteenth-century idea, and we are trying to transition into the twenty-first century [with] multiethnic states."[208] These and other declarations are taken as sure signs that an American project of constructing a universal and uniform New World Order is well under way.

U.S. military operations are viewed as implementations of the preexisting plans for the globalist plot. Le Pen denounced the first Gulf War as an attempt to "put in line" any nation that dares to challenge the new international system.[209] Similarly, the 1999 Kosovo intervention was taken as "proof of American domination of the world" in which "Europe has no say because it is governed by a globalist technocracy modeled on the United States."[210] Bossi saw the NATO intervention in Kosovo as part of an American plan to destabilize Europe by creating a "Muslim spinal column" on the continent.[211] Mégret's MNR proclaimed that the New World Order forces nations to submit themselves to the United Nations, NATO, and the WTO: "Misfortune befalls those that refuse. They will be smashed like Iraq and Serbia."[212]

In the literature of these parties, the European Union (EU) is consistently portrayed as an agent for the advance of the new global order, existing only to subsume the natural diversity of nations within an artificial internationalist system. As the program of the National Front states, a unified Europe will "destroy nations, abolish borders, and be the first stage toward a world government. It is not the interest of France that prevails but rather submission to globalist policies."[213] For Le Pen, the ruling elites of Brussels are aligned with the international oligarchy in a sinister scheme to promote massive immigration that will inevitably lead to multiculturalism in Europe and obliterate primordial national, cultural, and ethnic identities.[214] The Northern League has depicted the European Union (EU) as the "Europe of the Masons" in radical contrast to the "Europe of peoples, homelands, and traditions."[215] According to Mégret, the EU is a "globalist and bureaucratic construction [made in] Brussels . . . a Trojan horse for foreign interests."[216] The "Europe of Eurocrats" has also been denounced by Spanish nationalists as nothing more than a "necessary step to advance globalism."[217] The BNP condemns the "deceit and deception" of the internationalists' plans, "from the creation of a United States of Europe and embryonic One World institutions, to genocide through racial integration and the destruction of the manufacturing industries of the West."[218] And the Portuguese nationalists have bitterly repudiated the Lisbon accords as the "suicidal policies of mercantilists who sell out their homeland to satisfy unspoken interests."[219]

Opposition to an American-led New World Order has recently been complicated by another preoccupation of the nationalists: the threat to European identity posed by Islam. Ever since the 1990s, the increasing presence of Muslim immigrants in Europe has been represented as part of an American design to diffuse the primeval identities of European peoples. America's ongoing support for Turkey's EU membership has only confirmed the notion that "Islam" is a weapon being used against Europe by the hidden globalist conspiracy. One result has been a renewed emphasis on the "Christian" and "Western" roots of Europe, which the populists say must be marshaled in defense against the "ideologies of conquest represented by globalism and Islam." As Le Pen has baldly stated, the struggle now is against the "universalism of the market and the universalism of the sacred."[220] In Italy, the Northern League portrays itself as "the last obstacle to the progression of the universal American and Islamic empires."[221] According to a MNR member, "In face of globalism and Islamization, the national and identitarian forces must organize a political offensive" to save civilization.[222]

Citizens! Awake and Rise!

The populist-nationalist parties' general solution for the global perils that endanger the survival of the community is a "return to the people." This call is at the heart of a polarizing ideology built around a systematic separation between the *citizenry*, conceived to be inherently good and moral, and the *elites*, who are by nature evil and treacherous.[223] The defining idea is that for decades Western democracies have been usurped by a greedy, power-hungry clique— composed of mainstream left- and right-wing politicians and their financial and media allies—that always acts on behalf of the globalist conspiracy. These treacherous elites subvert the *real* interests of the people, who are kept in the dark and deprived of any significant voice in the destiny of the nation. Because they represent the last reservoir of human freedom and independence, populist-nationalist parties are relentlessly persecuted and demonized by the "system." As Le Pen states: "Hatred follows the National Front and its militants and officials because they constitute . . . the only link that binds the nation today and tomorrow, to the detriment of cosmopolitan interests."[224]

Herein lies the self-professed moral *exceptionalism* of these parties. They see themselves as the only ones who have not deserted the people;[225] only they have remained faithful to the mystical nation. As a Northern League senior member proclaims: "The League is the sole true party of the people, [a party] that has no interests behind it, small or large. The League is the guarantee of democracy and of a government by the people."[226] Similarly, the National Front sees itself as a "spontaneous expression of the people; it can unite them against a system that has confiscated power for its own profit."[227] The Spanish DN says it is the "only party in the entire nation that has raised and will continue to raise its voice against globalist colonialism,"[228] while the Portuguese nationalist leader asserts: "All other political forces cravenly collude in the destruction of Portugal. . . . Only the voice of the nationalists has been heard (in opposition). Our voice!"[229]

The nationalists argue that the only way avert the imminent debasement and eventual disappearance of national identity is revitalized popular participation. But achieving this goal is an arduous task because the masses are addicted to (and entertained by) a numbing culture of spectacle and anesthetized by relentless consumerism. As a result, the majority are totally unaware of the dangers besieging the nation and unwilling to fight against them. Today, "humanity has lost any link with culture, community, and land; human interests don't go beyond 'tomorrow'; the most lively of its interests, the only medium that humanity has to fulfill itself [and to] fill its interior emptiness, is consumerism."[230] In this, the "worst of all possible worlds," men and women are "connected to each other only by the economic nexus."[231] As Le Pen warns, the people are

> . . . stuck in the torment of doubt and materialism, their vital dynamism is crippled by demographic decline and migratory invasion, they are cut away from their spiritual roots, trapped by the illusions of Europeanism and globalism, betrayed by their elites and pushed around by lobbies. They are in great peril of destruction.[232]

To avoid this miserable fate, the populist-nationalist parties have embarked on a mission to *rescue* their compatriots. "We are the watchmen, those who awake our people, the voices in the night."[233] They will "open the eyes [of the people] about the reality of decadence and engage them on the path of renewal."[234] To "keep our country free from foreigner invasion and tyranny" the BNP calls for a "New Battle of Britain" to "win back the freedoms" our forebears fought to save.[235] The call to action and popular involvement for the defense of the community has a dual implication for the policies that these parties propose; they all advocate the principle of national preference (priority for national citizens in the job market, for example) to contravene the neglect fostered by antinational governments. The emphasis on national priority is complemented by widespread calls for the construction of a "new democracy" in which the people directly determine their own futures, rather being manipulated by the treacherous cosmopolitan elite. As the National Front program announces:

> In reality the system in which we live in is not one of freedom and democracy
> ... the legitimacy of the decisions [does not originate] in the sovereignty of the
> people. . . . For the supporters of the oligarchy, what is legitimate is not what
> the majority of the French want, but what conforms to the new official ideol-
> ogy, the globalist ideology.[236]

Populist-nationalist parties contemptuously dismiss the debates and policies of their respective national governments, portraying them as meaningless feuds among the already established dominant classes. To restore the people's immediate and real control over the nation that has been stolen from them, they favor the implementation of "direct democracy." For example, the Spanish DN, in its "Decalogue," calls for "new alternative forms of political representation" featuring citizens' referendums and initiatives.[237] Because "democracy and freedom are under attack" and "Big Brother [has] more power to snoop and interfere," the BNP also favors citizens' initiative referendums.[238] To these parties, the relative absence of such referendums over sensitive issues of immigration policy, military alliance, or the transfer of sovereignty to transnational bodies amply confirms that globalists and their minions have usurped the citizens' power.

This critique of modern democracy, like the critique offered by Chavéz and other antiglobalists, is not a trivial matter. It highlights a fundamental tension between the principle of immediate "power to the people" and the actual practice of representative democracy, which inevitably falls short of the ideal. For the nationalists the "crisis of representation"[239] is especially salient in a world battered by an assault on the mores and cultures of local communities. In response to this attack, they ardently hope to establish a pure form of popular sovereignty that will pit the immediate will of the disenfranchised people against the overwhelming power of the global elites. Articulating this perspective, Le Pen has declared, "I, and only I, incarnate democracy,"[240] while the BNP proclaims itself as "Britain's most democratic party."[241]

But mere bureaucratic electoral reforms promoting direct democracy do not suffice to awaken a populace that has been brutally torn from its cultural and spiritual foundations by its all-powerful enemies. More drastic measures are needed. This is why the populist-nationalists sacralize politics.[242] Their entire rhetorical and symbolic discourse is dominated by the notion of regaining "the transcendence and sense of sacred that, in all times and everywhere, has existed in our nations and has given them so much strength and humanity."[243] The monumental task at hand for the nationalists is to reenchant the world through myth, rituals, and a redemptive vision of hope. In this grand struggle, political action is never simply a matter of pragmatic interest. Rather, it is a spiritual struggle to vanquish evil, transform the dominant value system, and give an ultimate meaning to human existence. Acting within this eschatology, these parties emphasize their mystical attachments to the historical and cultural roots of the nation. Only these attachments can provide permanent moral and spiritual solutions to the fragmentation caused by the rampant globalist ethos of consumption and individualism.

The populist-nationalist sacralization of politics is expressed and embodied in a remarkable efflorescence of rituals reinforcing communal bonds and affirming the identity of each group as the "last of patriots." The rituals also symbolically support the epoch-making nature of their shared missions and the role of their leaders as charismatic spiritual/political guides. Ritual moments of communion and faith are generally performed in locations that awaken collective memory and testify to the nation's historical authenticity. For Le Pen the "sacred altar of the homeland" is the cathedral of Reims, where King Clovis I of Gaul was baptized, where later French kings were crowned,[244] and where Le Pen leads rituals affirming the members' loyalty to the National Front. Another ritual cycle begins with the party's annual parade through the streets of downtown Paris and culminates when Le Pen lays a wreath at the feet of the gilded statue of its patron-saint, Joan of Arc, the savior of France. Similarly, the Northern League organizes regular rituals in Pontida (in the Lombard region), where northern Italian communes swore to resist the invading troops of Frederick I Barbarossa in the twelfth century. The party also holds three days of rallies yearly in the Po River region, marking the boundary of its imaginary homeland of Padania.

Invented rituals celebrating a historic and personal connection to national roots are characteristic of all these European nationalist-populist parties. The Portuguese PNR, for example, consecrates June 10 (marking the death of Luís Vaz de Camões, the poet who immortalized Portugal's voyages of discovery) as their "national festival." The festival includes a "patriotic procession" culminating with a speech by their leader. The PNR also organizes a rally every year on December 1 to celebrate the restoration of Portugal's independence in 1640 after sixty years of rule by the Philippine dynasty. Portugal's loss of sovereignty and identity in the seventeenth century is specifically paralleled to the modern threat to the country's autonomy and culture. In a like manner, Spanish nationalists annually commemorate the death of the eleventh-century heroic knight El Cid, "the champion." Parades are organized in the medieval warrior's northern hometown of Burgos, where followers lay a bouquet at his statue. At one such occasion, Manuel Canduela, the party's leader, compared El Cid's struggles to the present, when the nation is once again threatened by the machinations of a treacherous political class.[245]

For the faithful, the historical persons invoked in these charged ritual performances embody national principles of freedom, independence, and historic greatness. These heroes are not imprisoned in historical time but remain alive as the unseen guardians of the righteous. As Le Pen declared: "In our march we have the company, invisible but omnipresent, of the saints, the martyrs, and the heroes of our long history."[246] The deeds and lives of these "invisible but present" heroic figures are enacted again in today's world. For instance, the sword-wielding medieval warrior Alberto da Giussano, who led the northern Italians in a rebellion against invaders, holds a central place in the mythology of the Northern League. Bossi is described by loyalists as "the man descended from Alberto da Giussano."[247] In France, equivalent fusions of past and present regularly occur. As the headline of a magazine sympathetic to the National Front sympathizers read: "Clovis–Joan of Arc–Le Pen: The Same Struggle."[248] In his speech at the annual National Front tribute to Joan of Arc, Le Pen specifically conflated the modern situation of France with the situation in Joan's era: "Today we live in an identical crisis of civilization, with completely comparable cultural and sociological consequences resulting from the corruption of power, the dissolution of customs, and preference for the material over the spiritual."[249] For Le Pen, the path to France's renaissance is to be found in recollection of "past ordeals, in superior principles, in the traditions of our people, in the example of its heroes . . . [including] the most emblematic and extraordinary of all: Joan of Arc."[250] The merger of past and present exists as well in Spain, where the nationalist leader told his followers that they incarnate the ideals of El Cid, who "will once again ride in the lands of Castile."[251] And in Britain, on the day of the 2008 local elections, the BNP website posted an article containing Tacitus's version of a speech by Calgacus (praised as the "leader of the ancient Britons") in which he exhorted his army to defend the freedom of the British Isles against foreign enslavement. The article concluded with a call for freeborn Britons to "join the ranks of these heroes of old . . . and make this land our home once again."[252]

The rediscovery of sacred history corresponds with an urgent call for the destruction of the ideology of the "Golden Calf"[253] of materialist values that have degraded human nature so radically that "the soul is banished, there are no inner values, sentiments are forbidden, there's no love, only selfishness."[254] Because spiritual emptiness is the source of modern decadence, society must not only be repaired but also purified through a fiery renewal. As Le Pen avowed: "Here and elsewhere, recovery will not be possible unless it involves the spiritual dimension of the soul."[255] Pervasive moral and spiritual decay is manifested in social pathologies that have turned contemporary society into a "state of living death." Under these alienating conditions, it is no wonder that "so many people in advanced Western nations suffer so much depression, drug addiction, and family breakdowns."[256] Hence, in radical contrast to the modern cult of hedonism, the populist-nationalist parties praise the virtues of suffering, asceticism, and sacrifice and glorify courage, honor, faith, and duty.[257]

The language in these panegyrics is often belligerent and apocalyptic. As Bossi announced: "Today our land is engaged in a mortal battle for independence,"[258] while Le Pen praised the "sacrifice of one's life for the defense of sacred notions,"[259] and Pinto-Coelho declared: "If necessary, we will fight . . . to defend Portugal as did the heroes of 1640."[260] The downward slide to decadence can be reversed through stimulating popular devotion to ancient values and through the exercise of sheer will power.

The arguments of the populist-nationalist parties ultimately rest on the assumption that globalism is an arrogant, abstract, and artificial human invention overturning and violating the natural order of things, introducing dangerous disharmony into the world. Only the emergence of a spontaneous natural reality can restore balance. The essence of this natural and deep reality is the resurgent nation, which is not a human creation but rather is a primordial and even biological essence, rooted in a deeply spiritual and physical continuity between the past and the present. This belief arises from the populists' adherence to a precontractual image of society. As the National Front platform asserts: "Under abusive and intoxicating universal changes, the great and profound law of immutability is hidden."[261]

In practical terms, this means that all policies emerging from a globalist standpoint must be vehemently rejected for fear of shattering the underlying cosmic harmony (which, despite its immutability, is also very fragile). As Bossi says: "We stand for what is natural. The Left, the caretakers of the occult powers and of the great international economy, are on the side of the artificial."[262] Le Pen concurs: "We refuse the constructivist ideology of the New World Order . . . We claim a natural order that respects the human being in his natural and living surroundings [which are] the family, the community, work, the province, the nation."[263] In the parties' rhetoric it is therefore quite common to find terms such as "antinatural" and "antihuman" applied in debates about economic policies, supranational bodies, or multiculturalism.

Though the issue varies in importance from party to party, environmental problems are understood as the inevitable consequence of the unbalanced relationship between humans and the natural order. In Le Pen's view, "ecology is the defense of the agreement between nature and human activity." This balance has been "destroyed by frantic materialism."[264] The BNP defends "econationalism" to counter the effects of capitalism and consumerism that "exceed the natural limits of the planet's environment."[265] Like the ENR, populist-nationalist parties also favor a "multipolar" politics based on respect for the separate identity of peoples, the absolute sovereignty of countries, and noninterference, in contrast to the universal world order dominated by America.[266] At a European level this stance translates into a total rejection of the European Union, which is condemned as a hegemonic superstate built "on artificial grounds and denying the reality of European Nations."[267] Though some parties' view of the European project has evolved (the Northern League, for example, initially thought to use the EU to bolster its case for "freeing" Padania by weakening the Italian state), at present all call for an alternative to the "totalitarian" project of Brussels, one based on the natural diversity and the historical/cultural distinctions of European peoples and nations. This vision is presented as a "Europe of Fatherlands" or a "Europe of Nations" in which many cultures could flourish.

Nationalists of All Countries, Unite!

While the attachment to an essentialized primordial nation is a driving force of populist-nationalist parties, a transnational mindset has unexpectedly emerged from within their milieu.[268] This is because the "assault on nations" is understood as a global process, so that these parties can then conceive of their own problems and solutions on a global scale. Of course, expanding the local struggle into the global arena also greatly magnifies the importance of the nationalists and their leaders, who become actors on a much larger stage. What inspires them in particular is the specter of a New World Order and the demolition of European civilization at the hands of both U.S. and Islamic empires. They then portray the European fight against these hegemonic forces as an example for nationalists everywhere. As usual, Le Pen's words encapsulate this trend:

> Instead of opposing each other, [we] must make an effort to understand and to establish a united front against a common enemy—the "Big Brother" who wants to govern the planet, annihilate differences, turn the world gray and tepid, without roots or past, without memory or future. My rallying cry: "Nationalists of all countries, unite!"[269]

Using growing mechanisms for institutional cooperation and networking, the nationalists self-consciously constitute themselves as the last bastions of Western civilization against the onslaught of the barbarians. "Globalized nationalism" has been born.[270] Predictably, Le Pen has been especially active in this domain through his participation in the union of European nationalists (EuroNat), which was formally created in the 2005 during the traditional Blue, White, and Red party festival. As stated in the EuroNat website: "The time has passed when each of us would strive on our own . . . Mutual support is crucial in order to reverse the tide that threatens to destroy our entire civilization." EuroNat is the "one and only Nationalist platform to counter the creation and establishment of the dreaded New World Order."[271]

Despite that claim, the European National Front (ENF) has convened a rival network whose founding declaration calls for the "patriotic forces of our nations" to cooperate for the "development and defense of our common values," which are "under huge pressure by New World Order forces straining to destroy our Christian civilization."[272] Populist-nationalist forces have also signed a Declaration of Patriotic and National Movements and Parties in Europe that affirms the "unifying struggle of European ethnic communities against the social and economic effects of globalization."[273] The pan-European confluence of nationalist sentiment has been felt as well in the European Parliament, where populist-nationalist parties from six member states convened a short-lived political group calling itself "Identity, Tradition, and Sovereignty" (ITS). Its founding principle was a "commitment to Christian values, heritage, culture, and the tradition of European civilization."[274] And in 2008 a group of leaders (among them Le Pen) announced plans to create a pan-European party, the European Patriotic Party, which will stand against globalization, immigration, and Islamization.[275] As Nick Griffin, the BNP leader, comments: "Nationalists must overcome their own ideological and historical differences. . . . If we fail to overcome our past our children will not have a future, so the effort must be made."[276]

Ironically, the establishment of these antiglobalization networks has benefited from the advances in the same communications technology that enables the spread of globalization. The increased connectedness brought about by the Internet has helped to bring nationalists together and made their voices heard in the international arena. As a result, "globalization's greatest critics have become globalization's biggest political beneficiaries."[277] However, the nationalists do not see this as a contradiction. Ultimately, because the repressive new world order has global roots, they argue that deliverance from its ills can be achieved only through entering into concerted horizontal communication (and communion) with other peoples who are victims too. "Globally we are not alone," Le Pen proclaims. "Dozens of peoples, millions of individuals, aspire to our ideal." Accordingly, the battle against the "universalization of identity" must be launched against both market and sacred (meaning Islamic) universalisms.[278] In this way globalized nationalism transcends the contradiction between the particular and the general by providing a nationalistic answer to the spiritual homelessness and misery of all suffering peoples everywhere.

After World War I, Paul Valéry wrote: "We do not know what is to come, and have some reason to fear it. We hope vaguely, but dread precisely; our fears are infinitely clearer than our hopes."[279] Both the European New Right and the populist-nationalists of our modern era share Valéry's tragic sense of despair and loss, coincident with reactive emotions of rage at their attackers and pride in their idealized past. Yet, they also have faith that their actions can right the balance and bring a new and better world into the light. And they are ready to act to make that dream come true.

4 GLOBAL MOVEMENTS TO TRANSFORM HUMANITY

*The everyday is never the same after one has tasted a moment
that is ruled only by freedom. Tasting such fruit is dangerous,
because it leaves a craving to repeat the exhilarating experience
again and again.*[1]

—Notes from Nowhere

*While "another world is possible" it may not necessarily be that
dreamt of by the anti-capitalist movement.*[2]

—Ronaldo Munck

THE MOVEMENT OF MOVEMENTS

Contesting the Way the World Is Run

The World Social Forum (WSF)[3] began as a parody. It was conceived in 2001 in the depressed and impoverished Brazilian city with the ironic name of Porto Alegre (Happy Port) when a group of disgruntled international journalists, leftist intellectuals, and other activists joined the powerful Brazilian Worker's Party (PT) in a satiric protest against the neoliberal economic policies, elitism, secrecy, and undemocratic procedures of the World Economic Forum, which was meeting at the same time in Davos, Switzerland. Unexpectedly, an enthusiastic crowd of 15,000 attended the discussions, lectures, and debates. Although originally conceived as a unique event, the forum has become a worldwide movement. The 2005 WSF (held once again in Porto Alegre) was attended by an estimated 155,000 participants, and subsequent forums, along with various authorized and unauthorized offshoots scattered across Europe and the Americas and extending to Asia and Africa, continue to draw large crowds.

According to its charter, the WSF is a loosely coordinated international meeting place for civil society activists who are "opposed to neoliberalism and to domination of the world by capital and any form of imperialism, and are committed to building a planetary society centered on the human person."[4] It has proven to be the most widely spread, well-known, and successful expression of what has often been called the "antiglobalization movement," though many members reject this label as too narrow and negative. Some prefer the "global justice movement," others the "movement for a global civil society," the "anticapitalist movement," the "world democracy movement," the "alternative globalization movement (alter-globalization for short)," or the "movement of movements." According to influential journalist and WSF supporter George Monbiot, perhaps the best descriptor would be: "a large number of people, dispersed among most of the nations of the world, who, in contesting the way the world is run, regard each other, most of the time, as allies."[5] For its supporters, the WSF is "the movement of the millennium,"[6] "the most important political development of the twenty-first century,"[7] and a crucial part of a "multicentric network of movements" engaged in a "world revolution" to reorient history and restructure the current world order.[8]

Like other alter-globalization movements, the WSF was greatly inspired by the success and philosophy of the Zapatistas, as we detailed in Chapter 1. But another major and more direct influence was ATTAC, a French-based collective of journalists, academics, and youth associations under the intellectual leadership of Ignacio Ramonet, an editor of the influential leftist periodical *Le Monde Diplomatique*.[9] Despite its aggressive connotations, ATTAC is an acronym for the rather more tame *Association pour la taxation des transactions financiers pour l'aide aux citoyens* (Association for the Taxation of Financial Transactions for the Aid of Citizens). Its practical goal is the implementation of the "Tobin tax" proposed by Nobel laureate economist James Tobin. It has defined itself as an "international movement for democratic control of financial markets and their institutions."[10]

After its first meeting in 1998, under the rallying cry of "the world is not a commodity," ATTAC quickly expanded its base, as members and affiliates used peer-to-peer networking and established a website that became a popular venue for publicizing a variety of protests and a platform for debating proposals for change. In its policies, ATTAC remained primarily reformative, not revolutionary. Compared to other alter-globalization protest groups, it was more centralized, more bureaucratic, and more focused on policy issues. At the same time, the ATTAC leadership realized that "the expressive aspects of protest had somehow to be incorporated within explanatory frameworks of collective action."[11] Following the model of ATTAC and of the Brazilian trade unions, the WSF originally consisted of a fairly conventional, hierarchical, pragmatic coalition of dues-paying activists, academics, and journalists who were seeking the practical reform of international financial transactions. Its policies and organization were "shaped by older, previously existing political cultures and forces."[12] But despite its conservative genesis, the WSF appealed to a new generation of anticapitalist and antiglobalist activists dispirited by the collapse of Soviet communism and uninspired by the tired oratory and regimentation of the traditional European socialist parties for whom "the only politics left was a politics of conserving and in some instances downright conservative resistance."[13]

In contrast to this dated approach, the WSF appeared to offer new ways to deflect and even overturn the worldwide march of capitalism toward the "end of history." Novel WSF practices included an open-ended horizontal organizational structure based on Internet networking; a transnational orientation, which removed it from any particular territorial identity; a strong sense of collective hope and solidarity engendered by participation; and the strategic use of theatrical performances, irony, and humor to attract media attention and arouse the enthusiasm of members.

The appeal of the WSF and of ATTAC was in part a reflection of the remarkable success of the iconic "Battle of Seattle"—the "coming-out party for a global resistance movement"[14]—which occurred in November 1999 when a surprising coalition of fifty to a hundred thousand protestors, chanting "This is what democracy looks like," forced the closure of the annual meeting of the World Trade Organization (WTO) and temporarily shut down Seattle's downtown. The effectiveness of the protest was remarkable enough, but what was even more extraordinary was the huge variety of activists who were brought together in shared distaste for WTO policies. In marked contrast to the uniformity of the WTO delegates in their monochromatic suits and ties, the antiglobalist protests in Seattle included "union members, farmers, landless peasants, people of faith, women's organizations, youth organizations, small business owners, artisanal producers, economic justice organizers, prison reform advocates, environmentalists, AIDS and other health activists, politicians, independent media organizations, civil servants, the homeless, peace and human rights organizations, gay and lesbian groups, intellectuals, consumer advocates, and even a few corporate CEOs of every age, religion, race, and nationality."[15] As one protestor shouted to the police: "You'll have to arrest the entire population of the world if you want to get us all."[16] For some, the multiplicity of participants promised the transformative arrival of a "new international" consisting of a "convergence of the struggles" against the global capitalist system and "open to all peoples from north to south, all social classes and popular strata."[17]

In spite of (or perhaps because of) its vast internal variety, and again in complete contradistinction to the WTO, the alliance of protestors functioned "without a central organization, leadership, or defining ideology."[18] Decisions were made within spontaneously organized "affinity groups" of five to fifteen trusted friends with "shared values and identities" who directly elected representatives to central planning but who acted "organically from the context of protest in which they were situated and from each organization's own traditions of protest."[19] The basic structure was one of consensus and open deliberation—an "ad-hocracy."[20] Participants also made extensive use of new networking technology to exchange information, rapidly adapt to changing circumstances, and organize themselves. There was a strong emphasis on symbolic and expressive actions such as "'radical jeerleading' and drumming"[21] that were designed to undermine the authority and legitimacy of the WTO and to involve protestors in exciting dramatic performances. Finally, in another conscious contrast to WTO secrecy, a noncorporate Independent Media Center (Indymedia) documented all phases of the protest for later public distribution. All of these practices would greatly influence later alter-globalization movements.

Also among the immediate precursors to the WSF was the Global Day of Action in September 2000 when the International Monetary Fund (IMF) meeting in Prague was besieged. Again, expressive theatricality predominated in the protests. "There are no borders to the imagination of those who take action in 110 cities in solidarity with the demonstrators in Prague. . . . IMF 'delegates' in pig masks play football with a globe and a capitalist monster covered in corporate logos eats people in the crowd."[22] And in July 2001 the Genoa Social Forum, supported by ATTAC, mounted a street protest of 100,000 against the upcoming meeting of the G8. The death of one of the protestors provided the new movement with its first martyr.[23] Earlier influences on the twenty-first-century antiglobalist social movements include the successful media campaigns of Greenpeace, the witty theatrics of Abbie Hoffman and the 1960s Yippies, and the revolutionary tactics of Guy DeBord and the Situationist International. In fact, the spontaneous spirit of 1968 is apparent in the exuberance, polarizing rhetoric, optimism, and theatricality of many of today's activists.[24]

The protestors who took part in all of these actions felt considerable pride in organizing and successfully carrying out their demonstrations, but a

> deeper imprint was left by the experience of the carnival—halfway between party and protest, resisting at the same time as proposing, destroying at the same time as creating. . . . Using rhythm and music to reclaim space, transform the streets, and inject pleasure into politics. . . . Who wants the tedium of traditional demonstrations and protests? . . . Instead why not use a form of rebellion that embodies the movements' principles of diversity, creativity, decentralization, horizontality, and direct action?[25]

This attitude was taken to its logical extreme by the Clandestine Insurgent Rebel Clown Army (CIRCA), whose mission was to ridicule and parody the capitalist order, using laughter as a weapon of subversion and as an example of an alternative world of free play.[26]

For many, participation in the carnival of rebellion[27] created "a break that exists to this day . . . it's only by focusing on this initial political fissure that we can see the slim utopian space, where, perhaps, we can truly be ourselves."[28] "For that moment, and truly forever, the power of people acting in peace had won a holy victory."[29] Those who had felt the thrill of direct confrontation were not willing to lend their enthusiasms to orthodox leftist political groups, with their dated rhetoric and bureaucratic structure. The burgeoning alterglobalization movement, as represented first by ATTAC and then by the WSF, appeared to offer a new, more empowering route to "a better world" and toward the ultimate goal of achieving "self-realization in everyday life."[30]

Fighting the Unholy Trinity

The WSF was only one of a number of antiglobalization groups that appeared around the same time. In Italy alone, they included the Black Bloc, the White Overalls, Rete Lilliput, and the Network for Global Rights. Each had different modes of action and goals and different attitudes toward violence. Rete Lilliput took a Gandhian approach, White Overalls practiced civil disobedience, and NGR used violence on symbolic targets, while the anarchistic Black Bloc were (in)famous for rioting and destroying property.[31] Despite marked differences in strategy, within the alter-global movement network boundaries between groups are blurry, and multiple memberships are normal. A survey at the 2005 Porto Alegre meeting of the WSF found that 70 percent of the respondents were involved in other activist groups, 40 percent in three or more.[32] As the Notes from Nowhere manual for rebellion explains: "Fuzzy borders favor the disenfranchised. If the Zapatistas had tried to hold their lines and fight they would have been defeated long ago. Their advantage lies in fluidity and lack of definitions."[33] For this reason, global justice activists are rarely affiliated with political parties—even those of the left. Unlike open-ended movements, parties are viewed as untrustworthy, unaccountable, rigid bureaucracies, driven by their leaders' desires for personal power and legitimacy, not by the real needs of citizens.[34] Worse, parties waste time drawing up rationalized plans for the future, ignoring the existential truth that the "revolution is . . . a process that begins right here, right now!"[35]

Regardless of their origins, alter-globalists profess to share a similar emotional reaction to the state of the world: "Faced with the mutilation of human lives by capitalism, a scream of sadness, a scream of horror, a scream of anger, a scream of refusal: NO."[36] And, whatever their political strategy, all the contemporary alter-globalists are united in their steadfast opposition to the evils of neoliberalism, which, as WSF activist David McNally writes, intensify "the historical legacy of colonialism, racism and imperialism that has marked capitalism since its birth."[37] According to the standard ideology, the globe is under the command of the "Unholy Trinity" of the World Bank, the IMF, and the WTO, which is "the actualization of every political activists' worst nightmare: an unelected, closed-door organization with the power to override national sovereignty in the name of profit."[38] The major political ally of the dominant corporate interests is the United States, whose power is "the central determinant of the neoliberal project"[39] and whose "foreign policy is a major obstacle to making another world possible."[40]

In a typical historical analysis provided by the International Forum on Globalization (IFG—an offshoot of the WSF), the conspiracy between big capital and American military power began when a new international banking system was secretly installed during the Bretton Woods conference just after World War II. This was the beginning of "forums for elite domination" such as the Trilateral Commission, which "help maintain 'stability' in global policies, but they also deprive the public of meaningful participation and choice—as some participants explicitly intend."[41] This secretive elite power structure has shifted power away from nations and toward multinational corporations, promoting hypergrowth; environmental exploitation; the privatization of public services; homogenization; consumerism; the conversion of national economies to harmful export oriented production; deregulation; the movement of capital across borders; increased corporate concentration; the dismantling of all public health, social, and environmental programs; the replacement of democratic systems by global corporate bureaucracies; and a host of other interlinked evils.

Because the ideology of neoliberalism privileges property over people, it turns everything into a commodity, including human relationships. In so doing, it also suppresses

> political, economic, cultural, racial, gendered, sexual, ecological, and epistemological differences. . . . Neoliberal globalization is not simply economic domination of the world but also the imposition of monolithic thought (*pensamento unico*) that consolidates vertical forms of difference and prohibits the public from imagining diversity in egalitarian, horizontal terms. Capitalism, imperialism, monoculturalism, patriarchy, white supremacism, and the domination of biodiversity have coalesced under the current form of globalization.[42]

This hegemonic doctrine cares nothing for dignity, love, identity, character, spirituality, or truth; nor does it have any interest in protecting the environment or maintaining the viability of the planet. The only goal is to "align all of the world's formerly disparate national economies behind a single formula" that will benefit corporations, regardless of the fact that global homogenization and rationalization will make millions homeless and devastate nature.[43]

Like the ENR theorists we documented in the last chapter, antiglobalization intellectuals—especially Marxists and socialists—generally recognize that the negative aspects of modernity are inevitable consequences of the contradictions of evolving capitalism. But this objective view coincides with a widely shared belief that predatory neoliberalism is an evil plot hatched by "globalists who meet in posh gatherings" where they secretly implement the "intentional actions of a corrupted political system awash in corporate money."[44] These schemes have a perverse spiritual foundation. As Susan George explains, "From a small, unpopular sect with virtually no influence, neoliberalism has become the major world religion with its dogmatic doctrine, its priesthood, its law-giving institutions and perhaps most important of all, its hell for heathen and sinners who dare to context the revealed truth."[45] For members of this all-powerful sect, the opening of markets is an act of faith, "like a catechism."[46] They justify their injustices and cruelty as necessary for maintenance of their sacred ideal: the unrestricted flow of capital.[47]

The case for a "religion" of capital is made even more forcefully by WSF intellectuals Michael Löwy and Frei Betto, who proclaim—with tongue in cheek but also with underlying seriousness—that the corporate elite "hold dear three great values and are willing to fight with any and all means to safeguard them—even by war, if need be. These three values of the Davos creed are at the heart of Western capitalist civilization in its current form. They are the dollar, the euro and the yen!" The divinities of this value system, Löwy and Betto say, are Currency, Market, and Capital; it has its church in the stock market; its holy office is the IMF and WTO; and it persecutes those who believe in other values. Like Moloch and Baal, the modern idols of capital demand human sacrifices. The ultimate sacred commandment, as set by Saint Adam Smith, is that "each individual must pursue, in the most implacable manner possible, her or his selfish interest, in utter disregard of their fellow men and women."[48]

The results of this faith are painted in dark colors by global justice activists such as David McNally, who fulminates:

> Behind their fluffy rhetoric about free trade and free markets lurks a hostility toward freedom for ordinary people—and a love affair with police and prisons. Their heroes are not sweatshop workers standing up for their rights, indigenous peoples reclaiming their lands, or homeless people who resist a police beating. Such people give them nightmares. Instead, they adore jackbooting police with automatic weapons who are so brave as to shoot unarmed protesters and beat the daylights out of youth of colour from the projects. Brutality, egregious violations of civil rights and freedoms, even murder are acceptable to them in the battle to utterly defend the "freedom" of propertied interests.[49]

According to prominent movement journalist Naomi Klein, citizen resistance to this ugly situation is well-nigh impossible because the state—particularly the American state—is thoroughly under the thumb of a "McGovernment" that "is biased at every level towards centralization, consolidation, homogenization." This unrepresentative system aims at "the privatization of every aspect of life, and the transformation of every activity and value into a commodity." Its policies consist of "a happy meal of cutting taxes, privatizing services, liberalizing regulations, busting unions—what is this diet in aid of? To remove anything standing in the way of the market."[50]

The consequences of the predominance of the neoliberal faith are dire:

> Having robbed our lives of meaning, capitalism pretends to sell it back to us in the form of things. . . . The more we pursue the things on offer in capitalism, the more estranged we become . . . Sacrificing ourselves for money warps and deforms all parts of our lives. Instead of a rich social life characterized by creative work, play and recreation, artistic expression, intellectual stimulation, love, solidarity and cooperation, our lives are impoverished. The rich diversity of human possibilities mindlessly reduced to one narrow, alienated goal: accumulating private wealth.[51]

The defining clash of our times is between "a delusional value system" that fetishizes money and overconsumption, versus a "value system centered around the biological realities of life's diversities . . . Life versus the doomsday economy. Hope versus extinction."[52]

As a result of this existential confrontation: "The modern world-system is in structural crisis, and we have entered an 'age of transition'—a period of bifurcation and chaos."[53] But structural crisis has its positive side, best articulated by movement ideologist George Monbiot:

> By forcing governments to operate in the interests of capital, (globalization) has manufactured the disenchantment upon which all new politics must feed. . . . But it has done more than that; it has begun to force a transformation of the scale on which we think, obliging us to recognize the planetary issues which bear on our parochial concerns.

As a result "a metaphysical mutation has arisen. . . . Heedlessly, it sweeps away economic and political systems, ethical considerations and social structures. No human agency can halt its progress—nothing but another metaphysical mutation."

Yet, the "metaphysical mutation" requires human agents for its realization:

> The world will not change until we seize control of global politics. . . . We must harness the power of globalization, and, pursuing its inexorable developments, overthrow its institutions and replace them with our own. . . . To be truly free, in other words, we must be prepared to contemplate revolution. . . . It depends on your preparedness to abandon your attachment to the old world and start thinking like a citizen of the new; to exchange your security for liberty, your comfort for elation. It depends on your willingness to act.[54]

But the price of freedom will be high: "We will know our approach is working only when it is violently opposed."[55]

Demand the Impossible

The slogan of protestors who took to the streets in Paris in the May 1968 was "Be realistic, demand the impossible!" It is often cited with approval by contemporary alter-globalists. But what are the "impossible demands," and how can they best be realized? In answer to the first question, the WSF charter insists on a "globalization in solidarity (that) will prevail as a new state in world history. This will respect universal human rights and those of all citizens . . . and will rest on democratic international systems and institutions at the service of social justice, equality and the sovereignty of peoples."[56] According to the IFG, this new global system must follow principles that are the "mirror opposites of the principles that drive the institutions of the corporate global economy . . . Instead of shaping all systems to conform to a global model . . . we must reshape our institutions to favor exactly the opposite."[57]

However, the charter gives no concrete instructions as to how to realize these "impossible" oppositional goals because the WSF "does not intend to be a body representing world civil society. . . . Meetings do not constitute a locus of power to be disputed by the participants."[58] Instead, the "movement of movements" must provide both an antiexclusionary space and a meeting ground where no person, program, or policy is privileged over any other, with the exception that global civil society "explicitly excludes reactionary—racist, fascist, or fundamentalist—organizations and movements."[59] Furthermore, all participants in the WSF must accept principles of nonviolence, oppose neoliberalism, and approve of "universal human rights."

In the antiauthoritarian environment of the WSF, sympathetic governmental leaders and other notables who attend the forum can do so only under the pretext of being ordinary participants, not representatives of the state. When Hugo Chávez spoke at the 2005 Forum, he introduced himself as follows: "I'm not here as president. I'm Hugo. The presidency is just a crappy job I've been assigned. I'm really just a peasant, a soldier, a man committed to the struggle for a better world."[60] But despite such disclaimers, many WSF participants have vigorously protested against the special attention paid to visiting politicos, against the privileges granted to wealthy luminaries from powerful nongovernmental organizations (NGOs) and academic institutions and against the authority exercised by the WSF's unelected governing body of the International Council (IC), which is made up of the prominent intellectuals, journalists, and unionists who were the group's original founders.[61] In 2002 young activists from the Intergalactic Laboratory of Disobedience, accompanied by a samba band, marched to the Catholic University where the official forum was being held and occupied the VIP room, proclaiming, "We are all VIPs!" And in 2005 there was massive protest from the rank and file when nineteen well-known WSF members issued a public manifesto without engaging in public debate or gaining popular consensus.

Internal controversies have also swirled around the manner in which the WSF meetings have been organized and coordinated. In the first Porto Alegre meeting, the Forum consisted of four panels and 420 workshops under four different themes: production of wealth and social reproduction; access to wealth and sustainability; civil society and public arena; political power and ethics in new society. The members of the panels were "leading names in the fight against the One Truth."[62] But the hierarchical organization and dry content of these panels and workshops was immediately decried as unrepresentative and tedious. In response, the organizers altered the structure of the meetings, permitting a much wider range of "thematic terrains" that could be initiated by the delegates themselves. For example, the fifth edition of the WSF had eleven themes under which more than 2,500 panels, discussions, and presentations were incorporated. These included: Defending Diversity; Assuring and Defending Earth; Communication; Sovereign Economies for and of the People; Arts and Culture; and Human Rights. Smaller venues were set aside for workshops on topics such as feminism and sexual repression but also included subjects like hip-hop and clowning. Many of the topics that had been promoted by the original leadership turned out to be of little interest to the rank and file, who were concerned about very different issues. In particular, many workshops dealt with spiritual themes and issues of identity.[63]

Despite the increasing emphasis on fostering a directly democratic and egalitarian ethos in the forum meetings, considerable disagreement remained within the WSF as to the best way to proceed. Some, notably trade unionists, members of NGOs, and more traditional leftist intellectuals and academics, cautioned that a hierarchical, representative organization is best able to engage with the existing nation-state and push it to adopt meaningful programs for change. But others—statistically much in the majority—viewed the state as an enemy and utterly rejected participation in electoral politics, preferring grassroots outreach instead. For insider commentators, "the two inhabited parallel universes."[64] As WSF theorist Boaventura de Sousa Santos documents, traditional leftists continued to use the old rhetoric of class struggle, power, state, reform, and rationality while their opponents referred to "love, dignity, solidarity, community, rebellion, spirituality, emotions and sentiments, transformation of subjectivity, 'a world to encompass all the worlds.'"[65] The second set of values is an example of shared assumptions common among civil society activists that appeal "to universal, transcendental, but ultimately mystical values—the values of the human rights movement and the 'innate' dignity of the person."[66] Accordingly, the cultural and epistemological rift within the WSF is a result of the emergence of new actors from "subordinate, indigenous, feminist, Asian, African and African-American cultures" previously ignored by the classical left.[67]

The emergence of these dissenting "new actors" is a consequence of a concerted WSF effort to establish a more "polycentric" organization able to reach the disenfranchised and excluded peoples of the nonwhite, ex-colonialized "global south." To achieve this end, the third WSF was held in three cities: Bangkok, Barcelona, and Florence; the 2004 meeting was in Mumbai, India; and in 2006 it spread to three cities on three continents: Bamako, Mali; Caracas, Venezuela; and Karachi, Pakistan. Meanwhile, many other meetings and actions, small and large, official and unofficial, have occurred across the globe.[68] For example, during the 2008 "Global Day of Action," coincident with the World Economic Forum meeting (January 22), protests and press conferences were scheduled in over thirty countries worldwide—though most were in Europe and Latin America. However, the number of people actually participating in these activities is impossible to estimate, as is the degree of commitment inspired. There have been complaints that the linkages forged at the meetings erode rapidly and that the main purpose of the WSF is to generate publicity for itself.[69]

Nor has the ongoing problem of incorporation and inequity been solved through expansion. As one young attendee of the 2007 WSF in Nairobi observed:

> There was a lot of confusion and complaints about Kenyans not being granted free admission, and there were food vendors who were kept outside the Forum for a few days. This seemed antithetical to the mission of the WSF in building a better community. . . . There were also many more middle-aged nonprofit and NGO workers and academics than I envisioned. The conference would have

been totally different with more representation of disadvantaged groups. It seemed to be conference goers were on the whole quite privileged.

Others at the conference complained about the number of corporate sponsors and attendees staying at four-star hotels and the gates, fences, and body searches that kept local people away from the meeting, which took place at the Moi International Sports Center, a venue associated with the elite.[70]

The fact of the matter is that the Forum's concerted efforts to include the ex-colonized, people of color, indigenous groups, and other marginalized and impoverished communities have not yet been successful. The majority of participants in the WSF are still white, young, educated, middle-class students, professionals, or intellectuals.[71] Most are what Tarrow has called "rooted cosmopolitans" (i.e., locally based activists working on "global" issues).[72] In light of these data, Rolando Munck asks: "Is the WSF a little bit too Western, too 'white' to understand the majority world where social, religious, and ethnic conflict is quite raw, immediate, and overwhelming?"[73]

Because of these failures, there is considerable internal disapproval of WSF efforts to broaden participation, encourage democratization, and increase diversity. For example, when the "Movement for Global Resistance" was invited to become a member of the governing IC, it refused, on the grounds that "a top-down process, involving a closed, nontransparent, nondemocratic, and highly institutionalized central committee will never attract collectives and networks searching for a new way of doing politics. This should be a space of participation, not representation."[74]

The Square without an Owner

This negative judgment ignores several important developments within the WSF. One is the rise of the International Youth Camp (IYC), which began in a public park as a way to house the young people who came to the first WSF meeting but soon grew to a kind of tribal gathering—a "temporary autonomous zone"[75] where transgressive behavior occurred. The IYC could easily be dismissed as "thousands of fresh-faced, body-pierced, tattooed, dreadlocked youngsters living in tents . . . (with a) bonfire in the middle of the central square, around which people gathered everyday at sunset to join the epitomic Mexican shaman Oscar."[76] Although it was disparaged as the Woodstock of the antiglobalization movement, the IYC proved to be a fount of energy and inspiration, overturning taken-for-granted modes of behavior, belief, and organization.

Members of the IYC were among the most prominent protesters against the privileges of elite delegates; using "vernacular technology," self-organized IYC groups built their own temporary housing out of recycled waste; the IYC accessed alternative open source media outlets, evolved its own internal currency, and prepared its own organic food. Publications of the IYC were the first to refer to the WSF as "a movement of movements" and the first to proclaim the WSF "not an event, but a process." In so doing, the IYC helped to initiate a shift "from the first, rigid model to a more fluid one" and provided an "innovative space for generating new forms of social, political, and cultural interaction."[77] By 2005, the IYC had grown enormously and had moved from the periphery to the center of the forum space.

Coincident with expansion of the IYC and other autonomous spaces within the WSF (a "Solidarity Village" or "Life Despite Capitalism," for example),[78] came greater support for carnivalesque creative performances. As Alisa Solomon documents, in the 2005 meeting in Porto Alegre, spontaneous musical, artistic, and dance productions appeared everywhere, so that

> to walk the sweltering trek from one section of meeting tents to another was to pass from the electric screech of a punk guitar to the mesmerizing repetition of indigenous chants to the melodic beat of two South African men rapping about HIV prevention. . . . A local samba school involved more than 300 forumistas, some of whom had attended its workshops, in a raucous street show . . . The mass inched rhythmically down the street . . . joined by all the standard elements of a samba team: dozens of young men pounding on drums, dervishing grandmothers in ruffled prom dresses, shimmying women in enormous heels, feather headdresses and sequined bikinis. This was high-spirited agitprop without a trace of sanctimony. . . . Interventions like the samba parade . . . not only added to the giddy assertion of public space. They offered a model for the doing of politics: groups of strangers coming together with common purpose and, with a little improvising, discussion, adjustment and trust, making something wonderful happen.

Such dramatic performances "captured the WSF's spirit: exploratory, capacious and more than a little chaotic."[79] The IYC and the new emphasis on ecstatic performance reminded forum participants that

> carnival and revolution have identical goals: to turn the world upside down with joyous abandon and to celebrate our indestructible lust for life, a lust

that capitalism tries so hard to destroy with its monotonous merry go round of work and consumerism. . . . It gives a glimpse of what is possible, igniting our imagination, our belief in utopia—a utopia defined not as no-place, but as this-place.[80]

From this perspective, the WSF can be described as "a form of *political improvisation* that mirrors jazz performances; players demonstrate the uniqueness of their instruments and their own creativity while maintaining rhythmic and tonal connections with the group."[81] As WSF founder and theorist Chico Whitaker writes, the improvisatory process flourishes when it "has *no leader*. It is only a place, basically a *horizontal space*. . . . It is like a *square without an owner*. . . . a space created to serve a common objective to all those who converge to the Forum, functioning horizontally as public space, without leaders or pyramids of power."[82] The square without an owner is congenial to open debate and democracy "based on social justice rather than formal elections."[83] In it, free exchanges of information link all those who oppose neoliberalism, imperialism, colonialism, and militarism. This fluid relationship provides a *real-life model* of another world, and its enactment actually *alters the consciousness* of participants:

> The experience of acting as human beings, not cogs, as members of a society of equals, is both exhilarating and transforming. Possibilities that previously seemed unreal, open up. Getting rid of "the muck of ages" becomes conceivable because the individual's behavior and sense of self is shifting, changing and developing so rapidly. . . . Listen. Hear the poetry of the future. Soon, those whispers may become a roar, declaring to all prepared to listen that another world is possible.[84]

At this juncture, the whispered "poetry of the future" that is being improvised in the "square without an owner" has not yet become audible to the general public, but certain key melodies can already be heard. Of crucial importance is the embrace of "the diversity of genders, ethnicities, cultures, generations, and physical capacities" that the WSF charter demands.[85] The Forum's approval of tolerance is not a platitude. Rather, within the WSF alternative framework utopia *is* multiplicity. As Simon Tormey remarks, "It is not coalescence of outlook that marks the politics of the alterglobalisation movement, but the multiplication of differences, positions and standpoints. It has also been marked by a recognition that such differences are intrinsic to understanding the strength and vibrancy of the movement and hence that any attempt to undermine it would change its character."[86] By extension, the WSF positive policy against proclaiming any positive policy is, in itself, the declaration of a new way of being that "says no to a single way of thinking and yes to equality and diversity."[87] The result, according to the Notes from Nowhere collective, is a "movement of pink fairies in solidarity with Indian farmers, of taxi drivers and graffiti artists issuing the same demands, of indigenous Ogoni identifying the same targets as pie-throwing utopians."[88]

The implications of the pursuit of infinite variety are profound. The emphasis on multiplicity (rather than homogeneity) is at the center of what Hardt and Negri see as the arrival of an "absolute democracy" of multitudes, "without boundaries and without measure": an "open network" of groups and populations cooperating in the construction of a new society.[89] As Naomi Klein writes, the nurturance of variety requires the construction of a global

> political framework that can both take on corporate power and control, and empower local organizing and self-determination. That has to be a framework that encourages, celebrates and fiercely protects the right to diversity: cultural diversity, ecological diversity, agricultural diversity—and yes, political diversity as well: different ways of doing politics. Communities must have the right to plan and manage their schools, their services, their natural settings, according to their own lights. Of course, this is only possible within a framework of national and international standards—of public education, fossil-fuel emissions, and so on. But the goal should not be better far-away rules and rulers, it should be close-up democracy on the ground.[90]

As Klein indicates, "close-up democracy on the ground" is an ultimate value for movement activists. William F. Fisher and Thomas Ponniah explain that a sweeping democratization of society is "the essential step for overcoming elite domination, technocracy, classism, racism, sexism and the apathy generated by bureaucratization and the current forms of representative democracy." The democracy required for this revolutionary change is direct, not representative; it is "a radical, participatory, living democracy (that) involves all citizens in the daily reconstruction of society. . . . decisions, in every sphere, are determined by directly democratic decision-making."[91] Representation is the "space of treason" of popular sovereignty while the "democratization of representation" is favored, which means that "the electoral mandates must be placed under constant citizen vigilance."[92] Voter withdrawal, passivity, or disinterest is apparently not an option in this directly governed, radically democratic new world. Although we do not as yet know what decisions will be made in the future "reinvented society," we can be sure that each decision will be made only after much debate and many, many workshops and meetings.

The requirement to protect diversity and preserve autonomy pointed to by Klein implies yet another central aspect of the movement's plan for the future: strong support for the rights and claims of local communities. This support is best exemplified in movement attitudes toward indigenous peoples ("First Nations") who are portrayed as "the oldest of globalization resistance actions." As founts of ancestral wisdom, environmental awareness, and revitalizing tribal consciousness, their practices of collective responsibility and stewardship, rather than ownership, of resources "fly directly in the face of the basic assumptions of neoliberal global capitalism."[93] For example, the IFG approvingly quotes a "call to consciousness" published in 1978 by the native American Iroquois Nation:

> Many thousands of years ago, all the people of the world believed in the same way of life, that of harmony with the universe. [But] the way of life known as Western Civilization is on a death path on which their own culture has no viable answers. . . . The traditional native people hold the key to the reversal of the processes in Western civilizations. . . . We are the spiritual guardians of this place. We are here to impart this message.[94]

A similar statement by Colombia's indigenous U'wa people, for whom "the money king is only an illusion," is also frequently mentioned in alter-globalization circles.[95]

The struggles of indigenous peoples for recognition of their autonomy and culture are understood as the most extreme instances of the universal human battle for dignity and identity that inevitably occurs under the alienating conditions of the neoliberal regime. For antiglobalization activists, the world "as it is" cannot offer anyone, anywhere, an authentic sense of belonging or being:

> Material success, no matter how sumptuous, does not by itself fully satisfy or meet the full emotional aspects of identity self-sufficiency. Burning underneath is the eternal thirst of respect for one's cultural identity and humanity, irrespective of times and space, so that s/he is no longer viewed and treated as the perpetual 'other' or simply as inferior, deserving little respect and dignity.[96]

Regretfully, the deracinated majority cannot reconnect to their authentic tribal roots and so must create social bonds through ramifying horizontal networks that "provide something of a counter to the social dislocations and displacements of globalization. . . . A collective identity that is not linked to state structures or the market."[97] The result is a new form of authenticity based on "the uprooting of activities and relationships from local origins and cultures."[98] The deterritorialized community will "abandon nationhood, just as, in earlier epochs, we abandoned the barony and the clan. It will compel us to recognize the irrationality of the loyalties which set us apart. For the first time in history, we will see ourselves as a species."[99]

The Curse of Realism and the Necessity of Miracles

The movement's pursuit of a generic "United States of Earth"[100] would seem to contradict indigenous claims for recognition as autonomous nations, solidly located in place, history, and practice; but, according to activists, the contrary is the case. "All that prevents the final destruction of most of the world's indigenous peoples is the support which they and their defenders can summon from beyond their own national borders. By appealing to universalism, they defend diversity."[101]

Support for the communal identities and cultural beliefs of the first nations and other local communities and a faith in the transformative power of direct democracy coincides with another fundamental principle of the alternative globalization movement. This is subsidiarity, defined as "a reversal of power, away from the global toward the local." Under the aegis of subsidiarity, "whatever decisions and activities can be undertaken locally should be. Whatever power can reside at the local level should reside there. . . . The principle of subsidiarity recognizes the inherent democratic right to self-determination for people, communities, and nations as long as its exercise does not infringe on the similar rights of others."[102] Ideally, the result is "a democracy which takes place on the stage of spontaneously unfolding life, not raised above the audience but at ground level, where everyone can be involved. There are no leaders, no spectators, no sidelines, only an entanglement of many players who do their own thing while feeling part of a greater whole."[103]

Squaring WSF support for "First Nation" autonomy and local self-determination with the WSF goal of universal human rights is easily accomplished under the Zapatista "one world that contains many worlds" slogan. However, the question of how a triumphant global movement might incorporate local cultures that are undemocratic, hierarchical, or intolerant is not seriously addressed. The assumption seems to be that, if protected from neoliberal interference and fenced in by the imposition of international standards of fairness, human beings will naturally act democratically to achieve what the WSF understands to be their fundamental rights, most importantly "the right to live in harmony with one another"[104]—a "right" that human history hardly confirms.

Intellectuals within the movement respond that such a criticism is guilty of mistaking what is for what must be. This is an instance of "the curse of realism" that "determines limits before these limits are themselves known . . . (and) denies the fact that change is cumulative, not sequential, that the present is always conditioned on the future."[105] Critics should realize that the WSF is an improvisation, making up new worlds as it goes along. In the performance of spontaneous and protean activism, "what is realistic is what happens. The moment we make it happen, it becomes realistic. As the other possibilities fall away, a global democratic revolution is, in both senses, the only realistic option we have. . . . Why not embrace those proposals which give us what we want, rather than just what we imagine 'the authorities are ready to consider?'"[106] So, instead of disallowing alternatives out of hand and becoming complicit in the world order, we must be "prepared for and . . . expect 'miracles' in the political realm."[107]

As Jackie Smith and her collaborators explain in their historical review of the WSF, the future can be imagined and objectively realized through "'prefigurative politics'—or the enactment of the world we envision . . . Social forum events are attempts to create miniworlds, models the forum process hopes to export around the globe." This

> new form of politics challenges the visions of history that emphasize chronological chains of processes where all that happens is the logical consequence of its context and its immediate past. . . . The continuity of corporate globalization is now in question. By challenging the relentless progression of privatization, trade liberalization, consumption, and individuation, the rebellion has created another temporality within which the WSF is clearly situated.[108]

That is why alter-globalization activists frequently define their work in terms of "dual politics": They *simultaneously* engage the system (by protesting against it) and distance themselves from it by creating defiant networks and spaces in which the world they are struggling for (diverse and radically democratic) is realized and experienced.[109] Hence the importance of "liberated spaces" for the practice of alternative ways of life,[110] such as the Zapatistas' caracoles, urban squatter networks, or the communities of the landless movement in Brazil.

The cumulative effect of such logic-challenging, history-altering participatory experiments is a cascading personal and collective experience of transformation that cannot be captured by rational analysis. "To feel part of this global movement that transcends boundaries of language, culture, distance and history, is empowering beyond words. . . . A trickle can become a flood: Raindrops coalesce, tributaries join. Our movement is like a river. A fractal network of converging and anastomosing [sic] channels, defying straightforward analysis, and rising from a thousand distant sources." Immersion in the flood requires "letting go of our precious identities, letting go of our egos and our subcultures." When the self and its cultural context have been dissolved in the torrent, then we will "have the courage to demand . . . everything for everyone, the courage to keep the spaces that this movement of movements has created, radically open, rebelliously inviting, and profoundly popular. . . . For when 'we' are truly everywhere, we will be nowhere—for we will be everyone."[111] No wonder that "in facing the global crisis, the most powerful weapon that we have is our imagination."[112]

Ecstatic merger in a revolutionary communion is not just the dream of a few impassioned activist youth. The hardheaded George Monbiot has a similar vision. As he writes:

> We can, quite rationally, subordinate our desire for liberty to our desire for security. Or we can use our agency to change the world, and, in changing it, to change ourselves. We will die and be forgotten with no less certainty that those who sought to fend off death by enhancing their material presence on the earth, but we will live before we die through the extremes of feeling which comfort would deny us.

This is because

> there is, in collective revolutionary action, something which appears to be missing from almost every other enterprise in modern secular life. It arises, I think, from the intensity of the relationships forged in a collective purpose concentrated by adversity. It is the *exultation* which Christians call 'joy,' but which, in the dry discourse of secular politics, has no recognized equivalent. It is the drug for which, once sampled, you will pay any price.[113]

It seems that the WSF, and the alter-globalization movement in general, offers much more to its members than the reform of the tax system.

SLOW FOOD AND SLOW LIFE[114]

Revolutionary Pleasure

While global justice activists are inspired by the ecstasy of revolutionary action, Slow Food appeals to the ordinary pleasures of eating a good meal in good company. And, unlike the aggressive antiglobalization organizations, movements, and parties we have already documented, Slow Food has a nonconfrontational approach to transforming the world. But its ambitions are no less total.

Slow Food, which claims 80,000 dues-paying members in 126 countries, is the brainchild of Carlo Petrini, who was born in 1949 to a family of socialist greengrocers in the provincial town of Bra in the Langhe Region of Northern Italy. Bra is an economically depressed industrial backwater well known for leatherwork and its leftist voluntary associations. Like many other young activists of the 1960s and 1970s, Petrini was disenchanted with the compromising politics and bureaucratic structure of the old left but repelled by the violence and extremism of the Italian radical parties. In response, he and his colleagues organized a political club (the Circolo Leonardo Cocito—named after a local hero of the Italian resistance to fascism) and supported their grassroots efforts by starting a cooperative grocery store (the Spaccio di Unità Popolare or "Store of Popular Unity"). The club soon joined ARCI,[115] the Italian recreational association of the political left. Petrini also held a seat on the city council as member of the Proletarian Unity Party (PdUP) from 1975 until 1980. In addition to his political activity, Petrini was deeply engaged in organizing and acting as master of ceremonies in local folk music festivals. Serious debt obliged him to "set aside songs and politics." He "resigned from his seat at the city council . . . and began getting involved in catering and social tourism," establishing several restaurants serving traditionally prepared local food. In 1981, Petrini and his cronies formed the "Free and Praiseworthy Association of the Friends of Barolo,"[116] with the aim of increasing awareness and consumption of the indigenous fine wine. Italy had long been the home of gourmet societies, but this was something new. Where the earlier groups had been transitory apolitical clubs exclusively for gourmandizing elites, Petrini's Association united a leftist ecological, antiglobalist agenda with the message that authentic local food production would promote a healthy and egalitarian lifestyle based on the enjoyment of "life's pleasures: good wine and food." Their slogan, "Barolo wine is democratic, or at least it can become so," reflected their pleasure-based, populist philosophy.[117] The tireless and charismatic Petrini also organized a cooperative advising local businesses,[118] which sponsored rural summer camps for children so that they could learn firsthand how their food was grown. These initiatives presaged the unique Slow Food combination of dedicated pursuit of gustatory pleasure, social activism, the cultivation of tradition, and pragmatic commerce.

From its inception, the Arcigola combined its program of political/ecological activism with an aggressive and quite successful local campaign to draw tourists to the Langhe region by publicizing wine and food tastings and local festivals. Guidebooks were written to educate the public about the quality of regional wines, produce, and restaurants. Its pedagogic and profit-making initiatives expanded to include Arcigola-sponsored guidebooks about food and wine in all of Italy and then later to other areas where a "convivium" (a Slow Food voluntary collective) was located. In what has been called "the gourmet community's equivalent of a world social forum,"[119] the international network of Slow Food activists gathers together in a biennial conference—entitled Terra Madre (Mother Earth)—which draws thousands of food producers and "co-producers" (Slow Food language for consumers) to Turin, where they "explore important issues and share solutions to common challenges of producing food in a sustainable manner."[120] It is, as one activist says, an "Earth democracy" that combines both a "planetary consciousness and a local embeddedness."[121]

This event occurs in conjunction with the Salone del Gusto: a mammoth five-day celebration of regional food, cooking, and eating. During a recent Salone "a Japanese sake-maker discussed Internet marketing with a Bolivian llama herder. Bakers from France and Italy compared notes on stone-ground flours. Everywhere you looked, someone was turning the principles of Slow Food into profit."[122] This heterogeneous entrepreneurial-cum-revolutionary festival has drawn over 130,000 participants since its inauguration in 1996, all affirming the uniqueness of their own specific local "Food Communities" while simultaneously mobilizing against the global food industry. As Petrini exhorted the Salone del Gusto in 2004, "When you return to your villages . . . you will know that you are no longer alone." Instead, you are "brothers from all over the world" united in an "international alliance of the Earth's caretakers" battling against the evils of agribusiness.[123]

Because "virtuous globalization" requires knowledge as well as organization, Slow Food has initiated a variety of educational projects, including the establishment of a University of Gastronomic Sciences (UNISG) in Italy, outreach programs on taste education in primary and secondary schools, and increased connections to college students worldwide to promote a holistic "eco-gastronomic" approach to food production, preparation, and consumption. From the Slow Food perspective, gastronomy is a uniquely unifying discipline that "entails a broad knowledge of botany, genetics, physics, chemistry, agriculture, zootechnics, agronomy, ecology, anthropology, sociology, geopolitics, political economies, trade, industry, cooking, physiology, medicine, and epistemology, as all these subjects relate to food."[124] Furthermore, in conjunction with the Region of Tuscany, Slow Food has developed the nonprofit Foundation for Biodiversity, whose "mission is to organize and fund projects that defend our world's heritage of agricultural biodiversity and gastronomic traditions."[125]

Slow Food also has initiated the "Ark of Taste," which catalogues foods that are "threatened by industrial standardization, hygiene laws, the regulations of large-scale distribution, and environmental damage."[126] And it supports a myriad of locally organized "Presidia" to protect and promote the endangered food products included in the Ark of Taste. The Presidia work to "promote artisan products; to stabilize production techniques; to establish stringent production standards and, above all, to guarantee a viable future for traditional foods."[127] The purpose of all this activity is to "spread—according to local culture—our message of peace, well-being, innovation, tradition, pleasure, happiness, and our desire that Good, Clean, and Fair food be available for everyone."[128]

Slow Food promotes its "defense of pleasure" by a remarkably effective communications and propaganda network that makes extensive use of the Internet;[129] by its own publishing house (Slow Editore) that produces a wide variety of reports, studies, guidebooks, memoirs, surveys, newsletters; and by a quarterly magazine (*Slow*), which is written in six languages and distributed to members worldwide. Petrini and others in the movement have written books for both the mainstream and alternative press. Each national association also has its own websites and blogs producing a flood of information on its activities, inviting response and participation at every point. Furthermore, Petrini urges "all convivia to construct and strengthen their own local communities . . . beginning with widespread involvement, with producers' communities, knocking on the door of local institutions to raise awareness, organizing markets, initiating small projects in the area, contributing to the international association's communication with news and issues to bring to the world's attention."[130] The result, Petrini writes, is a "communication strategy that makes it possible to 'sell' the world a complex image combining history, landscape, wine, cuisine, and a style of welcome."[131]

Healthy Craziness

Organizationally, Slow Food radiates from the outsized personality, inexhaustible energy, and inspirational pronouncements of its charismatic founder, Carlo Petrini, whose plans are implemented by an impressive bureaucratic apparatus and a daunting profusion of statutes, articles, and provisions that codify every aspect of the organization's structure. The most recently ratified international statute is forty-five articles long. But, like other such transformative collectives, Slow Food also wishes to constitute itself as a decentralized and democratic "horizontal" structure—much like the communications network that has helped to make it so successful. Thus the local convivia are given very considerable autonomy. The paradoxical mixture of a charismatic centralization with egalitarian democratic local activism is frequent in aurora movements. Zapatismo is the type case.

As we have also seen in other cases, the inevitable tension between centralized structure and horizontal spontaneity[132] is eased through the cultivation of an atmosphere of informality and celebration, actualized in the Salone del Gusto and in other mass meetings, where Petrini can apply his old training as master of ceremonies and where music, feasting, and other pleasures act as garnishes to make the centralized structure and bureaucratic apparatus surrounding it more palatable. As Petrini told his audience during the opening speech at the 2007 Slow Food International Congress:

> Many say that being an association means assigning a rational agreement among citizens who agree upon a common objective. We are here because we have common objectives, but this is the tip of the iceberg. Being in an association means a rational project, but often pushed by non-rational impulses. The wish to access life, to have a hope in life, the need to socialize, to be useful, to react to injustice. . . . Being in an association has a seed of foolishness, craziness, and we should nurture this. This healthy craziness, we need just a little of it.[133]

According to Petrini, the Slow Food combination of a little craziness and a lot of rationality can "create an original and unusual social group that would be open, democratic, and uncontaminated by particular interests and that would avoid making itself ridiculous with rites, protocols, and trappings."[134] The struggle against pretension may be a losing battle, at least on the local level, as there is much that seems bombastic and absurd (at least to an outsider) about a movement whose members spend an evening solemnly sampling thirty different kinds of salt, painstakingly marking scorecards to be compared and tabulated at the end of the exercise. As one friendly critic warns, "The Presidia products, or even the simple discourse of Slow Food, can be utilized to bring a good conscience to an approach more closely resembling snobbism than social engagement. One cannot underestimate this risk, but it is inherent to the decentralized nature of the movement."[135] It also must be kept in mind that the ultimate purpose of the tasting exercises is to increase the members' capacity for awareness, pleasure, and solidarity. Convivium, Petrini reminds us, "means conviviality . . . it is a tool for freedom. It means that we have to all respect each other."[136]

According to Slow Food ideology, the need to cultivate liberation and mutual respect is great because "this age of globalization, the postindustrial age," which "the world system seems unlikely to tolerate for much longer,"[137] is "dominated by hegemonic forces that are threatening to turn it into a desert."[138] The Slow Food manifesto, ratified by members from fifteen countries in 1989, stated: "Fast life . . . disrupts our habits, pervades the privacy of our homes and forces us to eat Fast Foods." Symptoms of the disease include the introduction of a "distinctively 'American' way of eating—the idea that food is something to be consumed as quickly, efficiently and inexpensively as possible."[139] Slow Food is adamantly opposed to a Americanized homogenization of taste. Slow Food is also against the "absurd idea" of industrial agriculture, which is derided as "a form of cultural annihilation that has affected the countryside of every part of the world, on a scale that is unprecedented in human history."[140] Slow Food challenges the authority of an "official" science engaged in a "demented drive toward a world of tomatoes that don't go bad and strawberries with salmon genes."[141] Slow Food has been accused of utopianism, but (like other alter-globalizing movements) it argues that mainstream scientists are the real utopians because they "think that by applying industrial techniques to agriculture it would be possible to solve the problems of hunger, profitability, the wholesomeness of food and the conservation of the environment."[142]

Instead of science, only "suitable doses of guaranteed sensual pleasure and slow, long-lasting enjoyment" will "preserve us from the contagion of the multitude who mistake frenzy for efficiency"[143] and offer "the world the hope of a future different from the polluted and tasteless one that the lords of the earth have programmed for all of us." To achieve this goal, Slow Food has promoted a long-term strategy of supporting

> food that is ethically produced, with fair treatment of workers, equitable relationships with farmers (locally and abroad), and humanely treated animals. It's food that is environmentally sustainable—grown without chemical pesticides, large-scale mono-cropping, or huge carbon footprints. Real Food is food that tastes good, builds community, and has the potential to inspire broad-scale social change.[144]

The Slow Food policy is symbolized in its snail logo[145] and by its slogan of "Good, Clean, and Fair."

Of central importance in the Slow Food strategy has been its effort to save "historical and localized" producers, foster good taste, educate the public, and "reconstruct the individual and collective heritage."[146] This effort begins with "respect for traditional knowledge" that is not controlled by scientific experts. Ancient wisdom is "in the hands of humble people, of farmers, fishermen, [and] food producers."[147] The argument is that industrialized fast food is of course nasty, impure, and dangerous; but even worse, under modern conditions commensality "is rendered banal, functional, or literal and increasingly reserved for the diversions of private life."[148] The retreat to the homogenized and mechanical isolation of fast food ruins genuine communal identity and the legacy of history, which is retained in the venerable food traditions of the countryside. If we do not eat proper food grown, prepared, and served in the original manner, we cannot experience the powerful ancestral links that bind us together; nor can we realize our own authentic personal identities, which are intertwined with our shared history and experience. Fast food and existential anomie go together, as do Slow Food and authenticity. From this perspective, enjoying a McDonald's hamburger is not only a moral failing; it is also a lapse of taste, a betrayal of the self, and evidence of bad faith:

> When we pledge our dietary allegiance to a fast-food nation, there are also grave consequences to the health of our civil society and our national character. When we eat fast-food meals alone in our cars, we swallow the values and assumptions of the corporations that manufacture them.[149]

Slow Food does recognize that taste is learned and culturally specific. As Jean Lhéritier tells Siv Lie:

In my region there is a tradition of putting a little piece of rancid fat in traditional dishes. . . . I wrote an article about this rancid taste in our newsletter, in
which I said that a history and a social group, a population has validated this
culinary culture. There is no reason for someone who is not used to this taste,
who considers it a defect, to dismiss it.

The difference between the rancid fat enjoyed by Lhéritier and a McDonald's
hamburger is the connection the first has with an ancient and authentic local
tradition, while the second is manufactured and homogenous, without cultural specificity. Therefore, taste workshops are conducted by convivia "so
that people can understand why a certain taste is particular, so they can learn
about it and appreciate it. But one has the right to not like something. What
we're concerned about is the culinary culture of a social group."[150]

Despite its preoccupation with resuscitating tradition and maintaining
authenticity, Slow Food does not favor returning to the localized rural world
of yesterday, when people ate the same things throughout their entire lives.
Though healthy, that would be just as tedious as a diet of McDonald's hamburgers and would destroy one's sense of taste, defined by Petrini as "a rest-
less creature that thrives on diversity, works retroactively to revive memories,
and goes forward blindly, promising virtual pleasures."[151] Because habit is
the enemy of taste, the Slow Food initiate must always seek diversity. Petrini
proclaims "to eat a different kind of food in every street in the world is the
best answer to fast food."[152] For the Slow Food gourmet, only a certain type
of variety will do if a newly discovered taste is to be truly delicious and not
indulgently clever and therefore inauthentic. In the first place, whatever the
revolutionary pleasure-seeker swallows, it must be made with the highest-
quality, certifiably purest ingredients and cooked in a traditional, simple,
unpretentious, and *authentic* manner reflective of the unique terroir where
it belongs.[153] Proper consumption also requires extensive knowledge of the
varied historical, cultural, and ecological backgrounds of local comestibles.
As Petrini informs us: "In order to learn how to find slow pleasure, one has
to travel, read and taste, abandoning the temptation of entrenched isolation."
After cultivating diversity and exploring exotic traditions the worldwide association of self-aware gastronomes then become "allies who think alike while
respecting one another at a distance." They are members of a new form of
collective that is "heterogeneous but strongly cohesive . . . an elite without ex-
cluding anyone." The hoped-for end result is a plural community that "singles

out, highlights, and values difference" and is unified by a shared appreciation for ecologically sound, aesthetically satisfying food production, preparation, and consumption.[154]

Sublime Life of Wonder

There are many criticisms of the Slow Food "revolution." Some say it returns women to their traditional role as kitchen drudges; others complain that it transforms cheap local food into expensive international products,[155] has a simplistic and unrealistic view of "authenticity,"[156] "is a grassroots movement of influential urban elites,"[157] and cannot spread beyond its food-loving Italian base.[158] Nonetheless, many activists have committed themselves to its message. For example, the prominent West Coast restaurateur Alice Waters believes that eating natural food is not just an aesthetic experience but also a way to save the planet and oneself. In a mission statement for her Parisian restaurant, she says a "restaurant must feel human, reflecting the spirit of the farm, the *terroir*, and the market, and it must express the humanity of the artisans, cooks, and servers who work there."[159] Similarly, the Los Angeles–based Viand collective asserts that "pleasure and quality in everyday life can be achieved by slowing down, respecting the convivial traditions of the table, and celebrating the diversity of the earth's bounty."[160]

More importantly, the Slow message has been expanded to apply to areas far removed from food. For example, Cittaslow (or Slow Cities) was directly inspired by Slow Food and is "committed to ecological preservation, sustainable development, and . . . quality of life." From Italy to Korea, Cittaslow activists search for a slow-paced life.[161] Other slow associations include the Transition Movement (toward sustainable communities), the Car-Free Movement, the Sloth Club and BeGood network in Japan, the Long Now Foundation in the United States, the European Society for the Deceleration of Time, Slow Travel, Slow Design, Slow Money, Slow Schooling, Slow Housing cooperatives, speeders anonymous, Slow Music, superslow weight lifting, slow therapies like reiki healing, chi kung, yoga, and even a slow sex movement.[162] Slow Food, in these instances, has become the bearer of a generalized message inspiring a multitude of believers to transform their ways of thinking and living. Petrini is not hostile to this mutation: "We don't have the ambition to be a political party . . . We should not be scared of people stealing our ideas."[163]

The Slow Food philosophy therefore goes far beyond contempt for industrialized hamburgers. For many, it has become a call to radical insurgency.

According to the author of *The Revolution Will Not Be Microwaved*, a new wave of "resistance movements . . . reject dead, industrialized, homogenized, globalized food communities in favor of real, wholesome, local, unadulterated food." Instead of falling back into consumerism and "all the other alluring empty promises of globalized corporate food," this "food-related political activism" builds alternatives that "transform the world one bite at a time."[164] The Italian "Land and Liberty/Critical Wine" movement, which was founded to defend wine producers and traditions from the homogenization of global taste, now sees itself promoting a planetary revolution against the "reduction of life to a machine" and for freedom, joy, and a "new alliance" between humanity and Earth. If the revolution fails, the result will be the inevitable "suicide of the [human] species."[165]

Other enthusiasts see Slow Food as the source of a powerful philosophy of "slow life" that penetrates into and transforms every aspect of society and self by reversing the present direction (and pace) of history. As Cecile Andrews proclaims:

> People are beaten down, overworked, stressed, and depressed. . . . We need . . . joie de vivre, the state of feeling vital and alive. Of being caught up by exuberance, enthusiasm and excitement—high spirits and high energy. Of recapturing those youthful moments when life seemed wonderful and all you felt was yes, yes, yes! . . . Enjoyment must be our guide. . . . S-L-O-W stands for Sublime Life of Wonder. . . . The Slow Life engenders a "culture of connection," a connectedness to life—to yourself, to others, to the planet, to the universe. . . . How do we know when we connect? . . . You get a sudden burst of energy, and things start popping to the front. There's light and movement. That's what happens if you connect with life. If you don't connect, you feel dull and dead; if you do, you feel alive and energetic. It's being in tune with life.[166]

In the same vein, Carl Honoré writes:

> Fast is busy, controlling, aggressive, hurried, analytical, stressed, superficial, impatient, active, quantity-over-quality. Slow is the opposite: calm, careful, receptive, still, intuitive, unhurried, patient, reflective, quality-over-quantity. It is about making real and meaningful connections—with people, culture, work, food, everything. . . . it strikes at the heart of what it is to be human in the era of the silicon chip. . . . We need to go further and rethink our approach to everything. . . . Decelerating will be a struggle until we rewrite the rules

that govern almost every sphere of life—the economy, the workplace, urban design, education, medicine. . . . The big question now is when the individual will become the collective. When will the many personal acts of deceleration occurring across the world reach critical mass? When will the Slow movement turn into a Slow revolution?[167]

To this question, Petrini gives a cautious reply: "We are not trying to change the world anymore, just to save it."[168] Nonetheless, the dreams of Slow Food are very ambitious. In its own self-description, implementing its program will lead to greater pleasure, deeper knowledge, and shared social responsibility for the environment because "for a true gastronome, it is impossible to ignore the strong connections between plate and planet."[169] More importantly, a Slow revolution will expand and soften human sympathies. As Petrini puts it, "We catch barely a glimpse of the fundamental concept that ought to underlie all these projects: that of 'feeling good' with oneself and with others."[170]

THE RAVE AT THE END OF TIME
Attaining Cyborg Subjectivity

Attending an illegal all-night party in an abandoned warehouse where stoned young people, dressed outrageously, sucking pacifiers and waving phosphorescent glowsticks, dance and stomp to ear-shattering music may not seem to be an alternative to globalization. But it is.

The global rave counterculture is a mind-bending mix of music, drugs, trance, dance, and travel. It has no central leader, no active political program, no clear membership; it is based primarily on expressive performance and ecstatic experience and is resolutely anti-intellectual. This amorphous collective is founded in a multimedia and transformative dance event, which, as ethnographer Anthony D'Andrea puts it, "reshapes self-identities in consonance with destabilizing effects of globalization upon tradition, identities and subjectivities." Rave arose alongside New Age religious movements in the 1980s "at the confluence of new digital technologies, globalized exchanges and neo-liberal exploitation."[171] It is both a reaction to, and an amalgam of, all these influences. Its heritage also reaches back to San Francisco in the 1960s when Ken Kesey and the Merry Pranksters, along with the Grateful Dead and other psychedelic bands, staged all-night LSD-fueled dance parties that were meant to liberate consciousness. As we shall see, for practitioners, it has a much longer lineage, dating back to prehistory.

The music igniting rave is techno—a combination of a Teutonic man/machine aesthetic with the sensual funk and house music of the post-Stonewall black and Latino gay clubs of New York City, Detroit, and Chicago.[172] Techno is an umbrella term covering a constantly evolving variety of electronic dance music (house, jungle, Goa, trance, ambient, and the like) in which sophisticated digital technologies produce powerful repetitive beats and swirling randomized sequences that weave "psychedelic squelches through the mass of electronic sound."[173] During a rave, techno music throbs nonstop, while the DJ seamlessly slides one track into another, building to repeated crescendos. Lacking lyrics, techno relies on sampling for verbal content, and the result is a bewildering and intoxicating mélange of random voices and cries laid over a pulse that builds to produce "a euphoric catharsis . . . comparable to a roller-coaster ride, where the car pulled to its highest point, people bursting with suspense, higher, higher . . . and then let loose to the forces of gravity with thundering abandon."[174]

In the 1990s, techno-trance music and dance were exported to the United Kingdom, where unused industrial storage space was illegally appropriated for all-night parties that were frequented by brightly costumed young people, often high on LSD (acid), cocaine, marijuana or—especially—the "love drug" MDMA (ecstasy).[175] The phenomenon soon entered the mainstream and moved from its original illicit sites to "super clubs" located in London and other urban settings worldwide and also to youth-oriented vacation centers where many thousands of transitory "neo-nomads" and holiday makers flocked to party without inhibition. For some, rave "became the most dynamic digital counterculture of the 1990s,"[176] "the first counterculture to have emerged under the direct impact of global processes,"[177] and "the largest popular cultural movement of the 20th century."[178]

It is true that rave and its offshoots constitute one of the biggest modern social movements. For example, the Love Parade in Berlin is said to attract a million people; Earthdance joins even more enthusiasts through worldwide Internet linkages. Huge venues such as Space in Ibiza can hold up to 10,000 ravers, and it is only one of many operating every night during the holiday season. But if the numbers are large, the commitment demanded is small. Most who participate are "weekend warriors" or tourists simply looking for a temporary escape from the drudgery of their ordinary lives; the rave experience apparently makes little difference in their daily routines. The vast majority go back to work after their mind-bending vacations or wild nights. However, even for those seeking only temporary diversion, rave can be surprisingly important for the construction of a valued and ecstatic (if transitory) alternative identity that offsets the alienating environment of the everyday.

The first steps toward formation of an alternative rave identity occur prior to the experience itself. In its earliest incarnations, a rave was held only for the cognoscenti. It took place in a hidden and remote spot that required time and effort to locate; the site was often communicated through coded messages decipherable only to insiders, confirming their membership in a special club. The event itself was organized by volunteers and was—at least ideally—not a commercial enterprise. As one DJ states: "What attracted me in the beginning of electronic music was that it didn't reflect the Western mentality. I am not really interested in any music . . . where consumption is the basis of the mentality."[179]

Even when raves became both very public and very profitable, they retained a countercultural aura. For example, gaining entrée still required the right "look," which meant dressing up in colorful, humorous, infantile, and sexually suggestive outfits, replacing suits with swimwear, cigarettes with pacifiers, pens with glowsticks. The donning of outrageous clothes symbolized the adoption of a "*nocturnal self*" that is seen and experienced as freer, more vivid, more expressive, more emotional, more erotic, and more *authentic* than the daytime workaday self.[180] Inside the rave site, whatever remained of normality was obliterated on a dark, murky, immense, crammed dance floor (there is no stage) where speech was drowned out by the pulverizing techno beat. The steps of the dance are simple, mechanical, and repetitive. Energized by the trance-inducing music, the ecstatic crowd, and (often) by the effects of mind-altering drugs, the ravers dance into the morning, pushing themselves to the edge of collapse and sometimes beyond.[181]

One commentator describes the experience as follows:

> A pulse like mother's heartbeat give(s) an androgynous "pre-Oedipal" framework . . . in which the dancer loses a sense of self, however temporarily, whilst feeling safe. Such a repetitive musical structure synchronizes the crowd, affecting the body's own pulses, which can produce a profound experience of transcendental universality, where time seems suspended, a forever here and now. . . . The continuous exercise, sometimes for hours on end, may stop an awareness of the limited body and self. This is combined with the ritualistic

predictability of the DJ-led dance event. . . . As the crowd moves in unison, the individual could gain an experience of being absorbed and becoming part of a larger timeless organism. . . . Hooked chemically and sensorially into the machine pulse of techno, the post-industrial alienated individual sacrifices the self ritually to achieve a spiritual transition into a cyborg-like subjectivity.[182]

According to participants, going to a rave, even a commercial rave at a club, is both disintegrating and empowering because the intensity of the experience shatters personal identity while simultaneously stimulating strong feelings of equality, vitality, and "merging into the crowd, in a process of de-subjectification."[183] Through this process, a new temporary collective ecstatic identity is shaped:

> It was people who counted above everything. A rave was always about community. . . . Going to a rave is . . . just like you're all sharing the same kind of feelings. You've got this one thing in common. . . . The music, the dancing, lifts you onto another plane where everyone feels the same.[184]

The Raver's Manifesto puts it this way:

> We came to accept that we are all equal. Not only to the darkness, and to ourselves, but to the very music slamming into us and passing through our souls: we are all equal. . . . Pushing us to turn to the person beside us to join hands and uplift them by sharing the uncontrollable joy we felt from creating this magical bubble that can, for one evening, protect us from the horrors, atrocities, and pollution of the outside world. It is in that very instant, with these initial realizations that each of us was truly born.[185]

For one writer: "Rave is more than music plus drugs, it is a matrix of lifestyle, ritualized behavior and beliefs. To the participant it feels like a religion; to the mainstream observer it looks more like a sinister cult."[186] For another: "Rave is the space of 'awakening' . . . the edge of the dance floor is 'the edge of a vast remembering' upon which the physical earthly realm merges with the heavenly . . . to be a party to this experience amounts to *rapture*."[187] Or, from a more political perspective,

> It could be said that rave culture is essentially a revolutionary political movement in that it represents the will of a significant portion of society to organize and gather for the purposes of creating a new community model and that these activities are carried out despite fervent opposition from governing bodies. . . .

A rave makes the political statement that we are all equal, and that no matter how different we may think we are, on a more tribal level, we all have the same basic needs as human beings.[188]

As mentioned above, not everyone is allowed to participate in what D'Andrea has called the "globalizing *digital art-religion*" of rave.[189] Those without the proper "look" are kept out. But all those who do manage to get onto the dance floor are welcomed. Tolerance is possible partially because the ravers are "alone in a crowd" and don't interact with their fellows except insofar as they all are engaged together in the same intoxicating activity.

The central rave value of "unity and acceptance of diversity" is symbolized in the initials often emblazoned on the dancers' bodies and clothes: PLUR—Peace, Love, Unity, Respect.[190] Therefore, before and during a rave all sorts of transgressive alternative identities can be safely unfurled and flown in full color, in the sure faith that they will not be rejected. In fact, the more extreme the look and behavior, the more it is approved—though violence is strictly prohibited. At the same time, it should be noted that the overwhelming majority of ravers worldwide are middle- or working-class urban unattached white youth (forty seems to be the upper age limit), mostly from Europe, Australia, and North America, although quite a large rave community exists in Israel, and smaller ones can be found in the industrialized centers of Japan, Korea, and elsewhere in Asia and South America.[191]

Toward Gaian Holism

For most, the rave is a utopia that exists only in the moment and only in the body; it is a pure instance of what the often-cited anarchist/Sufi/philosopher Hakim Bey (also known as Peter L. Wilson) has called a temporary autonomous zone (TAZ), which he defines as a "fleeting moment where fantasies are made real and freedom of expression rule before external reality intervenes." The hyperreal but fleeting TAZ is portrayed as the polar opposite of the mundane world of stability, hierarchy, family, structure, and rational action. Rather, it is

an affinity group, the initiates sworn to a bond of love. The band is not part of a larger hierarchy, but rather part of a horizontal pattern. . . . it envisions an *intensification* of everyday life, or as the Surrealists might have said, life's penetration by the Marvelous . . . in which all structure of authority dissolves in conviviality and celebration.[192]

Some of those who have experienced the TAZ of rave find that the humdrum world they had previously taken for granted is now no longer acceptable or even palatable. "The first time you rave, you go in blind. You come out and you can see. . . . Everything's fucked up. Nothing's right. Why is the news always bad? Rave is just generation of kids who don't know what the future is. We're waiting for the Earth to explode."[193] As Hakim Bey asks, in this dire situation,

> Are we who live in the present doomed never to experience autonomy, never to stand for one moment on a bit of land ruled only by freedom? Are we reduced either to nostalgia for the past or nostalgia for the future? Must we wait until the entire world is freed of political control before even one of us can claim to know freedom?[194]

The answer is no. According to the rave prophet and proto-shaman Terence McKenna, humanity is "in a state of transition; we have arrived at nothing less than the end of history."[195] As the advance guard of human transformation, ravers "seek liberation from the contaminating effects of society and culture; seek genuine experience; seek to express all that one truly is at a spiritual being; and—for many—seek to experience and nurture all that is embedded within nature, beyond the reach of the artificial, the power games of the lower self, the destructive implementation of the technological."[196] As McKenna explains, this quest will succeed because

> large groups of people getting together in the presence of this kind of music are creating a telepathic community of bonding that hopefully will be strong enough that it can carry the vision out into the mainstream of society. . . . The new rave culture is the cutting edge of the last best hope for suffering humanity. . . . We're leaving this world behind, for a brighter, better world that has always existed; in our imagination.[197]

McKenna's words are echoed by others for whom rave is "an epicenter from which to spread the positive and powerful vibrations . . . out into society at large."[198] "As the depression in the dominator system deepens into final collapse, the co-operative free/fiesty/rave/squatter/new new age/techno tribal traveler cross-over counter-culture will grow unstoppably into the new dominant goddess-worshipping techno-tipi dwelling eco-culture that will inherit a cleaned planet."[199] The task of McKenna and other rave performers and DJs is to "act as exemplars, by making this cosmic journey to the domain of the Gaian ideas, and then bringing them back in the form of art in the struggle to save the world."[200] The loving artist/shaman/DJ is the missionary hero of the coming rave world, replacing the cruel patriarchal warriors who rule by fear.

For rave's proto-shamans and ecstatic dancers, world redemption is closely connected to the development of computer technologies, which permit the instantaneous sharing of information and the evolution of a shared planetary consciousness, unfettered by space and time. Hallucinogenic drugs also are thought to facilitate a return to a primitive unity between human beings and reconnection to Earth itself, as well as instigating a metaphysical fusion with the superhuman extraterrestrial "Others" who are guiding humanity toward what McKenna calls a "Gaian holism" that "will be tribal in character. The next great step toward a planetary human world with the archaic matrix of vegetable intelligence that is the Overmind of the planet."[201] Fraser Clark, the founder of London rave club Megatripolis, made the connection between rave and "Gaian holism" clear in a lecture to an audience in Stanford:

> We're all in this together. This is our planet. She is indescribably beautiful, gigantic. We are atoms of that living Goddess. Personally, I can't see a better way to help people to learn a love, respect and reverence for Nature than the classical open-air all-night Rave. Can you imagine what it felt like with 20,000 people going for it and actually feeling together, and the power of a people together . . . and then dancing the sun up? It is awesome, it is religious, and it is life-changing.[202]

> Local rave is the real opening point . . . [in] the battle to save the planet and ourselves.[203]

In the digital art-religion of rave, salvation of the planet and of the self can be achieved by resurrecting ancient tribal rituals. Dancing the sun up

> has roots in prehistory. It's like one of these big dance sessions where they would chant all night long. . . . I really think they're tapping into something really deep in the psyche. . . . The sounds are the new epic poetry of this century. . . . The knowledge is beyond consumerism and materialism, and associated disaffected, alienated and generally self-destructive style of the industrial being. . . . It's the re-discovered language of transcendence. . . . The "coming of age" ritual which Western culture has long forgotten.[204]

Many ravers believe they are

> in some way connected to prehistoric tribes of nomads who had celebrated music and dance thousands of years ago in the same surroundings; that free parties were shamanic rites which, using new musical technologies in com-

bination with certain chemicals . . . preferably in settings of spiritual significance, could reconnect urban youth with the earth to which they had lost
contact, thus averting imminent ecological crisis.[205]

The all night dance ritual is a memory that runs deep within us all; a memory
that takes us back to a time when people had respect for our great mother
earth and each other. Dancing was our rite of passage, our shamanic journey
into altered states of reality where we embodied the Great Spirit and the magic
of life.[206]

Rave "is a form of meditative collective spiritual worship. It is a reconnection
with the elemental, primordial rhythms of organic, cosmic life force."[207]

Psychedelic Guerillas

For most members of the rave community, ecological and personal wounds
are healed—at least temporarily—through their occasional rapturous mind-
meld with tribal/primal Gaian consciousness. Having "reconnected with the
elemental" the dancers return to daily life until the next redemptive party. Life
is an oscillation between dull anonymity in the workaday world and immediate ecstatic "savage" merger in the alternative rave world. The hope is that the
latter will gradually spread to engulf the former.

But for a minority, the ecstatic reconnection with the elemental results in
a permanent "derailment" of consciousness that propels them into the "negative diaspora" of permanent nomadic neotribalism; a "trans-ethnic dispersion
of peoples that despise home-centered identities."[208] These self-exiled *psychedelic guerillas*[209] have "relinquished all idea, desire, or nostalgia for fixity" in
favor of "an identity made of transitions, successive shifts, and coordinated
changes, without and against an essential unity."[210] For converts to *nomadic
spirituality* and *psychic deterritorialization*,[211] personal experience is the only
possible arbiter of "what we can be." Therefore,

> As soon as the subject believes that a specific practice no longer provides the
> expected returns in terms of insight or behavior change, this will likely be in-
> terpreted as a moment to move on. . . . Affiliations are thus better understood
> as being adverbially temporary: "*Yesterday* I was into . . . , *today* I am into, and
> *tomorrow* I may want to try . . ."[212]

In a real sense, the new psychedelic nomads are the logical products of the
modern message of emotive individualism, finding significance only in fleeting
moments of experiential embodied revelation.[213]

Observers have described these deterritorialized collectives of "inner worldly" mystics as "effervescent, ascetic, oriented toward the past or the future; they have as their common characteristic on the one hand, a breaking with the commonly held wisdom and, on the other, an enhancing of the organic aspect of the social aggregation."[214] They are held together not by interests, but "by a certain ambiance and a state of mind. Solidarity is expressed through lifestyles that favor appearance and form."[215] In particular, "it is the shared consumption of music and an appreciation of its inherent semiotic meaning, and its ability to link individuals together, that not only validates the individual's self identity but also helps to coalesce and create a neo tribe."[216]

In the late 1990s and into the twenty-first century, the most sought after "mythic" destination for these hypermobile neotribal "expressive expatriates"[217] was Goa, the former Portuguese colony in India,[218] which is portrayed and experienced by the neotribal seekers as the reverse of Western commercial, rational culture—a sort of permanent TAZ:

> Goa is a melting point for East and West, and already India is the only country in the world that is female, round, and the karma yoga is instantaneous. Most of West is a macho robotics, man-made world where feelings are secondary. It makes them candidates for ulcer, cancer, and other consuming illnesses. India is still a country where people smile at you in the street. They look in your eyes, which is like catching a glimpse of the soul, and everything is possible. It is the total opposite of the Western squareness.[219]

In Goa, rave took on an overtly religious character: "Goa trance was mystical music, a rave was a *satsang*, the DJ was a guru."[220]

Surviving on remittances, drug dealing, the manufacture of arts and crafts, provision of alternative healing practices, and other marginal enterprises, the psychedelic guerilla vanguard live clandestinely in "a vanishing culture requiring countermeasures of mobility and stealth against commodification and repression."[221] Valuing "not sameness but continual variation, not local roots but translocal interests," the expressive expatriates "do not want to be recognized by their pasts, constructed under social conditions imposed on them, but rather in relation to a drive for autonomy by which they feel free to fashion their own self-identity, as purified New Agers or transgressive trance freaks."[222]

But despite their strategic withdrawal into the periphery, the wandering psychedelic guerillas have not lost their millennial hopes and continue to see themselves as "people outside the system who will bring about the New Age."

Their hidden yet pervasive benevolent power is manifested in the healing ritual of the trance party, which—according to one believer—"creates a vortex of energy that spirals up into the sky, attracting our alien brothers from the Pleiades, and they come to watch us. The better the party, the more energy it concentrates. When everybody is on acid, the vibration has a higher frequency, and this brings transformation!"[223] Healing love energies accumulated in the party can then be transmitted to the core of the planet to be redistributed where needed, worldwide. The continued existence of human misery is only an indication of the inability of the majority to open themselves up to transformation. Nonetheless, hope springs eternal. As Hakim Bey remarks: "Let us study invisibility, webworking, psychic nomadism—and who knows what we might attain?"[224]

5 PURIFYING THE WORLD: THE GLOBAL JIHAD

*Jihad is an active holy war to eliminate un-Islamic systems,
to establish Islamic state rule, and to bring about a universal
revolution.*[1]

—al-Mawdudi

*... [I]n the West only two movements ... claim to be "inter-
nationalist": the antiglobalisation movement and radical Islam.*[2]

—Olivier Roy

THE MISSION OF AL-QAEDA

Origins of Jihad

On September 11, 2001, "everything changed." On that sunny day, enemies willing to kill and die for their cause attacked the symbols of American might. In our final case study, we will attempt to understand the ideals and motivations of the most infamous modern movement to overthrow modernity: al-Qaeda.[3]

Prior to 9/11, al-Qaeda was a thorn in America's side, but it was not seen as a major threat. Ironically, in a classic instance of blowback,[4] the clandestine American intervention in Afghanistan was instrumental in the development of the al-Qaeda network. During that struggle, many idealistic young Muslims, anxious to gain honor and demonstrate their piety, flocked to Afghanistan to fight alongside the Afghan mujahideen (warriors for God) against the communist invaders. For the Americans who supported the mujahideen, the campaign was part of a pragmatic geopolitical policy aimed at undermining the Soviet Union. For the Muslim volunteers, it was a holy war, and their experiences in Afghanistan eventually led them to export the battle into the heart of the "far enemy"—the "great Satan"—America.[5]

One of the early activists in the Afghan conflict was Dr. Ayman al-Zawahiri, who had already served as a leader of an underground Egyptian Islamist group. After the assassination of Anwar Sadat, al-Zawahiri was imprisoned and brutally tortured, which further radicalized him. Another Arab fighter in Afghanistan was Osama bin Laden, the scion of a fabulously wealthy Saudi Arabian family. When the pious bin Laden arrived in Peshawar, he became the disciple of Sheikh Abdullah Azzam, an exiled Palestinian religious scholar and charismatic public speaker who envisioned the war in Afghanistan as the beginning of a Muslim renaissance. His slogan was: "Jihad (holy war—'striving in Allah's cause') and the rifle alone, no negotiations, no conferences, no dialogues."

Azzam traveled throughout the Middle East, Europe, and the United States in support of the Afghan conflict, recruiting soldiers by proclaiming:

> History does not write its lines except with blood. Glory does not build its lofty edifices except with skulls. Honor and respect cannot be established except on a foundation of cripples and corpses. Empires, distinguished peoples, states, and societies cannot be established except with examples. Indeed, those who think that they can change reality or change societies without blood, sacrifices, and invalids . . . do not understand the essence of this *din* [Islam] and they do not know the method of the best of Messengers [Muhammad].[6]

Azzam's bloodthirsty rhetoric deeply influenced the later policies of al-Qaeda.[7]

After many internal intrigues, in 1988 bin Laden officially took command of an organization supporting Arab fighters in Afghanistan, with al-Zawahiri as his second in command. Both were passionately devoted to defending their religion, which they saw threatened by modernity; both were also strong believers in the importance of jihad, not only against Islam's external enemies but also against Muslims who had betrayed the faith. Bin Laden's nascent group (originally only fifteen men) was called al-Qaeda—the base, indicating its origins as supplier of training camps and guesthouses for fighters. It was then, and remains now, only one of a number of competing Muslim revivalist organizations. Some embrace violence in service of their mission; others propose more peaceful routes to the purification of Islam; and still others have moved from violence to accommodation.[8]

To begin to understand the theological and historical roots of jihadism, it is crucial to recognize that, like Judaism and Christianity, Islam believes in humanity's progressive evolution toward redemption. And, like Christianity,

Islam has the divine mission to convert the world to the true faith. Today, Islam has indeed become—by most estimates—the largest religion in the world, and it has a plausible claim to being the most universal of faiths, drawing people from every nation to the great pilgrimage (hajj) to Mecca. But, unlike the other Abrahamic faiths, in Islam the millennial dream of salvation appeared to have been actually achieved during the reign of Muhammad and the four rightly guided Caliphs (deputies) who succeeded him (Abu Bakr, Umar, Uthman and Ali). To put it in Christian terms, it is as if, instead of being crucified, Jesus had become the independent Emperor of Judea and was then succeeded in that post by Peter, Paul, Luke, and Mark, who conquered and ruled Rome. Muslims look back on this era as a period in which the believers lived in a kind of earthly paradise, under the guidance of the godly.[9]

Because the Prophet and his disciples actually did once rule, an overriding theological problem for Muslims is how to reconcile the tainted reality of the present with the shining glory of the past. For most, God's inscrutable will explains this disparity. In a corrupt world, ordinary human beings must accustom themselves to injustice and seek their own pathways to redemption through personal righteousness, assured that divine judgment will eventually condemn evildoers, apostates, and infidels to Hell. However, some zealots have always denounced this attitude as cowardly and un-Islamic. They say that true believers must be committed to permanent jihad against the enemies of the faith—including war against impious Muslims undermining the Islamic community (the *umma*) from within. Throughout history, these militants have been motivated by a deep sense of shame at the inability of their community to maintain its original state of grace, a fierce hatred of the forces they believe responsible for this failure, and an idealistic willingness to sacrifice all to regain Islam's original purity.[10] Their strategy, in the past, as in the present, has been to destroy the world as it is, so that authentic Islam may reign once more. Jihadis warn: "The war of cultures started long before the attacks and before Huntington and Fukuyama. This war existed since the existence of Infidels and Faithful."[11] The end result is not so much a commitment to the *clash* of civilizations (though modern jihadists very much approve of Samuel Huntington's theses)[12] but rather a fervent desire for the *crash* of civilizations, which must be wholly destroyed to build a better world—or, more accurately, to return the world to its prior ideal condition.[13]

Also prevalent in the jihadi narrative is the *hijra* (migration) of Muhammad, who was driven from Mecca, gained power in the marginal oasis of Medina, and returned to the Arab core as a conqueror. Ever since, opponents of the status quo have believed in emigrating from the corrupt center to create a refuge in the periphery, where a revolution of the righteous can arise. Following this model, many jihadis saw the rise of the Taliban in the Afghan hinterland as the inauguration of a new Caliphate. Similarly, the exodus of Osama bin Laden and other core members of al-Qaeda from Arabia to "a safe base in Khurasan, high in the peaks of the Hindu Kush" was proclaimed a "necessary migration" away from the authority of evildoers to establish a pure land from which the true Islam could rise again.[14] For this reason, the members of al-Qaeda are called *Muhajiroun*, like those who accompanied Mohammad to Medina, while Taliban and other local groups in Afghanistan are called *ansar*, like those who supported the Prophet in exile. When bin Laden rented a house in Peshawar he called it Beit al-Ansar—the place of the supporters of the Prophet, from which they could venture forth to defeat the infidel.[15]

Another theme that has been co-opted by the jihadis is the notion of the return of the redeemer (pervasive in Shi'ite salvationist theology, which is based on the existence of a hidden Imam). Although he himself never claims to be such a figure, Osama bin Laden has often been seen by others as the *Mahdi* (savior) who has come to rescue Islam and vanquish the infidels and apostates, or as the *mujaddid*—the renewer sent every hundred years by God to liberate the Muslim community.[16]

But for hostile outsiders, the most often cited historical precedent for the present day jihadis is the Nizari branch of the Ismaili Shi'ites, commonly known as the Assassins, who, at the end of the eleventh century, emerged from their remote mountain enclaves to attack the Seljuk Empire. Inspired by the charismatic theologian and mystic Hasan al-Sabbah, the "old man of the mountain," the Assassins consisted of tightly disciplined, centrally organized, closed communities of absolute believers who were willing to kill and die to bring the arrival of the redeemer. For this holy purpose, any means whatsoever could be employed, including clandestine operations by agents who remained hidden in place for years, awaiting the opportunity to murder (always with daggers) their appointed victims. Although the Nizari Assassins did not intentionally slay anyone but their targets, their tactics and their commitment are the antecedents of the suicidal bombers and terrorists of al-Qaeda, who call their fighters fedayeen, a term first used by the Nizari.

Less recognized as an inspiration for the jihadis is Sufism, wherein dedicated seekers seek mystical union with the deity through membership in hierarchical and often secretive holy orders (*tariqa*) gathered around charismatic spiritual leaders (sheikhs, *murshid*, or *Pirs*) whose word is absolute law. Sufi groups have long mobilized and inspired activists, and many Sufi orders have served as centers for resistance to colonial authority and as bases for opposition to the state. Yet, on the surface at least, jihadis have been very hostile to popular Sufism. Following the teachings of modern *Salafi* fundamentalists (from *salaf al salih*—the righteous predecessors), they maintain that the praise of Sufi saints and worship at saint's tombs are practices dangerously close to heresy. But despite their harsh ideological condemnation of Sufism, these radicals have nonetheless organized themselves in ways that very closely resemble Sufi brotherhoods.

For example, among Sufis, once the spiritual authority of the saint has been recognized, it is the duty of his disciples to emulate him and to offer him their complete devotion, like the original companions who gathered around the Prophet. In the tariqa, the devotees are taught esoteric doctrines and practices, study texts written or recommended by the saint, absorb messages conveyed in dreams and trance, and immerse themselves in techniques of self-loss. In exact parallel, Olivier Roy has observed that in radical Islamic parties, "the stages of 'initiation' are explicitly likened to a mystical initiation."[17] A jihadi group organized in this fashion is the equivalent of a Sufi tariqa; both are closed collectives wherein the soul is purified through submission to and imitation of the charismatic leader.

There is a major difference. While Sufis have usually been content to become peaceful virtuosos of the sacred, jihadis have voiced the Sufi *da'wa*, the "call," to the world. Those who do not hear or heed are, ipso facto, not Muslims and should be execrated and punished. As Devji remarks, "The 'final instructions' to the hijackers of 9/11 do not so much as mention any goal that they were to die for." Instead, hijacking was transformed into a sacred performance, with its own specific rites and prayers, closely resembling Sufi instructions for achieving mystical union.[18] The "martyrs" who blow themselves to bits in a suicide attack are likewise portrayed as initiates, disintegrating the mortal self in a cloud of blood and thus entering into God's eternal embrace.

Al-Qaeda also symbolically evokes traditional images of Sufism to validate its present. For example, bin Laden and al-Qaeda associate themselves with wilderness and ruins, in contrast to the urban world of orthodox scholars. Films and photos of bin Laden are usually shot in caves, conjuring up images of the isolated retreats of Sufi saints. The image is given more power because a mountain cave was the site of Muhammad's revelation and served as the refuge of the mystical seven sleepers of Ephesus. Like a Sufi saint, bin Laden's followers believe he has miraculous capacities, including the gift of prophetic dreams. Similarly, Mullah Omar, the leader of the Taliban, was inspired in a dream to rid Afghanistan of corruption—thus making theological knowledge irrelevant to his leadership.[19] Divine favor is also bestowed on the mujahideen, who heal quickly from or are unhurt by wounds that would kill others, and "emerge from battle looking like shining moons." Angels or mysterious strangers help the mujahideen to prevail against overwhelming odds; "fire from heaven will knock down enemy airplanes and helicopters"; dogs refuse to bark when the mujahideen pass; rain covers their tracks; food mysteriously arrives when most needed. The corpses of martyred mujahideen smell sweet, and white lights shine from their graves.[20]

In general, the mujahideen believe that they are both recreating and revitalizing Islam's past glories. A Muslim journalist visiting bin Laden's Afghan base of Tora Bora remarked that the al-Qaeda fighters around their leader "had all taken Islamic names, the most popular being those of the Prophet's companions, in particular those who were given the glad tidings that their places were guaranteed in Paradise."[21] The result is a sense of communion with the majesty and collective virtues of Islam in its original form. As a veteran of the Afghan war said: "Afghanistan reminded Muslims of all colors and races that what unites us is much more important than the superficial differences wrought by colonialism, secular nationalism, and other material ideologies. We felt we were on the verge of reenacting and reliving the Golden Age of our blessed ancestors."[22]

The Context for Terror

Like other jihadi groups, al-Qaeda works hard to legitimize itself within the mainstream of theological discourse. To understand this strategy, it must be kept in mind that there is no central authority in Islamic jurisprudence—no pope or supreme council—and so no necessary agreement among theologians beyond the general consensus of the community (*ijma*). Islamic law consists of sometimes opaque Quranic texts, a variety of often contradictory, recondite, or ambivalent traditions and a massive accretion of case manuals authored by various *ulema* (the learned, singular *'alm*) over the centuries.[23] A Muslim judge issuing a fatwa (legal opinion) justifies his findings by referring to and interpreting these multiple sources, which allows for room for dispute among jurists.

The flexibility of Muslim jurisprudence has therefore made it possible for al-Qaeda to enter the debate, reinterpret the textual corpus, and stake a claim as an authentic (in al-Qaeda's case, the *only* authentic) expression of Islam.

Ironically, the historical flexibility that has allowed it to enter the debate is precisely the aspect of Islam that al-Qaeda attacks. Tracing their intellectual pedigree to the modern fundamentalist Salafi movement, the jihadists argue that the meaning of scripture is obvious, eternal, and easily found in Islam's foundational texts, without any need for the "additions" and "innovations" of scholars, which only obscure or even subvert the truth.[24] The rejection of the religious status quo has been identified as a crucial dimension of the jihadist revolt.[25] Therefore, a layman like Osama bin Laden can ignore the traditions and findings of the learned, dismissing alternative opinions as false, corrupt, or sycophantic.

These responses coincide with a massive mistrust of state sponsored Islamic institutions, including educational institutions and their alumni, which are seen as irredeemably profaned by the decadence and blasphemy of official authority. Distrust of the state has a long history in Islam because all states are, by definition, disfigured and degraded versions of the original rightly guided Caliphate. Jihadi tracts regularly refer to leaders of the state as tyrants, traitors, and heretics.

The most influential modern spokesman for an unrelenting attitude toward the state and its minions was Sayyid Qutb, a leader of the Egyptian Muslim Brotherhood. Qutb was hung in prison in 1966, but not before he had composed *Milestones*, which is taken as a fundamental text by jihadis. As the editor's introduction to the English version states: "Sayyid Qutb concluded that the Egyptian government, along with all other governments in the Muslim world, were strictly comparable to pre-Islamic Arabia in its ignorance and disregard for divine precepts and that its state could therefore rightly be designated by the same term—*Jahiliyya*."[26] This term, used only four times in the Quran, is taken by the orthodox to indicate the state of ignorance of the Arabs prior to the advent of Muhammad, but jihadis have extended it to mean a lack of knowledge about Islam or the refusal to acknowledge Islamic principles. As the Pakistani theologian al-Mawdudi puts it, people in jahili society live in "the abyss of darkness," without knowledge or government and with no law except the law of the jungle, "reveling in adultery, gambling and drinking. Loot and plunder was their motto, murder and rapine their very habits."[27]

According to Qutb and those inspired by him, jahiliyya exists today as virulent contagion that is purposely being spread by the debased, materialistic, and individualistic culture of the West, aided and abetted by the hypocritical, sensual, and cowardly Muslim majority, who, under Western influence, have reverted to a jahiliyya state. The pious Muslim reaction to the depravity and dishonor of the modern world, Qutb says,

> takes shape in living souls, in an active organization, and in a viable community. It should take the form of a movement struggling against the Jahili environment while also trying to remove the influences of Jahili society in its followers. . . . It is necessary that this group separate itself from the Jahili society, becoming independent and distinct from the active and organized Jahili society whose aim is to block Islam.[28]

From its refuge, the vanguard group will then be able to undertake "a spiritual and moral quest to halt, *not* merely to moderate, the secularization of society."[29] This is the redemptive role that al-Qaeda seeks to fill.[30]

In the urgent battle for the soul of humankind, jihadis acknowledge that the odds are stacked heavily against them. "However far our capabilities reach, they will never be equal to one thousandth of the capabilities of the kingdom of Satan that is waging war on us."[31] "America has taken over the media sphere, manipulating in different measures these enormous powers as it sees fit."[32] Even within the Muslim world, those who struggle against sin are likely to be mocked and marginalized by the deluded majority won over by Western propaganda. But this does not dissuade the vanguard of the righteous. As an early proponent of the jihadi philosophy, Abdus al-Salaam Faraj, wrote:

> The truth is that those who will establish the Islamic State are a few believers, and those who stand straight on the way of God and the tradition of the Prophet have always been small in number. As Allah says: "But few of My servants are grateful. . . ." Also, victory does not come to Islam though large numbers because Allah says: "How often a small group overcame a mighty host by Allah's leave, and Allah is the patient."[33]

Large numbers are unimportant, and failure is irrelevant. "By establishing an Islamic nation we are carrying out the command of God. We are not asked to produce results."[34]

Having acted according to God's commands, the jihadi can remain serenely above the masses, certain of his own superiority:

> The society may be drowned in lusts, steeped in low passions, rolling in filth and dirt, thinking that it has enjoyment and freedom from chains and restrictions.

Such a society may become devoid of any clean enjoyment and even of lawful food, and nothing may remain except a rubbish heap, or dirt and mud. The Believer from his height looks at the people drowning in dirt and mud. He may be the only one; yet he is neither dejected nor grieved, nor does his heart desire that he take off his neat and immaculate garments and join the crowd. He remains the uppermost with the enjoyment of faith and the taste of belief.[35]

For these few virtuous heroes who know they are walking on the path of purity, the rewards of the mundane world are irrelevant. In Azzam's famous call for the believers to "Join the Caravan" of jihad, he specifically says that jihad is a "long path of effort, great sacrifice and serious losses, [but it] purifies souls so that they tower above the lower material world . . . and the Caravan moves on from the foot of the mountain top to the lofty summit."[36] As one militant explains: "We did not sacrifice the flower of our youth, the best years of our lives, in prisons to get jobs and earthly rewards. Our aim is to please God. The West cannot comprehend our spirituality and religiosity as long as it is blinded by materialism."[37] Osama bin Laden seconds this sentiment:

These young men . . . have left the material world and come to these mountains and this land; they have left their families, they have left their fathers and mothers, they have left their universities, and they have come here to face bombardment by American cruise missiles. . . . America, because it worships money, thinks that the people here are of the same persuasion. But by God we have not sent away a single man following this propaganda, because we do not doubt our brothers. We consider them best, and they are. God is their only reckoner.[38]

The rise of the idealistic, self-sacrificing, antimaterialist, anti-Western jihadi philosophy in the Middle East should also be understood in the light of the historical experience of postcolonial regimes that maintain their authority, in large measure, by coercion and terror. For example, during Saddam Hussein's reign in Iraq, it is conservatively estimated that over 100,000 citizens "disappeared"; the actual number is probably closer to 250,000.[39] Other Middle Eastern states have lesser, but equally horrifying, records, as witnessed by Ayman al-Zawahiri's account of his own experience in Egyptian prisons: "The brutal treadmill of torture broke bones, stripped our skins, shocked nerves, and killed souls. Its methods were lowly. It detained women, committed sexual assaults, and called men feminine names, starved prisoners, gave them bad food, cut off water, and prevented visits to humiliate the detainees."[40] According to one study,

"The bloody history of official torture and persecution perpetuates a culture of victimhood and a desire for revenge and enables the movement to mobilize young recruits and constantly renew itself. Arab/Muslim prisons, particularly their torture chambers, have served as incubators for generations of Jihadis."[41]

Hopes for a more just society, free from Western influence and local oppression, were raised momentarily in the Middle East by the appearance of the "alternative modernities" of socialism and nationalism; but these dreams were crushed by the ignominious defeat of Nasser's armies by Israel in 1967. The general sense of oppression, impotence, and shame; of having taken a wrong direction; of the vapidity of materialism and the meaninglessness of unfettered individualism, coupled with the collapse of viable alternatives, left a terrible spiritual vacancy, which, Sayyid Qutb believed, only Islam could fill. As he wrote in the famous opening passage of *Milestones*:

> Mankind today is on the brink of destruction, not because of the danger of complete annihilation, which is hanging over its head—this being just a symptom and not the real disease— but because humanity is devoid of those vital values which are necessary not only for its healthy development but also for its real progress. Even the Western world realizes that the Western civilization is unable to present any healthy values for the guidance of mankind. It knows that it does not possess anything which will satisfy its own conscience and justify its existence. . . . The leadership of mankind by Western men is now on the decline, not because Western culture has become poor materially or because its economic and military power has become weak. The period of the Western system has come to an end primarily because it is deprived of those life-giving values, which enabled it to be the leader of mankind. . . . The period of the resurgence of science has also come to an end. This period . . . does not possess a reviving spirit. The nationalistic and chauvinistic ideologies which have appeared in modern times, and all the movements and theories derived from them, have also lost their vitality. In short, all man-made individual or collective theories have proved to be failures and unsustainable. At this crucial and bewildering juncture, the turn of Islam and the Muslim community has arrived.[42]

Battling Darkness

And indeed, many new Islamic groups of various hues did appear in response to Nasser's debacle and Qutb's call, but the rise of al-Qaeda to prominence had to wait until the first Gulf War, when the Saudi Arabian regime chose to invite American troops into the Islamic holy land. This led to the following lament from bin Laden: "Is there any torment—in the world, in the spirit, or the senses—worse for any believer than the humiliation and weakness that his *umma* is experiencing, not to mention the defilement of her holy places, occupation of her land and violation and plundering of her sanctuaries?"[43] The al-Qaeda theoretician Abu Mus'ab Al-Suri, a former member of the Syrian Muslim Brotherhood and an Afghan war veteran, compared the consequences of the Gulf War to an "ideological and mental earthquake, particularly for the Arab-Afghan mujahidin." The war was seen as part of a wider plan of conquest: "It was abundantly clear that this was only a convenient curtain for new vicious crusader campaigns, which America, Western Europe and the Jews launched toward the midst of Islam's homeland in the Levant, Iraq and the Arab peninsula."[44] Under these circumstances, the philosophy of Salafi fundamentalism as interpreted by Sayyid Qutb was reshaped by jihadi theoreticians like Abdullah Azzam and his disciple Osama bin Laden into a justification for terrorism.

Their argument is as follows: It is assumed that all present governments in the Muslim world are in a state of jahiliyya. Therefore, their authority is abrogated. This was an idea that was already promoted by Faraj in his famous *Jihad: The Absent Obligation*: "The present rulers have apostatized from Islam. They have been brought up over colonial tables be they Christian, Communist or Zionist. What they carry of Islam is nothing but names, even if they pray, fast and claim to be Muslims." Today's rulers of the Muslim world are the equivalent of the heretic Tartars (Mongols) of the past.[45] Supporters or merely passive citizens of these illegitimate and ungodly nations are on the side of darkness because they have been blessed with the Prophet's message and have repudiated it through their cowardly acquiescence to evil—which, in modern jihadi terms, is equated with the United States and Israel. Thus Azzam angrily declared: "The Muslim umma is responsible for the honor of every Muslim woman that is being violated in Afghanistan and is responsible for every drop of Muslim blood that is being shed unjustly—therefore they are an accessory to these crimes."[46] Similarly, Osama bin Laden states: "Whoever cooperates with America—under whatever name or title—is an apostate and an infidel."[47]

According to bin Laden and the other contemporary jihadis, the only virtuous response to the present situation is a ceaseless and pitiless holy war against all that stands in the way of returning to the purity of the past. "Battle, animosity and hatred—directed from the Muslim to the infidel—is the foundation of our religion."[48] A war without mercy can and must be directed not only against the apostate rulers of Muslim states but also against the civilian populations who support them and who have thereby become heretics themselves. This unyielding stance is a reinterpretation of the traditional doctrine of jihad, which was divided into the categories of offensive and defensive. An offensive jihad of conquest and conversion can be initiated only by a Caliph who represents the whole Muslim community. Because no Caliph exists today, in principle no offensive jihad can be undertaken. Therefore, bin Laden always describes his jihad as defensive.

Operating under the assumption that Islam is under attack by Americans and Zionists and their allies, bin Laden argues that the faithful must defend their religion or else risk its destruction.[49] The solution—proved successful in the Afghan War—is for jihadis everywhere to unite. This explains al-Qaeda's support of Islamic radicals in places such as the north Caucasus (Chechnya), Iraq (where Zarqawi's network was called "Al-Qaida of Jihad Organization in the Land of The Two Rivers"), and Algeria, where the most important Islamist group merged with al-Qaeda in 2007.[50] The doctrine of self-defense justifies attacks on civilians in the United States, Europe, and other nations worldwide; on international organizations like the United Nations, the World Bank, and the IMF; and within the Islamic world—where in fact most of the casualties occur.[51] To Al-Muhajiroun ('The Emigrants'), an Islamic organization that operated in Britain, jihad was understood as the use of "military force, where diplomacy fails, to remove the obstacles the Islamic state faces in carrying its ideology to mankind." Accordingly, "the battlefield must not have any borders or nationality. The enemy is all over the world so we need to fight them wherever we meet them. We must revive the mentality of Jihad and the mentality to fight against the enemy."[52]

Given the postulate that the faith is under attack, jihad is no longer a collective political obligation requiring the command of the state (*farz kifaya*). It becomes instead a personal responsibility for all believers (*farz ayn*). There is "no doubt that fighting the enemy, whether the part which is near to you or that which is far away, is a duty upon Muslims."[53] According to al-Zawahiri: "Jihad always takes precedence over marriage and the pursuit of knowledge because it is a personal obligation."[54] And bin Laden adds that al-Qaeda "wants to keep jihad alive and active and make it part of the daily life of the Muslims. It wants to give it the status of worship."[55] Jihad is thus spiritualized and put on a par with, and even elevated above, the fundamental "five pillars" of Islam.

Orthodox scholars who oppose this reading agree that Islam will eventually fulfill its divine destiny as the dominant religion in the world, but for them violent struggle is not tactically appropriate or productive in the present situation. Rather, Muslims must gain victory gradually, by reason, example, and the promise of reward on Earth and in the afterlife.[56] Jihadi activists rebuke this as compromise with the devil. The holy war must be fought now, with total commitment and by any means, including the slaughter of noncombatants.

To make their case theologically, the jihadis resort to the theory of "progressive revelation" to argue that passages in the Quran that favor violent jihad take precedence over more conciliatory passages. Even more importantly, jihadi literature continually draws attention to Western aggression against Islam. "I write these lines to you," bin Laden says,

> at a time when even the blood of children and innocents have been deemed fair game, when the holy places of Islam have been violated in more than one place, under the supervision of the new world order and under the auspices of the United Nations, which has clearly become a tool with which the plans of global unbelief against Muslims are implemented. . . . The evidence overwhelmingly shows America and Israel killing the weaker men, women, and children in the Muslim world and elsewhere. . . . So in fact it is as if Israel—and those backing it in America—have killed all the children in the world. . . . Despite the ongoing American occupation of Saudi Arabia, America continues to claim that it is upholding the banner of freedom and humanity, yet it perpetrated deeds which you would not find the most ravenous of animals debasing themselves to do. . . . We ourselves are the victims of murder and massacres. We are only defending ourselves against the United States. This is a defensive jihad to protect our land and people. That's why I have said that if we don't have security, neither will the Americans.[57]

The importance and urgency of the times call for a redefinition of the meaning of "terrorism." Al-Suri, for instance, advocates "praiseworthy terrorism": "It is terrorism by the righteous that have been unjustly treated. It removes injustice from the oppressed."[58] Accordingly, "Yes, we are terrorists towards God's enemies . . . terrorism has been commanded in God's book, and in situations where the mujahidin are repelling their enemy and the enemy's terror through a defensive jihad."[59] In a video message dated from 2001 bin Laden proclaimed: "What we are practicing is good terror."[60] Therefore, the attacks launched on September 11 were the ultimate "pious actions" of noble martyrs.[61]

The battle against the pervasive influences of jahili is not won only on the battlefield. As Hasan al-Banna, the founder of the Muslim Brothers, asserts, the defense of Islam requires "stand(ing) against the flood of modernist civilization overflowing from the swamp of materialism and sinful desires."[62] All those aspects of present-day jahili society that stand in the way of realizing Islam must be stamped out ruthlessly. What this means is the elimination of beliefs and practices that place the wishes, thoughts, or imagination of an individual above the word of Allah, as revealed in the foundational texts (according to jihadi interpretation). This implies the "rejection of modern forms of sovereignty and of human claims to knowledge that sustain them, and an insistence that, by contrast, God's knowledge of the deepest meanings of human existence justifies divine rule over not only the moral but the political life."[63]

Democracy is one such modern form, disparaged as an infidel invention wholly alien to the spirit of Islam. As a jihadi theologian puts it:

> Anyone who seeks to implement a legislation created by someone other than Allah, is in fact a polytheist. . . . People have followed these legislators and agreed to make their legislation as a right and characteristic for them. . . . Therefore, the legislators became gods to every one who obeyed and followed them, or agreed with them in this disbelief and polytheism. . . . These representatives, in fact, are erected, engraved images and worshipped idols, and claimed gods that are set up and fixed in their temples, in their heathen sanctuaries (the parliaments). . . . Democracy originated in the land of disbelief and apostasy. It grew in the hotbeds of polytheism and corruption in Europe, where there was a separation between religion and life. . . . It permitted sodomy, wine, and many other scandals. . . . So this is the freedom of democracy: to be free from Allah's religion and His legislation and the exceeding of His limits.[64]

Al-Zawahiri agrees with this interpretation: "A secular constitution does not recognize shari'a as sovereign. . . . In addition, the word 'democracy' . . . has a specific meaning, namely, the rule of the majority, and it does not in any way [recognize] the authority of shari'a."[65] The essence of democracy "revolves around the whims and fancies of man, which are articulated in a number of ways, and which become the ruling godhead."[66] Therefore, bin Laden denounces the United States as "a nation who, rather than ruling by the shari'a of God in its Constitution and Laws, choose to invent your own laws as you will and desire. . . . This is a people whose votes are won when innocents die, whose leader commits adultery and great sins and then sees his popularity rise—a vile people who have never understood the meaning of values."[67] Because al-Qaeda takes democracy at face value, as the responsibility of everyone, every American citizen is equally culpable for the crimes the United States has committed and equally deserving of retribution: "Every American is our enemy, whether he fights directly or whether he pays taxes."[68]

Another Western heresy that must be jettisoned by Muslims is contained in the first article of Charter 91 of the United Nations, which says that people have rights simply because of their humanity. For the jihadis this is unacceptable because the article elevates an abstract and universal principle over the edicts of God, which divide human beings into those on the side of right and those on the side of evil. As bin Laden testifies:

> It is great error to posit that the religion (Islam) honors mankind. And "mankind" as presented in the declaration represents none other than the Western peoples. . . . But the religion (Islam) can never possibly honor the Western man who rejects Allah Almighty. Indeed, He describes him as a cow and He has cursed him and prepared the everlasting Fire for him.[69]

A further pernicious delusion promoted by the West is world peace, which bin Laden denounces as a "fairy tale . . . they foist on Muslims in order to ready and prepare them to be slaughtered. . . . As for the so-called 'Peace' or 'Peace award,' that is a gimmick that is given to the biggest bloodshedders."[70] In this, he echoes contemporary Muslim apocalyptic literature in which the arrival of the Antichrist is heralded by "calls for peace, peace conferences, peace agreements, peace cities, and peace palaces . . . the same time as humanity groans under the horrors of the war, overflowing with hatred in brutal tyranny and international control, in the shadow of the Islamic revival."[71]

The Ancient Conspiracy

For jihadis, the signs all point to the revival of a primordial struggle between good and evil. As Sayyid Qutb writes: "The truth of the matter is that the latter-day imperialism is but a mask for the crusading spirit, since it is not possible for it appear in its true form, as it was possible in the Middle Ages."[72] Nor are contemporary American policies simply reactions to specific situations; they are elements of a nefarious plot to destroy all Muslims. According to Azzam, those seeking to create a truly Islamic society "must comprehend the magnitude of international conspiracies against Islam."[73] As bin Laden informs his followers: "We should therefore see events not as isolated incidents, but as part of a long chain of conspiracies, a war of annihilation in all senses of the word. . . . (They are) part of the great series of fierce and ugly Crusader wars against Islam."[74]

George W. Bush unintentionally confirmed this suspicion when he referred to the American response to the 9/11 attacks as a "crusade." Bin Laden retorted: "Bush said it in his own words: 'crusade.' . . . Bush divided the world into two: 'either with us or with terrorism.' Bush is the leader; he carries the big cross and walks. I swear that everyone who follows Bush in his scheme has given up Islam and the word of the prophet."[75] The sinister conspiracy against the forces of righteousness dates back prior to the medieval era and existed even before the advent of Islam. In his 2004 audiotape, entitled "Resist the New Rome," bin Laden specifically frames present-day Middle Eastern politics as the continuation of a battle that began over 2,500 years ago, over a thousand years prior to the birth of Muhammad. Other jihadis push the timeline back further, so that the United States is the modern incarnation of the oppressive regimes of ancient Egypt, with the American president as the modern Pharaoh, declaring his own godhood to the world.[76] Bin Laden sums up the jihadi attitude as follows: "I say that the West's occupation of our country is old, yet new, and that the confrontation and conflict between us and them started centuries ago. This confrontation and conflict will go on because the conflict between right and falsehood will continue until Judgment Day."[77]

For bin Laden, the fundamental reason for this confrontation is obvious. The entire world is split into two camps: "one of faith, with no hypocrites, and one of unbelief—may God protect us from it!"[78] Or, as the author of *The Virtues of Jihad* has written:

> The simple understanding of the difference between the unbelievers and believers is similar to the difference of light and darkness, black and white or happiness and sadness. It is in the nature of the unbeliever to hate Islam and Muslims. They will do their utmost and their sole aim of living is to destroy or cause harm to the Muslims. This is why the unbelievers have always been fighting against the Muslims and will carry on doing do.[79]

In return, between Muslims and infidels "there is an enmity, evidenced by fierce hostility, and an internal hate from the heart."[80]

The identities of the evil adversaries in this millennial battle are not hard to discover: The first and foremost is the United States, reviled as "the great tempter, the cultural imperialist, the destroyer of tradition and family and taken-for-granted patterns of life."[81] According to bin Laden,

> After the end of the Cold War, America escalated its campaign against the Muslim world in its entirety, wanting to get rid of Islam itself. . . . The USA started to see itself as a Master of this world and established what it calls the new world order. . . . It wants to occupy our countries, steal our resources, install collaborators to rule us with man-made laws, and wants us to agree on all these issues.[82]

> Americans' intentions have also become clear in their statements about the need to change the beliefs, curricula, and morals of Muslims in order to become more tolerant, as they put it. In clearer terms, it is a religious-economic war. They want the believers to desist from worshipping God so that they can enslave them, occupy their countries, and loot their wealth. . . . The occupation of Iraq is a link in the Zionist-Crusader chain of evil. Then comes the full occupation of the rest of the Gulf States to set the stage for controlling and dominating the whole world.[83]

As another jihadi tract warns: "Our Islamic nation is morally superior to the West and the United States. We must not be deceived by American and Western propaganda about progress and civilization. We must not let America colonize us mentally. We are facing a brutal form of intellectual and ideological colonization."[84] Already in 1990 al-Suri delivered a lecture to the mujahideen in which he proclaimed that the defining "political equation" of our times would be the struggle between the "new world order" and the "armed Jihadi current."[85] As in so many of antiglobalization movements, the notion of a repressive New World Order is prominent in jihadi narratives. *The Global Islamic Resistance Call*, Al-Suri's most important contribution to the jihadist movement worldwide, is specifically written as a guide for action and martyrdom in these post–Cold War times dominated by a "New World Order."[86]

In the hated "New World," all forms of depravity flourish under the protection of the false gods of democracy, human rights, and freedom, American style. One of the first to make this case was Sayyid Qutb, who visited the United States in 1948. He was astonished

> to realize, despite his advanced education and his perfectionism, how primitive the American really is in his views of life. His behavior reminds us of the era of the "caveman." He is primitive in the way he lusts after power, ignoring

ideals and manners and principles. . . . It is difficult to differentiate between a church and any other place that is set up for entertainment, or what they call in their language, fun.[87]

Qutb portrayed America as the schizophrenic offspring of a marriage of sophisticated technology with the lawless individualism of the pioneer. "In America man was born with science and thus believed in it alone. . . . Since he received nature as an untamed, stubborn virgin, and fought to build his homeland with his bare hands, applied science was his greatest ally in his violent struggle." But the American scientific quest "narrowed his horizons, shrank his soul, limited his feelings and decreased his place at the global feast, which is so full of patterns and colors."[88] He concludes: "The real struggle in the future . . . will be between materialism throughout the world and Islam."[89]

An even more negative opinion is expressed in bin Laden's scalding litany of American sins:

> You are a nation that permits acts of immorality, and you consider these acts to be pillars of personal freedom. You have continued to sink down this abyss from level to level until incest has spread amongst you. . . . You are a nation that permits gambling in its all forms. The companies practice this as well, resulting in investments becoming active and the criminals becoming rich. You are a nation that exploits women like consumer products or advertising tools, calling upon customers to purchase them. . . . You have destroyed nature with your industrial waste and gases. . . . Your law is the law of the rich and wealthy who hold sway in their political parties, and fund their election campaigns with their gifts. . . . How many acts of oppression, tyranny, and injustice have you carried out, O callers to freedom? Let us not forget one of your major characteristics: your duality in both manners and values; your hypocrisy in manners and principles.[90]

According to the jihadis, the degraded American culture has already spread worldwide, due to the ubiquity of pro-Western propaganda, which has clouded the judgment of the masses with false promises and led them away from the right pathway. As Sayyid Qutb exclaims:

> Humanity today is living in a large brothel! One has only to take a glance at its press, films, fashion shows, beauty contests, ballrooms, wine bars, and broadcasting stations! Or observe its mad lust for naked flesh, provocative postures, and sick suggestive statements in literature, the arts and the mass media! And

add to all this, the system of usury which fuels man's voracity for money and engenders vile methods for its accumulation and investment, in addition to fraud, trickery, and blackmail dressed up in the garb of law.[91]

In the same vein, al-Muhajiroun asserts that

A brief glimpse at any Western society . . . run on values of freedom, secularism and democracy will reveal a complete breakdown in the social and moral fabric with homosexuality, pedophilia, adultery, promiscuity, fornication, pornography and abortion rampant, not forgetting all the sexually transmitted diseases that come hand in hand with such liberalism. . . . All of this exposes gross incompetence on the part of those ruling in looking after the welfare of the masses, in providing for their basic needs and in protecting the citizens from exploitation of their emotions and desires, leading to diseases, depression and uncontrollable crime reflected in the statistics for murders, thefts, suicides and rapes in the West.[92]

And al-Zawahiri laments that nowadays

The Prophet Muhammad, prayers be upon him, and even Jesus Christ, peace be upon him, are not sacred any more, while Semites and the Nazi Holocaust and homosexuality have become sacred. In France, a law was issued to prosecute anyone who (says) that the Nazi Holocaust against the Jews didn't happen while they forbid Muslims to wear the veils in their public schools. In France, a Muslim father cannot prevent his daughter from having sex because she is protected by the law, but this same law punishes her if she covers her hair. And in England they punish those who encourage Terrorism, yet, no one dare to punish those who are insulting our prophet.[93]

Inevitably, among the "most important military targets" identified by al-Suri are the "advocates of dissoluteness, wickedness and depravity, and institutions spreading indecency among the believers."[94] This view is ubiquitous. Iran's Ayatollah Khomeini was also appalled by the depravity of the modern world: "Wherever you go, and whomever you encounter, from the street sweeper to the highest official, you will see nothing but disordered thoughts, confused ideas, contradictory opinions, self-interest, lechery, immodesty, criminality, treachery, and thousands of associated vices."[95]

According to bin Laden and other jihadists, the degrading colonization of humanity is the product of the schemes hatched by powerful Jews, "who control (American) policies, media, and economy." Within this taken-for-granted scenario, the U.S. leaders are "under payroll of the Zionist lobby which serves the needs of Israel, which kills our sons and our children without right so that it can keep on ruling with total control."[96] These assertions coincide with the claim made by a modern Muslim apocalyptic author that

> The American people . . . toil and slave to fill the warehouses of the Jews with gold. Their lives are for the sake of the Jews, and they make war and die for the sake of fulfilling the strategic interests of the Jews throughout the entire world in general, and to protect Israel and its expansion in particular. They will live and die for the Jews. . . . The most amazing thing about this whole matter is that this people (the Americans), which is in a state of societal slavery, extols freedom and lifts its slogans up, and is a universal example of it."[97]

Like the apocalyptic writers whose ideology they share, most jihadis firmly believe that

> All of history has been controlled by a group of Jews who, because they knew more than anybody else and had unlimited amounts of money and unassailable positions of power, together with satanic authority and the monomaniacal purpose of subverting all humanity and driving it into hell, have directed all past historical events.[98]

According to bin Laden, "these Jews are the masters of usury and leaders in treachery. They will leave you nothing, either in this world or the next. . . . These Jews believe as part of their religion that people are their slaves, and whoever denies their religion deserves to be killed."[99] The same perspective is taken by a popular author: "Has not the wind (*rih*) of the Arabs and the Muslims gone during these days? Have they not fallen under the Jewish world domination and the powers influenced and dependent upon it?"[100] Why exactly Jews are so evil is not clear. Apparently, vileness is inherent in their nature.[101] In any case, they are the eternal enemy, to be destroyed only at Judgment Day. Westerners in general are their willing puppets and so must also suffer the same fate, as must all those who do not stand up against their despicable schemes. Within this worldview, it is no wonder that, in the words of bin Laden, "every Muslim from the moment they realize the distinction in their hearts, hates Americans, hates Jews, and hates Christians. This is a part of our belief and our religion."[102]

Equality, Freedom, Obedience

The degradation of humanity, legitimized through the Jewish-Christian ideology of universal rights and human freedom, installed via sham democracy, maintained by capitalist usury, and imposed by brute force, can only be offset by jihad. But the jihadi message is not merely negative. As Sayyid Qutb argues:

> To attain the leadership of mankind, we must have something to offer besides material progress, and this other quality can only be a faith and a way of life which, on the one hand conserves the benefits of modern science and technology, and on the other fulfils the basic human needs on the same level of excellence as technology has fulfilled them in the sphere of material comfort. And then this faith and way of life must take concrete form in a human society. In other words, in a Muslim society.[103]

What this new society entails is outlined by bin Laden, who describes Islam as

> the religion of the Unity of God, sincerity, the best of manners, righteousness mercy, honor, purity, and piety. It is the religion showing kindness to others, establishing justice between them, granting them their rights, and defending the oppressed and the persecuted. It is the religion of enjoining the good and forbidding the evil with the hand, tongue, and heart. It is the religion of jihad in the way of God so that God's Word and religion reign supreme. And it is the religion of unity and agreement on the obedience to God, and total equality between all people, without regard to their colour, sex, or language.[104]

The fundamental promise is that "Islam establishes a new social, economic and political system, in which the dream of the freedom of man is achieved in practice."[105] However, Western readers should be warned that freedom has a particular meaning for the jihadist. According to al-Zawahiri:

> The freedom that we want is not the freedom of lowly rascal America. It is not the freedom of the usurious banks and the giant companies and the misleading Mass Media Organizations. It is not the freedom to ruin others for the sake of one's own material interests. It is not the freedom of AIDS and the industry of atrocities and same-sex marriage. It is not the freedom of gambling and wine and the breakdown of the family, and the freedom for women to be used as a commodity for bringing in customers and signing deals. . . . It is not the freedom of two faced principles and the division of the people into looters and looted.[106]

Rather, as Qutb makes clear, true freedom is only to be achieved through submission to the rule of divine law,

> [which] is a part of the universal law and is as accurate and true as any of the laws known as the 'laws of nature.' . . . Thus, the Shari'ah which Allah Almighty has given to man to organize his life is also a universal law, as it is related to the general law of the universe and is harmonious with it. Thus, obedience to the Shari'ah becomes a necessity for human beings so that their lives may become harmonious and in tune with the rest of the universe. . . . When a man makes peace with his own nature, peace and cooperation among individuals follows automatically, as they all live together under one system, which is a part of the general system of the universe. . . . Thus, blessings fall on all mankind, as this way leads in an easy manner to the knowledge of the secrets of nature, its hidden forces, and the treasures concealed in the expanses of the universe. Man uses these for the benefit of all mankind, under the guidance of the Shari'ah of Allah, without any conflict or competition.[107]

In the ideal world proposed by Qutb, all invidious human distinctions are eliminated in the embrace of the Islamic community, which is based

> on the association of belief alone, instead of the low associations based on race and color, language and country, regional and national interests. . . . Among the concrete and brilliant results of this attitude was that the Islamic society became an open and all-inclusive community in which people of various races, nations, languages and colors were members, there remaining no trace of these low animalistic traits. The rivers of higher talents and various abilities of all races of mankind flowed into this vast ocean and mixed in it.[108]

The promise of a tolerant and inclusive society has always been a major ideological factor in Islam's expansion, and the elimination of distinctions under the authority of God has continued to be the ideal of the jihadis today. As one fighter explained: "Forget about personalities; we are God's instruments and a community of believers. We are all foot soldiers in this epic struggle. There are no hierarchies of class differences that separate from one another. We are an egalitarian community."[109] Similarly, a telephone message justifying suicide bombing and other terrorist acts in Lebanon stated: "We are the Soldiers of God. . . . We are neither Iranians, Syrians, nor Palestinians, but Muslims who follow the precepts of the Qur'an."[110] Following this principle, the Muslim Brothers promoted the solidarity of all workers and employers, regardless of class, in a relationship of organic unity governed by the principle of "mutual social responsibility."[111]

Under the universal and egalitarian regime of Islam, which "speaks to all humanity together, and does not refer to them in any other way than as individuals of the human race,"[112] nationalism has no place. Quoting Qutb once again: "What is acceptable to Islamic consciousness is its belief, the way of life which this belief prescribes, and the society which lives according to this way of life. The soil of the homeland has in itself no value or weight."[113] Nor is culture of any special worth. In fact, according to Qutb, the notion of culture as "the human heritage" is part of the Jewish conspiracy "to eliminate all limitations, especially the limitations imposed by faith and religion, so that the Jews may penetrate into body politic of the whole world and then may be free to perpetuate their evil designs."[114] Islamic society, in contrast, "incorporates and builds upon a plurality of histories, cultures, and identities united by each individual's equal relationship with the Creator."[115] True acceptance of difference exists only when each person is free to choose salvation and to follow the shari'a. This freedom is possible only under an Islamic regime. Again, Qutb puts the position clearly:

> There are many practical obstacles in establishing Allah's rule on earth, such as the power of the state, the social system and traditions and, in general, the whole human environment. Islam uses force only to remove these obstacles so that there may not remain any wall between Islam and individual human beings, and so that it may address their hearts and minds. After releasing them from these material obstacles, and then leave them free to choose to accept or reject it.[116]

Or, as he states elsewhere, "Only under Muslim rule can humanity be truly free to choose between Islam and infidelity."[117]

From a comparative point of view, the jihadi struggle is "the radical conclusion of a more widespread conviction that contemporary life is plagued by a multifaceted alienation requiring redress." It is "part of the larger attempt among various groups and theories to 're-enchant' a world characterized by the experience of disenchantment."[118] The effort to reenchant coincides with the pursuit of a viable identity and a meaningful mission in life, one that stands opposed to the status quo and the alienating forms of identity normally on offer. In this respect it is significant that the great majority of the original Arab-speaking recruits into al-Qaeda did not fit the taken for granted model of the potential fanatic; they were not downtrodden or marginal, nor were they traumatized or neurotic. Rather, "the data suggest these were good kids who liked to go to school and were often overprotected by their parents."[119] The core Arab leaders were so wealthy that they were sent abroad for their educations; the rest tended to be middle-class, pious, college-trained, upwardly mobile young professionals, with expertise in technical fields. Many had traveled considerably and spoke several languages. At bin Laden's Afghan base at Tora Bora, a visiting journalist "found it remarkable that so many of the *mujahedin* possessed the very highest academic qualifications. There were doctors, engineers and teachers among them, people who had left their families and jobs to join the *jihad*."[120] In Marc Sageman's sample of 165 al-Qaeda members, 115 were recruited in a country not their own; 78 percent were cut off from their cultural and social origins.

Although the recruits had marketable skills, few were employed full time. Sageman argues that underemployment and a relative lack of achievement led to considerable frustration among these ambitious young men. Furthermore, their experiences abroad, cut away from their families and their collective moorings, made for deep feelings of insecurity, discrimination, and humiliation. Beset by spiritual isolation, the absence of a mission, and deep-seated resentment, "they sought a cause that would give them emotional relief, social community, spiritual comfort, and cause for self-sacrifice."[121] Under the influence of the propaganda campaign of Abdullah Azzam, they found significance and respect by joining the mujahideen, journeying to Afghanistan, swearing a formal oath of loyalty to al-Qaeda and to bin Laden, and entering the training camps to be transformed into zealots willing to die—and kill—for the cause.

Crucial in this process were the strong ties of affection and belonging that existed between the recruits—75 percent had preexisting social bonds to others in global jihad, while others joined alongside groups of friends and relatives. Very few, if any, joined as individuals. Sageman concludes: "Social bonds predating formal recruitment into the jihad seem to be the crucial element. . . . social involvement preceded ideology."[122] These affective bonds were then greatly intensified by the rigors of the training process and the camaraderie of battle. They became even stronger in 1991, after the struggle against the Soviets in Afghanistan was over, when bin Laden and his closest comrades went into voluntary exile in the Sudan, breaking off any alternative loyalties to homeland or community—leaving them with only their brethren in al-Qaeda to fall back on. Disconnected from home, family, and culture, they became an intimate, battle-tested, inwardly turned, nomadic collective bound together by shared grievances, by absolute faith in bin Laden and his mission, and by strong feelings of love for one another. Rather than a political party based on practical action, al-Qaeda (and other jihadi organizations) is much more like an antiestablishment religious sect, where true believers gather around a charismatic leader who "demands conversion, and not membership, and replaces political action by the display of his own behavior."[123]

The second generation of al-Qaeda members and supporters have somewhat different profiles, but they too are driven by the same volatile psychic constellation of resentment and hope, hatred and love, anomie and idealism, execration and transcendence. Even more than their predecessors, they are cosmopolitan nomads who have moved away from their ancestral homelands and lack any strong ties to a specific place or culture. In this, they are like approximately one-third of all Muslims today, for whom the umma is no longer territorial, the West is no longer "other," and Islamic identity no longer self-evident. Instead, faith now must be expressed explicitly in a world where differences are blurred and space is fluid.[124] In an increasingly virtual context,

> the quest for authenticity is no longer a quest to maintain a pristine identity, but to go back to and beyond this pristine identity through an ahistorical model of Islam. . . . The construction of a "deculturalised" Islam is a means of experiencing a religious identity that is not linked to a given culture and can therefore fit with every culture, or, more precisely, could be defined beyond the very notion of culture.[125]

For uprooted and alienated youth, ahistorical and universalistic revitalization movements such as al-Qaeda offer structure, meaning, identity, and emotional release. Seeking a lost ideal, "they become embedded in a socially disembedded network, which, precisely because of its lack of any anchor to any society, is free to follow abstract and apocalyptic notions of global war between good and evil."[126] This transformation often involves adopting and displaying a new set of identifying symbols—such as growing a beard, wearing stereotypical "Islamic dress," and so on. However, the internal alteration may not be externally obvious. The July 7, 2005, British suicide bombers, for instance, were apparently well integrated in British society and looked "Westernized."[127]

Like the first generation, the second generation consists of young men (bin Laden has stated that the best fighters are close friends and kinsmen between the ages of fifteen and twenty-five who are free of family responsibilities). They are united in small, egalitarian, closed, face-to-face collectives where "social implosion" occurs, extreme beliefs flourish, outsiders are easily dehumanized, and acts of terror become plausible. As with the older generation, most of these new jihadis are well educated, and many have college degrees or better.[128] According to al-Suri, the most important features for a potential jihadi are "talent, a broad general culture and acquired skills and preparation." For him, "talent for terrorism is like talent for poetry, music, painting, and different aspects of the arts, literature and hobbies."[129] The men responsible for the failed 2007 car bombings in London and Glasgow were doctors and engineers, invariably described as "intelligent" and "brilliant."

The Community of True Believers

Among these inwardly turned idealists, fantasies of revenge and triumph are continually reiterated and ratified, given form by Internet propaganda, validated in the fiery sermons heard in radical mosques, and eventually realized through the training, financing, contacts and information provided by al-Qaeda. The end result is a new counteridentity that condemns the Western values that were once longed for. As a jihadi activist imprisoned in France says:

> Before, I bore within me the despising gaze of the French and the Westerners and I despised myself despite myself. . . . I wanted to conform to the image of the average Frenchman, to be like them, to make myself in their image. But at the same time I had the feeling that this was more or less impossible: they didn't want me, even if I had citizenship and all the rest. They looked down on me, they treated me like I was nothing, they despised me. This contempt was killing me. Were we really so despicable? . . . I went back and forth between what I was and what I wanted to be: a little Frenchman. Whereas I was an Algerian. . . . Islam was my salvation. I understood what I was: a Muslim. Someone with dignity, whom the French despised because they didn't fear me enough. . . . Now we are respected. Hated, but respected.[130]

For this man, and others like him, the jihad is both a recapturing of what is genuine and authentic and a repudiation of the false gods of the West. As another interviewee says: "I had the choice between schizophrenia as a Frenchman and the recovery of my identity in struggle against this society that denies me my dignity and the most ancestral part of my identity."[131]

The pursuit of dignity and respect underlies the jihadi ideal of self-sacrifice, as this testimony from a member of Hizbollah attests:

The Americans pretend not to understand the suicide bombers and consider them evil. But I am sure they do. . . . What is so strange about saying: "I'd rather kill you on my own terms and kill myself with you rather than be led to my death like a sheep on your terms?" I know that the Americans fully understand this because this is exactly what they were celebrating about the guy who downed the Philadelphia flight on September 11. . . . They made a hero out of him. The only hero of September 11. They are hypocrites, the Americans. They know as much as we do that as a human being we all have the capacity to rush enthusiastically to our death if it means dying as a dignified human being.[132]

A readiness to die because life is not worth living in shame reflects cultural contexts in which honor is a central value. It is telling that bin Laden, when asked in a 1998 interview what message he would like to give to the Islamic world, said "We believe strongly . . . that they want to deprive us of our manhood. We see ourselves as men, Muslim men, committed to defend the greatest house in the universe, the holy Kaaba, which it is an honor to die for and defend.[133]

The internal structure of these redemptive jihadi groups is remarkably like that of some of the other social movements we have observed so far— very loosely organized, based on personal networks and informal connections made at hubs from which information flows. Hierarchy is minimal, and the local cells are relatively free to follow their own initiatives, inspired by the rhetoric and example of bin Laden and by the deeds of the heroic martyrs, as conveyed over the Internet and in communiqués to the media. It is a horizontal virtual community, everywhere and nowhere, without any actual base (an irony, since al-Qaeda means "the base") or constituency beyond the abstract community of the righteous believers. Membership is blurry; many who claim to be members are actually only sympathizers who have no real contact with the core. It is, in fact, very difficult to join al-Qaeda because of the personal and intimate nature of the organization. New recruits are almost always close friends or relatives of long-time members. Yet would-be al-Qaeda are almost as dangerous as real members because they follow the message of terror and self-sacrifice as preached on the Internet and can and do organize to act, though without the expertise and financing provided by the center. They operate as a "leaderless resistance."[134] The 2005 London terrorists, for example, were not actually al-Qaeda members but believed in and carried out al-Qaeda's mission.

It should also be pointed out that the idea of individual or small unit terrorism is strongly advocated by prominent jihadi strategists. Al-Suri proclaims that the activities of "small resistance units" are crucial for the "global Islamic resistance call" against the New World Order. Two forms of jihad should complement each other: the "individual terrorism jihad and secret activity of small units separated from each other" and "open front jihad." To him,

> While it is possible to perform individual jihad anywhere in the Arab and Islamic world, even all over the world, because this is not dependent on certain conditions where it takes place, the Open Front Jihad is dependent on strategic preconditions that are necessary in order to succeed, after success has been granted by God the Almighty and Supreme.[135]

Regardless of strategic discussions, at the center of this diffuse network is Osama bin Laden himself, who is recognized as the amir and the spiritual head of the movement in all its manifestations.[136] He is supported by his second in command, Ayman al-Zawahiri, and by a council (*shura*) of about a dozen close friends and comrades (mostly Egyptians) who fought alongside him in the Afghan struggle. They are divided into four committees: finance, military, religious, public relations. Beneath this very simple organization, there are four main groups and then many small cliques and clusters of members and helpers. Control from the center is generally limited to providing advice and financial aid, which allows the organization to evolve organically and quickly adapt to local circumstances. Authority at every level is consultative, with the members of each group deciding for themselves who will fill leadership roles.

This bottom up form of "direct democracy" is based on the notion that local individuals know one another's abilities and moral character best. Ideally speaking, the governing body taking power after the final victory over the evildoers will be based on the same principles. A consultative assembly will nominate candidates for amir, who will be selected by the acclamation of the whole umma, after which he will chose an executive governing body. Of course, the ultimate basis of the amir's authority must be his knowledge of and adherence to the holy text, in combination with his exemplary character. There is no room for a Western-style representative democracy in which the people themselves decide on the content of the law. The many problems involved in the actual implementation of this vague formula are little discussed in jihadi or salafi literature. As Oliver Roy remarks, the ideal solution "would be for the amir to be *index sui,* his own indicator. . . . The only criterion for designating an amir would therefore be the man himself, his virtue, his personality."[137] Or, as Mawdudi writes, pious believers will naturally and spontaneously recognize their leader from among the adult Muslim men who are healthy, who have gone on the pilgrimage to Mecca, who fear God, who are wise and trustworthy, and who do not aspire to the position. Once selected by acclamation, this religious cum political leader will be a living example of proper Muslim behavior, with the implicit right to interpret the law.[138]

Such is the case with Osama bin Laden. His mentor, Sheikh Abdullah Azzam, recognized his pupil's charismatic potential when he wrote that: "Osama bin Laden . . . is a whole nation embodied in one man. He shoulders the nation's cause,"[139] that is, the cause of the universal nation of Islam. Abu-Jandal, bin Laden's personal bodyguard, provides more concrete examples of bin Laden's appeal:

> I never saw him pay attention to what he wore or to his personal belongings. . . .
> He used to sit with us and eat and drink with us. . . . Imagine a man with the kind
> of resources he had, the cause he embraced, and his stature as a leader—sitting
> with us and eating rice and potatoes. I remember that at one point we ate only
> dried bread and water. . . . So we never really felt afraid as long as we were with
> that man. . . . I used to hear him telling his sons, "Your father's millions about
> which you hear are not for your father to use. This money is for the Muslims and
> I hold it as a trust for the cause of God. Not one riyal of it is for you."[140]

Bin Laden's rejection of wealth and his embrace of poverty and simplicity, his heroic self-sacrifice, his unyielding moral stance, and his contempt for the corruption of the state authorities all fit with a long-standing Middle Eastern image of the saint, which, as we have already mentioned, is symbolically conveyed in his public self-presentations, austerely dressed in white robes and seated in a stony cave.[141] Through bin Laden's public persona the advice of Azzam has been realized: "The vanguard must rise above the vanities of this world and distinguish itself through its asceticism and frugality."[142] The failure of the U.S. government rewards program to provide any significant clues regarding the whereabouts of al-Qaeda's leadership stems from the difficulty of suborning a community of true believers.[143] Loyalty, in these circumstances, does not have a price.

As we have seen, the jihadis are devoted to the realization of the Islamic ideal, as they understand it. "Wherever you turn your gaze to Islam, You find it as a bird with broken wings," says a popular jihadi tract.[144] The holy warriors have the duty to heal and redeem Islam's broken condition. But they also wish to free the world from enslavement to the West and its individualistic and materialistic worldview. As Ayatollah Khomeini declared:

> Islam is champion of all oppressed people. . . . We shall export our revolution to the whole world. . . . Islam is the religion of militant individuals who are committed to truth and justice. It is the religion of those who desire freedom and independence. It is the school of those who struggle against imperialism.[145]

With the attacks of 9/11, bin Laden saw this revolutionary dream becoming reality:

> As the twin towers of New York collapsed, something even greater and more enormous collapsed with them: the myth of the great America and the myth of democracy. It became clear to all that America's values are the lowest, and the myth of the "land of the free" was destroyed. . . . The attacks revealed the American wolf in its true ugliness. The entire world woke up from its slumber.[146]

Similarly, al-Zawahiri called on

> all the weak and oppressed around the world to stand with us in confronting the Great Satan and in confronting this criminal Western civilization which has committed outrages never before committed in the history of mankind, and to take advantage of the mujahideen's attacks on America to rain their blows upon America until the symbol of tyranny in human history falls.[147]

This call has not fallen on deaf ears. As one young European sympathizer remarks: "A religion that denounces the imperialism of the white man can't be all bad."[148]

6 BETWEEN DOOM AND REDEMPTION

For we act only under the fascination of the impossible: which is to say that a society incapable of generating—and of dedicating itself to—a utopia is threatened with sclerosis and collapse.[1]

—E. M. Cioran

There cannot be a nation of millionaires, and there never has been a nation of Utopian comrades; but there have been any number of nations of tolerably contented peasants.[2]

—G. K. Chesterton

A COMMON GROUND

We began our book by repeating an old saying about how terrible it is to wander without direction in times of chaos. However, the different movements whose ideologies and practices we have outlined do not believe they are lost; each believes it is carving a path through the wilderness; each is tenaciously striving—in its own specific way—to save humanity from the evil forces of globalization and capitalism. Although we hope the reader has been struck by how similar the premises and claims of these combatants are, we also hope that their variety and difference has not escaped the reader's attention. We are not referring to their geographic dispersion. We mean that some—the World Social Forum, ATTAC, Slow Food, and even rave culture—can be loosely defined as social movements operating outside of ordinary political/institutional frameworks. But the European New Right is a school of thought, the Zapatistas are a guerrilla movement, al-Qaeda is a millenarian terrorist organization, the European populist-nationalist groups are oppositional political parties, and the Latin American cases are incumbent governments.

Further, as we stated in our introduction and as has become evident in the preceding chapters, the ideological and philosophical backgrounds of many of these groups are markedly distinct. Le Pen and Marcos would probably not willingly sit together at the same table, just to give a striking image of *difference*. And it is even harder to imagine either of them having tea with Osama bin Laden or Carlo Petrini or Terrance McKenna (miraculously descended from whatever higher plane he now inhabits). But let's imagine such a meeting takes place, if not in the steamy Lacandon jungle of Chiapas, or in the mountains of Afghanistan, or on the beaches of Goa, then perhaps in an air-conditioned Parisian restaurant (one serving authentic French cuisine from the countryside—or perhaps one specializing in Middle Eastern dishes). The meeting would most likely be an uncomfortable experience but, nonetheless, a revealing one. After initial animosity arising from their different visions of the future and disagreements over how to proceed toward it, they would soon discover (to their surprise or chagrin) common ground in their critiques of the liberal-capitalist system that they see as ruling planet Earth. Let us sketch out what this common ground consists of before analyzing variations, paradoxes, ironies, and potential future scenarios.

As we mentioned in our introduction, while history may not be quite over in some of the more remote redoubts of the Third World, the general consensus among intellectuals has been that everywhere else the "grand debate" over the best system to rule human affairs has been concluded.[3] The dominant ethos of today's world is still—stubbornly—based on the "Fukuyamaian" belief that liberal capitalism is the ultimate and only possible formula for the future of humanity.[4] Yet, even though the consensus is that the future is permanently preordained, the movements, parties, and individuals that have filled the pages of our book have resisted closure with every ounce of their strength. While only the WSF slogan proclaims that "another world is possible," all the groups we documented firmly *believe* this to be the case and, in their disparate ways, they all intend to change the course of history in order to take the world to the new, better future that they envision. Furthermore, regardless of their differences, all fervently believe that the radiant peak promised by neoliberalism is actually an abyss. Instead of achieving the best of all possible worlds, humankind is diving headlong into Hell.

The image of a deluded humanity poised on the brink of destruction coincides with another shared and deeply held belief: The world is going through a *crisis* of cosmic proportions. Without action, it will be destroyed utterly. As the Nobel Prize–winning novelist José Saramago warns: "We are reaching the end of a civilization and the times of darkness are coming . . . there is not a lot of time left to change the world."[5] Saramago's words could have been uttered by any of those leaders we have referred to. The apocalyptic scenarios are framed in different ways, but they all prophesy the cessation of cultural diversity, authentic traditions, ethnic and cultural roots, and the possibility of redemption. We are witnessing the destruction of civilization, the debasement of humanity, the rape of nature, and even the degradation and ruin of Earth itself.

Recognition of the coming apocalypse is not an excuse for inaction. Rather, awareness of the rapid approach of complete catastrophe urgently demands *rebellion*. To save the world, the status quo must be overthrown, and quickly. All these movements see themselves as engaged in a last-ditch war against the "system," a war waged by writing books, calling meetings, creating "spaces of resistance," convening new collectives, altering individual and collective consciousness, by political action, by riots, by protests, and, in the case of jihadists, by bombs.

Obviously, the more terrible the trajectory of the world, the more important are the movements (and the people) struggling to change that trajectory. Thus, even though their ideology of egalitarianism and participatory democracy obliges some of the groups (especially the Zapatistas) to deny that they constitute vanguards in the battle against neoliberalism, nevertheless all of these groups think and operate as if *their* decisive action is necessary for salvation. As we've seen, those actions can range from creating alternative communities, to refinding indigenous roots, eating purer food, entering into entranced communion with aliens, and blowing up the World Trade Center. Despite the variety, in every case, the sense of *transition* is omnipresent. From Left to Right, from politicians to ravers, all those engaged in the uprising against globalization adhere to the belief that humanity is living through an interval, "moving the center" away from the "old world" (ruled by brutal free-market fundamentalism and a soulless technocratic society) to the "new world" (which is framed in different ways but is always imagined to be a paradise of lasting peace, plenty, and harmony where difference is valued but also subsumed within the larger unity). That is why, as we observed in our introduction, in terms of their motivations and ultimate goals, the collectives in search of a new world could well be defined as "aurora movements." The intellectuals, activists, and quasi-mystical leaders of these movements are prophets of both doom and rebirth. They see themselves hastening the twilight of the old to bring the dawn of the new. And they all believe that powerful reactionary establishment forces will resist this transformation with all their might.

Mere moral force cannot prevail in this combat; only violence can displace the armies of the night. The required violence is often symbolic, expressed in harsh critiques of the status quo and its supporters, but at other times it is all too real. And the anger of the oppositional vanguard is real also, justified by the urgent belief that the authorities defending the power structure are thwarting the birth of a new "axial age" destined to revitalize humanity.[6] Though the means to achieve renewal differ, as do the moral limits on action (the extremes are the WSF, which prohibits violence, and al-Qaeda, which embraces terrorism), there is a crucial element of zealotry in all these movements. The logic is that the final battle is being fought today and that all hope for the future will be shattered if the righteous do not stand up. Friends must gather and ready themselves for combat; enemies must be identified, ridiculed, protested against, forced to recant, or, in the most extreme cases, eliminated; moderation is derided as capitulation. Collective action must adjust to the imperatives of the times. To defeat entrenched resistance, the struggle must be undertaken *now*, and commitment must be *total*. In this context, action itself is idealized. The struggle against the evil system, despite overwhelming odds, and at the risk of isolation, mockery, or punishment, is a value in itself. A loss is never a loss if one knows one is right; even defeat is a moral victory if it occurs in defense of the eventual dawn of a better world.

No compromise is possible because, for the aurora movements, American-style neoliberal-capitalist globalization represents a dark power of indignity, disenchantment, homogenization, and debasement. It is not just flawed or mistaken; it is *evil*. Within this worldview, the struggle for the world pits right against wrong, true against false, human against antihuman. The forces of evil are pervasive, as witnessed in the degradation caused by the commodification and disenchantment of the spiritual and natural world, which has become simply an object to be manipulated and marketed by heartless and soulless entrepreneurs. Though the accusatory tone may be more or less severe, more or less abstract, in general there is broad agreement on exactly who the enemy is. The forces of destruction are led by the United States in alliance with perfidious and pusillanimous local elites, all dedicated to implementing and maintaining a hegemonic "New World Order" based on the wholesale destruction of all that is holy, humane, and authentic. Every time the leaders of the Western world, knowingly or not, with good intentions or not, refer to a coming "New World Order," they only confirm the aurora movement's narrative of a coordinated global assault.

America (sometimes envisioned as acting under the hidden command of an insidious conspiracy of financers and plotters) is not only identified as the ultimate source of the vile disease of the free-market ideology that threatens the survival of humankind and the future of planet Earth, it is also (but crucially) the home of a degraded "philosophy of life" that has infected the entire planet. All these movements would agree with the New Right belief that a person does not need a passport to be an "American." Rather, an "American" is anyone with an "American" attitude toward society and the world; that is, an attitude based on commodification and consumption. At the same time, Americans are pitied as victims of the system—their sensibilities deadened by pervasive commercialization and the overwhelming influence of the mass media. Because of the awesome power of conditioning into consumerism, American resistance to the status quo can arise only under extraordinary conditions. Although leaders may change, and some of the more repressive American foreign policies may be reversed, ultimately America is reviled for what it *is*; its essential faith in capitalism and individualism is the source of the world-engulfing virus that thrives on human ignominy.

ORGANIZE FOR VICTORY

A bleak view of the world is not limited to the movements we have discussed; pessimism is widespread in the anxious modern era. For the majority of the population, such pessimism is probably cyclical, interrupted by periods of relative contentment; most of us simply wait and hope that things will eventually improve without any major disruptions to our lives. Some of the truly gloomy and cynical have isolated themselves in hopes of avoiding the coming catastrophe. Survivalists, for instance, believe that they know full well what the future will bring and are busily getting ready for inevitable global devastation, storing food, stashing weapons, and building their fortresses deep in the woods where they can defend themselves against the starving masses. In the spirit of the increased popularity of acronyms, they are preparing for what they call TEOTWAWKI ("The End of the World as We Know It").[7] The people in the movements we have studied also believe TEOTWAWKI is looming ever

closer. But, unlike the survivalists, they have not resigned themselves to a di-
agnosis of current ills and a retreat to the remote hideaways to await the end.
Nor, like the majority, are they willing to simply shift the political ground a
few points or to accept symbolic changes. Rather, they offer a panacea for the
maladies of the era—a strong medicine that will require a complete reversal of
all that presently exists.

Obviously, such Earth-shaking goals cannot be accomplished without
method and organization. All the movements struggling for the world have
attempted, with some degree of success, to set up networks that can support
global rebellion. For example, in Latin America the Zapatistas, the Bolivarian
revolution, and Evo Morales's government have all created alternative media
focused on the news and history hitherto "suppressed" by the global corporate
media they revile as tools of the oppressors. In the same way, the New Right
and Populist European parties have created their own alternative communication networks, including many publications, magazines, and newspapers that
aim to circumvent the censorship imposed by "the system." Alter-globalists
are famous for their indictment of corporate media and have created sophisticated communication networks to give voice to the voiceless, exposing the
unreported inequalities, injustices, and indignities perpetrated by the neoliberal world order. Slow Food also has an extensive publication empire, promoting its philosophy worldwide, while the jihadis have been hugely successful in
spreading their message via their own media outlets. Even ravers, notoriously
disinterested in print culture, are linked internationally by media publicity
and by the circulation of music and shared communication among travelers
following well-worn pilgrimage routes.

All these networks of rebellion are intimately connected with the World
Wide Web. It serves as a crucial source for propaganda, recruitment, coordination and fund-raising. This is nowhere more obvious than among the Zapatistas, who used the Internet to stimulate global support for their movement,
tying the hinterlands of Chiapas to the international universe of activists and
intellectuals. With the Zapatistas, "resistance" was put online. The same is
true of the WSF. Without the Internet, its goal of mobilizing disparate protestors in many nations to create "another world" would be impossible. Populist-
nationalist parties and their followers across Europe are known for their antisystem virtual activism, in the form of websites, blogs, and media-sharing sites
as well as intense participation in forums. Slow Food devotees also proselytize
in the blogosphere and have a developed network of websites. The Internet

speeds their message of slowness. Ravers too communicate extensively on the web, giving directions to events and spreading the transformative message of PLUR ("Peace Love Unity Respect"). Modern times may be godless, but global jihad takes full advantage of the benefits of the revolution in communication technology. As bin Laden remarked, "These days the world is becoming like a small village."[8] Jihadis regularly run websites, publish articles, and debate doctrine online. Al-Zawahiri, for example, has regularly made himself available on the Internet, where he participates in live forums and answers questions from people all over the world. Often aurora groups use and experience the Internet as a transformative space that subverts the oppressive system *and* serves as a decentralized, diverse, and radically participative model of the world to come. Sometimes this subversion takes the form of cyber attacks against the infrastructures of the enemy. Nevertheless, the jury is still out on whether the Internet will fulfill its promise of liberation or instead legitimize new forms of enslavement.[9]

The communications battle and the use of the World Wide Web together comprise only one aspect of a wider organizational strategy shared by all these groups, which have developed loosely linked horizontal and egalitarian international networks of mobile activists. Geographically dispersed like-minded individuals, and groups opportunistically join forces for the common fight against the unidimensional model of society, economy, and culture of the mainstream. This pattern is most immediately clear and pronounced in the leaderless, decentralized, highly mobile, amorphous, and performative rave subculture. But it is evident elsewhere too. As we have seen, the Chiapas experience has developed into a worldwide solidarity movement known as International Zapatismo. Following that example, the alter-globalization movement promotes its inherently decentralized and horizontal ad hoc nature as major source of its strength. The WSF presents itself as an open space, a "square without an owner," all-inclusive, ruled by consensus, with no center of authority. Its lack of formal hierarchies is a point of pride, though in practice it does have an unelected governing body of elite intellectuals, who are sometimes opposed by rank and file. A diffuse, horizontal local/global web of activists is also a defining feature of jihadi movements, which are made up of numerous local hubs informally bound together in loose networks of independent cells, characterized by minimal hierarchy and in many cases inspired by rather than commanded by a charismatic central leadership. In fact, many devotees have no contact at all with the core and get their directions only from examples publicized on the Internet and elsewhere. Similarly, the personality-driven, hierarchical Slow Food organization is based on egalitarian local convivia, each following its own pathway, unhindered by central directives. Over time, the Slow Food message has expanded beyond its original organization, becoming a totalizing movement based on slowness as a way of life, which anyone can join simply by changing pace. And the ENR has its own diffuse horizontal network of committed intellectuals across Europe and beyond.

Even within the more centralized and vertical structures of governments and political parties, links have emerged with other individuals and communities that transcend the local or national level. For example, although the organizational framework is institutional, both the Bolivarian Revolution and Morales's government have inspired a dense and diffuse solidarity network across continents (illustrated in the formation of an international network of support to Chávez's revolution and in the global indigenous organizations and Western progressive groups that back Bolivia). At the same time, populist and ultranationalist European parties—aware that the assault on their communities is global and therefore they must act together—have built new forms of horizontal collaboration among diverse groups across national borders in the hope of creating a globalizing network that can unite them in their shared defense of local distinction. Though it is not a uniform process, this interaction between local or national struggles and growing global coordination explains the high level of deterritorialization manifested in all these movements, no matter how much they praise the authenticity of the local. It seems inevitable that the struggle for the world must increasingly seek its base in mobile international networks, which themselves have no roots.

Paradoxically, the widening spread of horizontal and decentralized organizations does not preclude the existence of strong, charismatic leaderships. As noted, in many cases a central leader, inspiring followers by personal example and devotion to the cause, embodies the mission of the entire community. Marcos may rail against the development of charismatic dynamics around him, but he is nonetheless the one and only leader of the Zapatista vanguard that will bring a new tomorrow. Chávez and Morales are the exceptional figures leading the struggle of the oppressed against the global forces of rapaciousness. All leaders of the European populist-nationalist groups have a devoted following, and a pervasive cult of personality surrounds them. Slow Food is a creation and reflection of Carlo Petrini. Osama bin Laden's exemplary character and self-lessness are the major sources of his charismatic authority inspiring al-Qaeda and all jihadis worldwide. Though it is not a formal organizational structure, the European New Right owes much of its appeal to unelected "strong" intellectual leaders from de Benoist onward. Similarly, even movements like the WSF and ATTAC that proclaim themselves independent of "old-style" leadership paradigms are indebted to the doctrines announced by charismatic left-wing intellectuals and journalists such as Ignacio Ramonet, Chico Whitaker, Naomi Klein, Walden Bello, or Samir Amin. In their different ways, these ideologues anticipate and exemplify the world to come. The same can be said about those ravers who follow the gospels spread by public shamans and mystic thinkers such as Terrance McNally, while also worshipping the DJs who unite them on the dance floor.

The larger point to be made is that, regardless of the degree of importance each movement officially gives to hierarchies (formal or informal) or to horizontality, there are individuals who "incarnate" the true spirit of the community and whose contribution, either through action, the word, or both, is seen as crucial to the ultimate success of the message. In fact, it can be argued that the vague doctrines, loose organization, and egalitarian ideology typical of aurora movements are conducive to charismatic leadership because lines of authority at the local level are amorphous and constantly contested. Under these conditions, a leader's personal appeal coalesces the inchoate group, offering direction and a point of focus—providing what Émile Durkheim called the "lens" that ignites the consuming fire of an effervescent collective.[10]

Such a lens is required because the organization and activism of each aurora movement must be quickened, sustained, and propelled by the emotional commitment of a devoted core community of true believers for whom activism is more than just a strategy; it is a way of gaining a meaningful identity, proving one's worth in life, and transcending the dehumanizing distortions of the neoliberal nightmare. The struggle for the world is no place for the lukewarm. The exemplary leader provides an example of dedication for the faithful to emulate. The intensity of commitment is heightened in the close-knit emotional communities of believers who are bound together not only by shared beliefs and experiences but also by righteous anger about what should be self-evident for everyone: Destruction rages, humanity is at risk. Obviously, everything must change. Collective action must adjust to the urgency of the times. The battle to overthrow the status quo, by itself, provides a release for the frustrated ire of activists who are not at home in this world.

This is clear in the case of jihadis. The holy war is the means through which a counteridentity is achieved; self-disgust overcome; lost manhood, dignity, and respect regained among Muslims who feel themselves marginalized. But if we pay attention to the activities and statements of members of other groups, we note a similar sense of self-empowerment and self-realization through ardent devotion to an overriding goal. One may be a nameless Zapatista, a "heroic son" of the Bolivarian Revolution, or a struggling Indian in Bolivia; a lone European intellectual resisting Western globalization or a foot soldier of a popular-national vanguard; a WSF activist debating means for achieving an alternative globalization; a Slow Food devotee resisting the homogenization of taste and of life; or even a raver experiencing a new world in the ecstasy of the moment. In all cases, members feel they belong to a community in pursuit of a transcendent cause; in the process, their entire lives are injected with a renewed meaning and sense of purpose. Their identity as meaningful beings is reinforced; their struggle *becomes* their spiritual and psychological home.

Ritual is one of the major mechanisms for inspiring members to the requisite strong identification with the organizational and ideological framework of each movement. Through repeated festivals and ceremonies, the participants in aurora communities reinforce their emotional ties and immediately experience the authenticity, diversity, solidarity, and humanity that they feel is denied to them in ordinary life. The world as it should be—the subjunctive— is realized in ritual moments of communion and celebration that provide an opportunity for ecstatic reenchantment.[11] The Zapatistas, for instance, are famous for ritualizing joy, holding many festivals and dances, and celebrating the richness and complexity of life in opposition to the colorless drudgery of capitalism. Alter-globalization activists also turn the world upside down in their chaotic carnivalesque gatherings that use street theater, artistic performances, and dances to protest against the system; such occasions are seen as the last bastions of human vitality and spirituality, a bright spark flickering in the cold winds and gray skies of neoliberal globalization. Raves, of course, are felt and understood to be collective rites that create rapture through immersion in ecstatic rhythm, restoring ancient and authentic tribal consciousness. Convivia and international gatherings assume a crucial role in the Slow Food movement as places where free, true, and diverse identities are experienced and celebrated. Collective rituals are also a mainstay of all the nationalist movements we have surveyed in this book. From Venezuela to Bolivia, as well as in the populist-nationalist European parties, a great emphasis is put on parades, pilgrimages, and rallies at "sacred" sites where heroes and histories of old are commemorated, roots and bonds reaffirmed, and the symbolic conquest of an evil and unjust world is momentarily achieved. Jihadis' mission and zeal are also embedded in ritual performance. The Quran is the timeless inspiration for the warriors invested with the mission of recapturing the golden age and reenchanting the world, while terrorist actions are understood both as a reiteration of battles of the past and as symbolic protests against the evil that currently rules planet Earth.

Ultimately, during these times of cosmic crisis, the militancy of each movement offers *the* model of commitment and engagement that in due time must be followed by the rest of the population. The aurora movements' self-perception as vanguards (although this perception is not always publicly acknowledged) is based on a fundamental belief that they have a unique historical mission to convert the masses to their cause. Even if the people do not know it, the goals of the vanguard *must be* the goals of society as a whole, if redemption is to be found. Ultimate success in the struggle against evil depends on mobilizing the desensitized populace to the cause. This is a tall order because the general population is thought to be easily seduced by propaganda and mesmerized by the shiny goods offered by the neoliberal Moloch. But the salvation of the community and of the entire world depends on ending this trance and stimulating popular empowerment and participation. Change need not be cataclysmic. As long as individuals and groups keep committing daily acts of defiance and subversion, as long as the cause keeps attracting new members, the system will be gradually subverted from within. In this case, people will notice the revolution has occurred only after it is already over. But, in general, the future is portrayed in a more apocalyptic light. Destruction spurs revelation.

Many movements, from European nationalist parties to the governments of Chávez and Morales, as well as the alter-globalization activists, herald direct democracy as *the only way* to circumvent the rule of the powerful and give the people the power they need to usher in a radically new social, economic, and political policy. Time is running out; everyone must be involved. However, participation does not necessarily require a passionate defense of "true" democracy. As we have seen, jihadi doctrine rejects democracy as the worship of popular whim. At the same time, jihadis place great emphasis on the duty of *all* true Muslims to participate in the struggle of our times. Jihad is a personal responsibility for every believer, while the democratic consensus of the faithful is the only way in which the true imam can be selected. In all cases, these movements' fervor, moral outrage, and intense involvement in the battle for the world sets the standard of behavior for the majority who are still, frustratingly, uncommitted.

There is also an undeniable intellectual dimension to most of the aurora groups. Many Western intellectuals have given their enthusiastic approval to the socioeconomic and cultural changes in Venezuela and Bolivia. Others are confidants of both leaders and are quoted in the regimes' sharp criticisms of Western imperialist globalization. Created by intellectuals, the WSF still has a highly educated membership. In the pantheon of the Slow Food movement, intellectuals, philosophers, and writers have a prominent place. The European New Right, of course, defines itself as an intellectual vanguard engaged in delegitimizing the philosophical and cultural foundations of the West. They have also heavily influenced core ideas of populist-nationalist parties. Al-Qaeda's propaganda owes much of its appeal to the previous intellectual labor of a number of writers, educators, and religious leaders. Sayyid Qutb, bin Laden, and al-Zawahiri are not only men of action but also men of letters.

Crucially, in all the movements, these intellectuals are rebels against the existing system, which they reject as oppressive, unjust, artificial, inauthentic, and—particularly in Latin America and in the Middle East, but also in Europe—externally imposed. Today's movement intellectuals are the modern equivalents of the "men of words" famously described by Eric Hoffer: journalists and scholars who prepare the ground for revolution by undermining whatever is taken for granted.[12] A number of reasons may explain the devotion of so many Western intellectuals to movements at war with capitalist globalization. In many cases this struggle is a continuation of older Cold War battles. At a deeper level, it may also represent the current form of an intellectual, mental, and moral disposition for revolutionary projects that aim to erase the evils of history once and for all. Why live a bland, ordinary life when the world is waiting to be transformed? By commitment to the creation of a new existence, the ordinariness, vulgarity, and pains of daily life are cancelled, even if only briefly, in ardent pursuit of a not-yet-realized project. Or, following Brinton, their resistance may be a frustrated reaction to the minor roles that intellectuals presently play in world affairs.[13] In any case, the organization and direction of the majority of these movements cannot be fully comprehended without paying attention to their intellectual appeal.

In sum, for the aurora movements, the dawning of new day entails a dispersed, digitally connected, diverse but also somehow united, enthusiastic core of warriors, buttressed by solid intellectual armor and solidified by charismatic leadership. But organization is not sufficient if a movement does not provide a vision of the alternative future, an inspiring glimpse of the coming dawn.

A NEW TEMPLE

There is a timeless wisdom to G. K. Chesterton's comment that "if there is one thing that men have proved again and again is that, even when they furiously burn down a temple, they like to put another on top of it."[14] All of the groups analyzed here are busy burning down the temple of free-market globalization. They all want to transcend the oppressive here and now and inaugurate a radical departure to a new future, which they all imagine in strikingly similar ways.

First and foremost, these movements preach *universalism*. They may be ardent combatants at a local or national level, but they all link their local struggles to a battle to liberate the whole world. Resistance goes beyond national or ethnic borders. From early stages, the Zapatistas have framed their struggle as encompassing humanity itself. In his version of socialism, Hugo Chávez sees the twenty-first century remedy applying not only to Latin America but also to a suffering world. The struggle of the first indigenous Bolivian president can be won only by recovering, at a global level, ancestral links to nature and tribal roots. The European New Right network is ultimately engaged in a universal quest for emancipation, transcending all states; liberation from the homogenizing "American dream" will purify humanity and revalue the planet. Even populist-nationalist parties overcome their particularistic concerns by pursuing a universalism of identity—victory can be achieved only by fundamental changes at a global level. If corporate power and the global free market breed misery and destroy humanity, then the WSF promises a solution through the globalization of solidarity. For local and authentic traditions to survive, the Slow movement pursues a new alliance between humanity and Earth. Even global nomads believe that by channeling cosmic energy, they will bring transformation: The rave is a battle for the planet. The ideal jihadi world extends beyond Muslim lands, bringing divine justice, equality, and harmony with the universe through the implementation of sharia law under the spiritual authority of the anointed imam.

Because they are galvanized by potent "images of the future,"[15] by a "desire for an elsewhere that nevertheless would be realized here and now,"[16] it is accurate to say that these movements are *utopian*. They want to "leap onto a new state of being in which contemporary values . . . are totally transformed or turned upside down."[17] Sociologist Alberto Melucci's emphasis on the primacy of the "utopian appeal" and "quest for transcendence" in contemporary collective action is indeed well placed.[18] This is so even though some groups reject outright the utopian label (for example, the Zapatistas or the European New Right), while others welcome it (Hugo Chávez and many activists and theorists of the alter-globalization movement).[19] Nevertheless, for all of them, a better world, a "new temple," *must* be built. The shape of this new reality varies according to the narrative of each group. If the Zapatistas and the WSF militants want a world that includes all worlds, Chávez and the Bolivarians strive to inaugurate a socialist kingdom, while in Bolivia a world ruled by tribal ancestral ways is sought. The European Right refinds roots and cultivates diversity, while jihadists want a universal empire of the faith. Ravers find their answer in ecstatic dance; Slow activists hope to change the world by changing its tempo.

But these "temples" are built, in each case, on mythical narratives. Initially, there is a *myth of origins*. The world to come must be constructed from the value systems and images of previous golden ages. Hence the importance that the Zapatistas, Evo Morales, and the WSF give to indigenous societies; hence the central role given by the European New Right to pagan times and the sacralization of historical periods and figures by populist-nationalist parties; hence the ravers' passionate apotheosis of and identification with the primitive; hence Slow Food's effort to recapture authentic traditions. The Bolivarian Revolution is understood to be a continuation of the glorious times of Bolívar, while jihadis recall the era of the Prophet as a pristine and timeless inspiration, to be revived and relived. Overall the aim of the aurora movements is not to simply turn back the clock or to "end" globalization. Rather it is to adapt globalization creatively according to their own goals, shaped by the sacred narratives of the past. For this purpose, reference to a mythical source is insufficient; there must also be a *myth of a new beginning*. That is why the literature in all these movements is full of narratives of rebirth, transformation, mutation, the resumption of harmony, the creation of new human beings, and the purification of nature and of humanity. In each movement, these myths of origin and of regeneration propel their utopian visions.

As has no doubt become clear, the sought-after solutions for the evils afflicting the world do not stop at instrumental or piecemeal adjustments. The primary interest is not inaugurating changes within the system; it is instead the manufacture of a wholly new universe completely at odds with the one existing today. Ultimately, a *new civilization*, rooted in ancient wisdom, while simultaneously creating a new cosmology and a new way of living, must be built.[20] When the first great recession of the twenty-first century irrupted the sociologist Robert Castel lamented that—because markets are an essential component of modernity—the only realistic solution was to rein in global capitalism, even though it was not a "heroic solution" that promised "tomorrows that sing."[21] But aurora believers will not easily accept a small and dim vision of a silent tomorrow. As an antiglobalization activist proclaimed: "The future is up for grabs and the potential for a better world is within our grasp . . . All we have to do is change everything."[22] This enthusiast is not alone in his belief and intention; it is widely shared. In the struggle to change everything, improving material conditions, though important, is secondary; what takes priority is a larger, profound reversal in humankind's attitude toward the self and the world. If humanity is to survive, a *spiritual change* must be accomplished first; materialism must take a backseat, and the current value system based on greedy individualism must be inverted.

This redemptive aspect becomes evident when we notice that aurora movements are generally not against commerce and business per se. They are neither communistic nor even completely socialistic. For example, as the Bolivarian revolution demonstrates, at least for the time being, capital may be used as long as it is applied properly, in the name of "good" and "morally" correct ends, as defined by the leader. Similarly, jihadis repudiate usury and unfair trade but are far from embracing any form of redistribution.[23] Slow Food has no problem with capitalism and in fact sponsors a global gathering of entrepreneurs specializing in "good, pure, and fair" products. The WSF is heavily invested in NGOs that aim to promote more just exchange; ATTAC wishes to install a more equitable taxation regime. In this new century, populist-nationalist parties tend to be protectionists without wanting to get rid of the market economy. For all these movements, the fundamental goal is not simply to overthrow the Anglo-American free-market order, but rather to reestablish the equilibrium among humanity, society, and nature. To achieve that great goal, the separation between politics and the economic and financial world, propelled by a culture of unbridled materialism and a value system that appeals to the basest instincts of human beings, must be brought to an end. A sustainable world demands the arrival of a new ethos. The declared enemy is not enterprise but a contagious and virulent form of capitalism without limits or ethics that wreaks misery and eats away at the soul. However, the suspicion remains that if aurora movements had total control, the survival of capitalism, at least in any recognizable form, would be doubtful. The implication—not always stated and more obvious in some movements than others—is that the revolutionary logic of total transformation would eventually lead, in the long term, to a postcapitalist future of communal sharing and blissful unity.

As premonitions of the ultimate aspiration, and as inspirational nodes for transformation, temporary autonomous zones (TAZs), liberated from the oppressive global order, have to be created. The terminology comes from ravers and their allies, but all the aurora movements aim at creating their own versions of independent spaces, regions, or geopolitical blocs. Zapatista communities, pan–Latin America projects, a "Europe of Peoples," the WSF "square without an owner," the jihadi cells, and many others, all constitute temporary autonomous zones (some more plausible than others). Such liberated spaces anticipate a wider imagined community of the soon-to-be liberated. It is no wonder that the proliferation of such spaces is the confirmation for some that the revolution is *already* under way: In autonomous communities, constituted against global and state power, one acts "as though one is already free." They represent revolutionary arenas in which the future is shaped and experienced in the present.[24] The ultimate goal is to break the spell of "Weber's curse," redeeming a world that since the dawn of modernity has become a wasteland under the authority of a tyrannical bureaucratic-technical rational impersonal system engulfing all the authenticity and creativity of human nature and erasing the richness of diversity. In contrast, aurora movements offer wholeness, smoothness, and concord. A *totalizing view* is at the very center of all these gospels of liberation. The ideal alternative universe is diverse, just, unified, organic, participatory, emancipated, vital, and joyous. Human dignity is regained. To the European New Right this state represents a return of the gods. But to all of the believers, the redeemed world would certainly be, once again, an enchanted place, in which ugly divisions, inequities, and disproportions would be permanently erased and where beautiful harmony would forever resound.

TROUBLES IN PARADISE

There are a number of issues, paradoxes, and ironies within the aurora movements that our research has brought to light. First, even though the movements we have surveyed often claim to be wholly new,[25] it is nonetheless the case that efforts to bring a "radical break between the present regime and the promised land," opposing "the corrupt world of today to the transfigured world of tomorrow,"[26] have been recurrent in Western history. Moreover, the revolt against the excessive rationalization of modern life—envisioned as destructive of human depth, creativity, and all that it is natural and holy—parallels the prophecies of many nineteenth-century dreamers. The importance of imagination, idealism, and attachment to transcendent goals of harmony and beauty that are present in today's activists—as well as their feelings of estrangement from the ways of the world—seem only to confirm their status as modern romantics. The twentieth century witnessed other similar moments of idealism corresponding with an ethical, aesthetic, and intellectual search for redemptive alternatives: Nonconformists, from across the ideological spectrum, left their mark in the 1930s and 1960s when they sought ultimate answers for appalling human conditions. Therefore, in more than one sense, aurora movements are not new; they embody and continue older struggles—some very ancient, some more contemporary. Corporate-driven, free-market, or neoliberal globalization is, in its essence, only the current incarnation of an older evil that plagues humanity; i.e., a materialistic and morally hollow orientation toward existence. That is why, as has become clear throughout this book, a primal struggle for the soul of humanity and for the world itself looms behind the indictment of globalization.

This realization leads us straight into the ongoing debate about whether the standard distinction between right and left bears any weight in the struggle for the world. In other words, are these movements *fundamentally different* because they originate from either extreme of the political spectrum? Surely for many of the militants involved the distinction is very much alive. With some exceptions (jihadis, Slow Food advocates, and ravers, for example), they all proudly announce their leftist or rightist credentials (although, as in the case of the ENR, they may often cross over into enemy territory). Even the more peaceful (though often no less militant) world of academia has increasingly accepted the idea that the clash between left and the right is rapidly expanding to cover the whole globe.

But what does the distinction actually mean? Some commentators have asserted that what distinguishes the contemporary left is its opposition to purely market-oriented approaches to globalization, its rejection of the triumph of market democracy, and its search for a new value-system where humanity is free at last from the chains of an out-of-control capitalism.[27] From this perspective, any opposition offered to globalization from the right is a mere barricade against a changing world, one that utterly fails to provide an alternative vision for the globe. According to one analyst, on the antiglobal right, "only jihadis" have a global imaginary.[28] If, after all these pages, the reader does not question these statements, then we have failed to capture the self-understanding of aurora movements—whether right wing, left wing or no wing—which, in their different ways, totally reject a world dominated by a destructive and soulless market. All of them, whatever their avowed political ideology and tactical disagreements, propound new values that transcend individualism and consumerism; all of them seek to reenchant the natural world and redeem a fallen humanity. They see themselves as guides in a world that has lost its way. Certainly we do not advocate the abandonment of the left–right cleavage in the study of movements that are in search of another world. The dichotomy remains useful, but we do not see it as a *dominant* feature: It is *part* of a larger redemptive worldview. A famous motto of neoliberal capitalism is that free markets and free trade create a rising tide that lifts all boats. But when all the boats are sinking—and for aurora movements this catastrophe is beyond dispute—finding a permanent and peaceful harbor is what truly matters.

One also may wonder whether these movements struggling for the soul of the world are equally substantial and serious—or are some of them merely trendy, or absurd, or fanatical? We make no final judgments in this matter. Regardless of the ways in which they manifest their rejection of this world—either by belonging to movements or parties that preach radical paths, by writing manifestos, by participating in forums, by seeking slow ways of living, by raving the night away in ecstasy, or by following an extremist religious path—the truth is that the actual experience of bringing another, better world into existence—if only momentarily—is characteristic of all of them. We may debate whether the goal of transformation is better met by writing a book, by dancing, by pursuing slowness, or in trying to bring down the WTO; we can debate as well whether the ideological foundations of some movements are more solid than are others. Certainly the Tobin tax proposed by ATTAC has a rational basis quite absent among anti-intellectual ravers, intent on communing with alien intelligences and pursuing ecstasy. But this does not mean that the first is feasible while the second is destined to vanish. Nor does it mean that the former is serious and the latter is frivolous.[29] Such accusations do not do justice to the actual understandings, experiences, and commitments of participants. In the end, we must admit that these movements all share a clear sense of their vital roles in the battle to bring the "transfigured world of tomorrow"; all have intimations of that coming world; all yearn for its arrival. Who is to say which has the mental map, spiritual motivation, or mode of action best suited to achieve the great transformation?

As we have argued, regardless of differences in the cures they prescribe, all aurora movements believe that the current world order stultifies human potential. Consent to the hegemonic system is, they believe, manufactured by a whole array of mechanisms, including omnipresent and overwhelming media propaganda. The aurora movements seek the emancipation of humanity from this coercive authority. The Zapatistas believe men and women can regain their dignity only when freed from the neoliberal prison; the Bolivarian movement intends to "establish the kingdom of heaven on Earth;" the Morales regime aims to reverse centuries of humiliation and disgrace for the aboriginal peoples; the European New Right wishes to emancipate the masses from the ravages of impersonal Western consumerism; alter-globalization movements pursue freedom from global exploitation and commodification; the Slow Food philosophy promotes the production and consumption of pure and natural food as the best route to salvation; in raves, dancers experience ecstatic release from alienation; the jihadis want to rescue the faithful from the rampant sin and degradation spread by the West.

Even though they all wish for peace and unity in diversity, these different totalistic visions of worldwide liberation have a danger inherent in them. This danger is most evident in the case of the jihadis: Nonparticipation, for whatever reason, in the holy war is interpreted as treason to the higher cause—a crime punishable by death. This is a radical example, but the totalitarian temptation is nevertheless present as a possibility in all movements that are *certain* the world is crumbling and *know* the cure for its ills. To bring about the needed new order, participation *must* be absolute and enthusiastic; anger and devotion are *required* to save the world. People *must* be involved; they *must* choose sides. The movement prescribes how members *should* live their lives; it is *certain* of the morally right path to follow and *clear* about what "true" humanity is and is not. Significantly, there is little discussion in the aurora movements about leisure or sports, nor is there much place for individual pleasure. This claim may sound contradictory to the reader who noticed the central role that joyous celebrations and rituals play in so many of these movements. But these are embodied ideological and political performances that cement individuals into a collective unity. In such celebrations, personal pleasure is for the sake of the group. And if there is no allowance for individual joy, there is certainly no room for apathy or withdrawal, no space for those who eschew the promised redemption, who do not fall into line, or who refuse to "share" their consciousness with others. If this is indeed the case, paradise is lost before it has been gained.

In the path of struggle, some movements are much more violent than others. As we have mentioned, in many of the aurora discourses violence is mostly symbolic; their talk is full of the images of destruction, chaos, and misery required for the transition from the bad world to the good one. But while some seek to accelerate this process through purifying acts of terror, as in the case of jihadis, others, notably a majority of Slow Food activists and ravers, work peacefully for the birth of the new, eating or dancing the millennium into being. Others take the middle ground. The Zapatistas first chose to fight a war of resistance but subsequently adopted a less aggressive approach, hoping to inspire transformation by example. Some antiglobalization activists have engaged in violent clashes with the police, destroying property, protesting the WTO, G8 meetings, and so on. But the WSF specifically renounces violence in its set of principles. The "movement of movements" assumes that inclusion and continuous debate will, in itself, promote unity in diversity, though there are radical-leftist voices calling for "defensive violence" against capitalist power.[30] The overtly political paths taken by Chávez and Morales have inspired great devotion but also strong opposition, as have the nationalist programs of Le Pen, Bossi, and others. As a result, there have been occasional episodes of serious violence, particularly in Latin America, but no full-blown civil wars—at least not to date. Evidently, the potential for violence will depend on several factors, including the strategy adopted for change and the degree to which members feel alienated and disconnected from society, as well as the degree to which a catastrophic worldview prevails within these movements. These dynamics, for the most part, will determine the extent to which cleansing violence against the system and against perceived enemies is seen as just and unavoidable. And, of course, the same factors will determine how much violence the mainstream will direct against those who oppose it. Under uncertain conditions, the danger of an escalating dialectic of repression and resistance is vastly increased.

Another point to be made is that, despite their efforts to proclaim an open-ended future, the aurora movements do not escape the allure of the philosophy of "endism" that has characterized contemporary thought. The public intellectuals who announce the end of history have been met by movement philosophers and others, who equally confidently proclaim the end of free-market capitalism, the end of neoliberalism, the end of the American era, the end of the West, and the end of liberal globalization—even the "end" of the "end of history."[31] Whether or not any of these pronouncements will prove true is still unknown, though the failure of similar predictions in the past does not bode well for those of the present. But it is impossible not to note that the movements of our study wish to offer a final solution that will permanently settle all the distress, suffering, and oppression in the world. They believe their actions will lead to final stage of fulfillment in which a liberated humanity will live in a permanent state of solidarity, equality, diversity, and identity. The grand debate over what is the best system for humanity will be finally settled. Out of the neoliberal chaos a new "land flowing with milk and honey" will emerge, and history will finally come to its ultimate idyllic end.

CONCLUSION: BEYOND THE DAWN

Historians and social scientists know that predictions about future possibilities usually frustrate those who make them. Reality has a stubborn way of turning our forecasts upside down. Therefore we are cautious when postulating what the future may hold for aurora movements, which themselves are based on positing new tomorrows. Still, we can wonder what their most probable trajectories may be. Which of them are more susceptible to accommodation in the system? It seems likely that movements such as those gathered around the WSF and Slow Food may well, with time, become increasingly rationalized and attached to formal structures of power, especially if an increasing number of governments adopt the reformist measures that they support. The Zapatistas, as well as the government of Venezuela (and to a lesser extent in Bolivia), have developed enough relatively successful "autonomous" areas to convince many across the world that they are actually creating viable alternative realities. Both Chávez's and Morales's leaderships have served as examples and inspiration for the "left turn" in Latin American politics at the beginning of the twenty-first century.[32] Whether these projects will lose their momentum and their allure for their core constituencies of the poor and downtrodden will depend to a large extent on the capacities of their charismatic leaders, who must continue to live up to their past achievements while maintaining glowing expectations. Even if their projects do succeed, their examples may well be marginalized if the current globalization system as a whole survives.

The autonomous areas may then serve mainly as refuges for the alienated and the idealistic, much like communes left over from the 1960s. A similar fate is likely for the New Right in Europe, which will probably remain on the periphery of national politics, attracting a loyal minority but incapable of overturning the center. However, ENR influence, like the influence of the Latin American nationalist movements, would be greatly heightened if a complete economic, political, and moral breakdown were to occur; in that case identity-driven ideals of spiritual rejuvenation and geopolitical overhaul would certainly contribute to the emergence of a "new world." Already some of the ENR beliefs regarding immigration have influenced mainstream European parties. At the extreme we may well find the deterritorialized ravers in unlikely company with al-Qaeda as the elements least likely to be integrated and normalized. The rave lifestyle, although constantly metamorphosing, will retain its embodied appeal among nomadic youth yearning for the immediate experience of a psychedelic apocalypse; al-Qaeda, equally apocalyptic, also thrives on alienation and idealism. But where the ravers lose themselves in the temporary ecstasy of dance, al-Qaeda obliterate themselves in suicidal rituals of terror. However, before assuming eternal intransigence, it should be recalled that some jihadis, under pressure or not, have already reached accommodation with the powers that be.

Whatever trajectory a particular movement takes, in all instances, it is fair to assume that a number of activists will be incorporated by the mainstream, shedding their revolutionary past and youthful dreams for an all-too-human need for security and a career. This is a recurrent trend in history. But there will also be zealots who refuse any accommodation, furiously burning their bridges in an attempt to ignite a new dawn. This will be especially true if the world does not end after all, despite the prophesies of the aurora movements. In that case, it is a safe assumption that groups such as those we have described— which may have different names and will certainly have new leaders—will continue to appeal to all those who wish to experience a better alternative, whatever it may be. Fear and hope, as David Hume told us long ago, still are the primary motivators for human beings.[33]

We should also note that the world is not *literally* ending. Instead, from the highlands of Chiapas to the streets of Venezuela and Bolivia, from meeting halls in Europe and from social forums worldwide to the mountains of Pakistan, from organic farms in Italy to raves in Goa, what may actually be under threat is the dominant Western *narrative* of a universe inevitably evolving toward an unbalanced technocratic society of mindless consumers. While this vision does not exactly herald Hell on Earth, or the final collapse of humanity, aurora movements have made it ever more evident that the result is far from "progress" or "happiness." All the aurora movements, today and tomorrow, are trying to write a new story that can redeem the world from a pervasive sense of disillusionment. They will continue to exist, if only in scattered sanctuaries and temporary autonomous zones where they can reject the standard tale and live out their own myths, at least for a moment.[34]

At present, movements that see themselves as building a new world atop the ruins of the old are still a minority. While many citizens may be alienated, bored, or fearful, few are willing to destroy what exists—however distasteful—in the dubious pursuit of something wholly new but also wholly unknown. Obviously, as we have stated, this can change if there is the deepening of a global crisis, triggering the existential terror that the situation has gone irreversibly out of control. Fear of impending chaos can contagiously spread and make the gospel of the aurora increasingly appealing. The likelihood of an apocalyptic sensibility is intensified in the modern setting, where the globe itself has become a frame of reference for so many.

It is not uncommon for people throughout history to believe that *their* times are special times—either of unprecedented promise or impending collapse.[35] Our age is no different. Naturally, one does not need to be committed to an aurora movement to believe that the world as we know it *must* change for the sake of humanity. There are those who believe in the power of "minor utopias" to bring about peaceful and gradual change.[36] But the idea that the old order is rapidly fading has gained traction among myriads of academics, artists, priests, and pundits. Many of them—who are not necessarily zealots (or at least do not see themselves as such)—rejoice at the death knell of the Faustian belief in productivity and endless progress. They imagine a worldwide transformation in consciousness in which spirituality, heterogeneity, playfulness, emotional expressivity, and primal attachments to roots and territories (real or virtual) will take precedence over a dry and detached rationality devoted to endlessly calculating profits. For these hopeful Dionysians, the coming new era will be one of a newfound energy, vitality, and creative effervescence in human and social relations.[37] The critiques offered by aurora movements tap into these widespread attitudes and indicate their potential to gain converts.

But regardless of whether the paradigm is shifting or not, because people are now aware of what is happening in different parts of the world in an unprecedented way, consciousness of the potential for change has become uniquely widespread. In troubled times, across cultures, people now vacillate dramatically from widespread panic to unsettling euphoria. Together, humanity awaits the future with a mixture of anxiety and anticipation, wondering, with Yeats, "what rough beast, its hour come round at last, slouches towards Bethlehem, waiting to be born?"[38]

NOTES

Chapter 1

1. Hardy 1901: 217.

2. Carlyle 1853: 30.

3. This version of the well-known Chinese proverb is from Rohsenow 2002:98.

4. For three characteristic statements to this effect, see Held 2000: 4; Steger 2003: 1–2; and Ellwood 2001: 8.

5. A number of authors argue that many aspects of globalization existed prior to the present-day integration and interconnectedness. See Friedman 1994; Lang 2006; Chanda 2007; Cohen 2006.

6. In *Maps of Time*, David Christian's introduction to "big history," the author marvels at the "great acceleration," the "hurricane of change" of the twentieth century: "Change accelerated so rapidly, and the ramifications of change were so universal, that this period marks an utterly new stage in human history and in the history of human relations with other species and with the earth. Indeed, it may be no exaggeration to say that the twentieth century marks a decisive moment in the history of the entire biosphere." (Christian 2004: 441).

7. For opposing views see Friedman 2007 and de Blij 2008.

8. *Ejército Zapatista de Liberación Nacional* (EZLN) 2008.

9. Greider 1997; Luttwak 1999.

10. Mittelman 2004: 8–9; Juris 2008: 6–7.

11. Gauchet 2006.

12. Cohn 1984: 281.

13. For an engaging account of the rise and fall of the Anabaptist Kingdom of Münster, see Arthur 1999.

14. Hill 1972: 363.

15. Babeuf 1795: 219.

16. Michelet 1853: 20, 444.

17. Talmon 1960: 15.

18. Dostoyevsky 1872: 525. See also Billington 1980.

19. Griffin 2007: 6.

20. Zolberg 1972: 129.

21. Fanon 1961: 2.

22. See Worsley 1968. The term has come to refer to a variety of indigenous symbolic efforts to tap into the vast powers of modernity.

23. Price, Nonini, and Fox 2008: 127–159.

24. Popper 1947: 361–362.

25. Arendt 1958: 133.

26. Solzhenitsyn 1986: 78.

27. Aron 1955: 324.

28. Shklar 1957: vii.

29. Bell 2000: 393. Later, Bell softened his position, arguing that "the 'end of ideology,' as the great historic crossover of beliefs, has run its course, I think. It is now the resumption of history that has begun" (Bell 2000: xxviii).

30. Kirchheimer 1972. See also note 44.

31. SDS 1962: 9, 77.

32. Quoted on Libcom.org.

33. Berlin 1978: 47–48.

34. Kolakowski 1983: 247.

35. Turner 1977.

36. Huntington 1989.

37. The idea of an end to history was not novel. On this issue see Niethammer 1992.

38. Bonnett 2004: 137. Other authors who have remarked on the utopian character of economic growth and free market ideology are Polanyi 1944: xxv; Gray 1998: 203; Mittelman 2004: 89–90; Stoll 2008.

39. Fukuyama 1989: 18. For his later reservations, see Fukuyama 2006.

40. Goodwin 2001: 298; Snyder 1999; Sanderson 2005: 165–166. For an opposing view, see Foran 2000: 442–443.

41. Mueller 1989. This parallels arguments made by Angell 1933: 59.

42. Hobsbawm 1990: 191–192. For a criticism, see Smith 1995: 8–28.

43. Jones presided over the suicide of 900 members of his cult (Maaga 1998: 164).

44. Flanagan 2000: 14.

45. For examples, see García Márquez 1992: 237; Solzhenitsyn 1993: 601; Huntington 1993: 48; Huntington 2007; Kaplan 2000. For a later view see Turner 2007. For a philosophical argument in favor of the indeterminacy of history, see Bloch 1986.

46. Barber 1993: 62.

47. Furet 1999: 502. Furet's cultural pessimism echoes Nietzsche's evocation of the "last man" (1891: 6, 172) and Weber's gloomy image of a future bereft of meaning (2001).

48. Bauman 1999: 8. For an opposing view, see Freeden 2006: 141–142.

49. Jacoby 1999: 180–181.

50. Steger 2003: 113.

51. Gill 2008: xvi.

52. Steger 2008. See also Albrow (1996: 4).

53. Touraine 2007: 25.

54. Niezen 2004: 10.

55. For a survey, see Chase-Dunn and Reese 2007.

56. Tilly 2004: 114.

57. Polanyi 1944. For contemporary uses of Polanyi's theories see Chin and Mittelman 2000: 34–37; Kiely 2005: 160–162; Steger 2007: 380; Kahn and Kellner 2007: 670–671; Stiglitz 2001; Munck 2007.

58. Friedman 2005.

59. Negri 2008: 59. See also Hardt and Negri 2004. For a critique, see Kiely 2005: 215–218.

60. Kahn and Kellner 2007: 670–671.

61. Giugni, for example, notes the "striking similarities displayed by movements across countries" (2002: 26); Devji argues that global resistance movements, from environmentalists to jihadists, are a part of a worldwide reaction to "the fragmentation and transformation of politics itself" (2005: 132).

62. Exceptions are the New Social Movement theorists, represented by Alberto Melucci 1989 and Alain Touraine 1981. For a critique, see Price et al. 2008.

63. Gills 2000: 9.

64. Webb 2006: 136.

65. Adorno 1951: 247.

66. Rupert 2000; Munck 2007; Webb 2006.

For discussion of the antiglobal right, see Mittelman 2004: 94; Kiely 2005: 176–179; Gill 2008: 258; Steger 2008: 213–218. For the inclusion of jihad in the antiglobal camp, see Tarrow 2005b: 206; Steger 2008: 218–235.

67. Munck 2007: 110.

Chapter 2

1. Galeano 2000: 8.

2. Mariátegui 2005: 287–288.

3. Named after Emiliano Zapata, a peasant leader in the Mexican revolution.

4. The Zapatista movement began in 1983 when a very small group of indigenous and urban mestizos with Marxist-Maoist revolutionary ideas set up a camp in the

Lacandon jungle of the state of Chiapas with the goal of creating a guerrilla war to overthrow the bourgeois regime. Marcos—whose real name is Rafael Guillén—was part of this initial group (Henck 2007: 65–128).

5. Marcos 2001b: 18.

6. Zapatistas 1998: 31.

7. Zapatistas 1998: 59.

8. Marcos 2005b.

9. Marcos 2001b: 167.

10. Marcos 1997: 261–262.

11. Marcos, quoted in Mentinis 2006: 128.

12. Marcos, in Báez 1996: 169.

13. Mentinis, 2006: 140.

14. Marcos 2007a.

15. Marcos, quoted in Henck 2007: 227.

16. Marcos 2001b: 167.

17. Almeyra and Thibaut 2006: 85.

18. Marcos 2005b.

19. Zapatistas 1998: 37.

20. Zapatistas 1998: 12.

21. Marcos 2001a.

22. Marcos 2005a: 180.

23. Katzenberger 1995: ii.

24. Marcos 2001b: 185–186.

25. Marcos 2001b: 167.

26. Marcos, quoted in Ortiz, Brige, and Ferrari 2007: 179.

27. Quoted in Magallanes-Blanco 2008: 172.

28. Reitan 2007: 197. See also Olesen 2005.

29. Notes from Nowhere 2003: 21–24; 23–24. For more on the Zapatista's influence on alter-globalization movements see Steger 2003: 121–122; Olesen 2005; Ross 2006: 101; Almeyra and Thibaut 2006; Reitan 2007: 188–229; Fougier 2008: 18; see also Chapter 5. On the unintended commodification of Chiapas itself as a tourist attraction, see *New York Times* (NYT) 2008a.

30. Henck 2007: 231.

31. Cleaver 1998: 81.

32. Zapatistas 1998: 62.

33. Zapatistas 1998: 62.

34. Magallanes-Blanco 2008.

35. Marcos 2001b.

36. EZLN 1995.

37. Marcos 2005b. See also Marcos 2005a.

38. Zapatistas 1998: 36.

39. Marcos 2001b: 111–112.

40. Zapatistas 1998: 40.

41. Quoted in Ross 2006: 202. See also Zapatistas 1998: 36.

42. Marcos 2001b: 19.

43. Almeyra and Thibaut 2006: 50.

44. Marcos 2005a: 180–181.

45. Zapatistas 1998: 13; see also Ramírez 2003: 234 and Holloway 2005: 213–213.

46. The website of the festival is available at: http://dignarabia.ezln.org.mx/.

47. Quoted in Báez 1996: 76. See also Olesen 2006.

48. Durán 2001: 51.

49. Ramírez 2003: 163.

50. Stahler-Sholk 2007.

51. Baronnet 2008: 116.

52. Quoted in Báez 1996: 99. See also Marcos 2005b.

53. Marcos 2001b: 44.

54. Mentinis (2006: 142–150) sees a discrepancy between the discourse of equality and participation and the actuality of continued male hierarchical domination, as sanctioned by indigenous traditions. For a contrasting view, see Jung 2008: 209–212.

55. Marcos 2004a: 586–588.

56. Henck 2007: 226–240; Mentinis 2006: 148. Marcos sees the attribution of charisma to him as the result of an absence of meaningful references in society (Rovira 2003: 339–340).

57. A case in point is Ross 2009.

58. Marcos 2007a.

59. Marcos 2001b: 19. The autonomous education of the Zapatistas' schools focuses on retrieval of the collective memory of "invasion and oppression" (Baronnet 2008: 117).

60. Rovira 2003: 212.

61. EZLN 2003.

62. EZLN 1995.

63. See for example Marcos 2001b: 407.

64. Marcos 2007b: 91.

65. Henck 2007: 269–272; Ross 2000: 88.

66. Marcos 2001b: 19–20.

67. Rovira 2003: 206.

68. Quoted in Benjamin 2001: 447; Marcos 2001b: 20.

69. EZLN 1994; Benjamin 2000: 447.

70. EZLN 2001.

71. Ramírez 2003: 201; Marcos 2000b: 505.

72. Baronnet 2008: 119.

73. Marcos 2007a: 353–354.

74. British Broadcasting Corporation (BBC) 2003.

75. Rajchenberger and Héau-Lambert 1998: 33.

76. Quoted in Ramírez 2003: 103.

77. Zapatistas 1998: 29.

78. Marcos 2001b: 186; Olesen 2005: 12.

79. Quoted in Ortiz, Brige, and Ferrari 2007: 176.

80. Marcos 2005a: 292.

81. EZLN 2001.

82. Marcos 2005: 162.

83. Marcos 2000a: 168.

84. Marcos rejects the utopian label: "Ours is not a liberated territory, nor a utopian commune. Nor an experimental laboratory for nonsense, nor the paradise of an orphaned left" (2007b: 256). Regardless, many external observers view the Zapatista network of autonomous communities as containing the potential for transforming radical politics and putting utopian thinking "in motion again" (Mentinis 2006: 137–138).

85. Marcos 2005a: 291.

86. Marcos 2000a: 159.

87. According to Gilman-Opalsky, the Zapatistas' public sphere is neither exclusively national nor transnational but rather is "transgressive" (2008: 239).

88. Marcos 1997.

89. *Popol Vuh* 1986: 99–100.

90. Zago 1992: 109–110.

91. Chávez 2003c: 101.

92. Chávez 1999h: 221.

93. Chávez 1999g: 334.

94. Chávez 1999d: 290.

95. Chávez 1999d: 289.

96. Chávez 1999c: 483.

97. Chávez 2003d: 136; Chávez 1999a: 198.

98. Chávez 2003d: 136.

99. Chávez 2003b: 392–393.

100. Carrera Damas 2006: 398.

101. Chávez 2009; 1999d: 280; Analítica 2000.

102. For an example Chávez 1999b: 259.

103. For an example, Chávez 2003e: 103.

104. Chávez 1999d: 290.

105. Quoted in Gott 2000: 113.

106. Chávez 2001f: 166.

107. Chávez 2003a: 593–594.

108. Chávez 1999d: 290.

109. Chávez 2001c: 681.

110. Chávez 2001g: 94.

111. On Chávez self-characterization as the interpreter of the national will, see Eastwood 2007.

112. Hellinger 2001.

113. For an example, Chávez 2003f: 412.

114. Agencia Bolivariana de Noticias (ABN) 2007a.

115. Chávez 2001a: 598.

116. Chávez 1999a: 191; 2003h: 265.

117. Two percent of the population (Van Cott 2007: 128).

118. Giordani and Villalón 2002: 45.

119. ABN 2007b.

120. Chávez 2001a: 597.

121. Chávez 1999e: 399.

122. Chávez 2003e: 107.

123. Chávez 2003k: 205.

124. Chávez 2003m: 512

125. Chávez 2003e: 108.

126. Chávez 2001d: 620.

127. Chávez 2005g: 419.

128. Chávez 2004a: 14

129. Chávez 2005j: 427; ABN 2008b; El Nacional 2009. Chávez often lauds American antiestablishment political activists, old and new, from Martin Luther King Jr. to Harry Belafonte and Noam Chomsky. See Chávez 2005j: 441; Chávez 2005c: 601; Chávez 2006d.

130. Chávez 2005l: 723.

131. See, for instance, Chávez 2003h: 265. On the coup attempt, see NYT 2002; Ellner 2008: 198.

132. Chávez 2005j: 446.

133. Chávez 2005j: 427.

134. For an example, see Chávez 2005j: 68.

135. Chávez 2006d.

136. Agence France-Presse (AFP) 2007.

137. For examples, Ultimas Noticias 2006; 2008i. On the role of conspiracy theories in the political communication of Chávez, see Hernáiz 2008.

138. ABN 2007e.

139. Chávez 2001d: 525.

140. Chávez 2003e: 123.
141. Chávez 2003j: 626.
142. On anti-CNN comments, see Radio Nacional de Venezuela (RNV) 2007a, b.
143. ABN 2008c, l.
144. Chávez 2003j: 630, quoting the Brazilian educational thinker Paulo Freire.
145. Televisora Venezolana Social (TVes) 2007.
146. Chávez 2005c: 617.
147. ABN 2008d.
148. ABN 2005.
149. Agencia EFE 2006.
150. ABN 2006.
151. Garrido 2007: 58–60.
152. Bolivarian Congress of Peoples (CBP) 2004.
153. Chávez 2003k: 206.
154. Chávez 2003l: 498; Flores 2005: 6.
155. Chávez 2001b: 690; ABN 2008m.
156. Bossi 2005.
157. ABN 2007d.
158. ABN 2008e.
159. Chávez 2001c: 618.
160. Chávez 1999d: 291–295. Even before he came to office, Chávez promoted the idea of a "Bolivarian" Third Way.
161. Quoted in Muñoz 1998: 95.
162. Chávez 2003i: 527.
163. Chávez 2005f: 90.
164. Chávez 2005h: 473.
165. Chávez 2005d: 317.
166. For an example, Chávez 2005h: 473.
167. For example, Chávez 2006b; ABN 2007g.
168. Chávez 2006c, d.
169. ABN 2007a, c.
170. For an example, Chávez 2002b: 543
171. Chávez 2002b: 477.
172. Chávez 2002a: 149.
173. Chávez 2004c: 453.
174. For an example, Chávez 1999g: 338.
175. Zúquete 2008.
176. Chávez 2007b.
177. Chávez 2004a: 42.
178. Chávez 2005a.

179. Chávez 2007c; 2005k: 522.

180. Chávez 2006a.

181. ABN 2007c, 2008j.

182. Chávez hailed the victory in the referendum, saying that it "opened the doors of the future" (ABN 2009a).

183. *El Nacional* 2006a.

184. Chávez 2006c.

185. Chávez 2005e: 567. For a critical view, see Rodríguez 2008.

186. Chávez 2003g: 651.

187. Chávez 2007c.

188. Resistance to this plan is documented in *El Universal* 2008.

189. For an example, Chávez 2006e. Che Guevara believed that "society, collectively, must convert itself in one gigantic school" (Che Guevara 1965: 259). See also, Hernáiz 2008: 717–718.

190. Chávez 2007a.

191. ABN 2007c.

192. ABN 2008e.

193. ABN 2008c. One of the main slogans of the group is "Ready for combat, in defense of humanity, Chávez, revolution, and the people" (Frente Francisco de Miranda [FFM] 2008).

194. Ministerio del Poder Popular para la Participación y Protección Social (MPS) 2008.

195. Chávez 2006d.

196. See Rosen 2005.

197. Arenas and Calcaño 2006: 374–375.

198. *Gaceta Oficial* 2006.

199. ABN 2007f.

200. Fehrer 2007/2008, 29.

201. Aporrea 2007.

202. To Sonntag (2006). "The same fascism of the thirties has returned but in a more modern edition."

203. For an example, Chávez 2001c: 620.

204. For an example, Chávez 2006d.

205. Hands Off Venezuela (HOV), for example, is present in more than thirty countries and campaigns to "defend the revolution" and its "struggle to liberate the oppressed" (HOV, 2002).

206. Chávez 2006a.

207. Chávez 2003c, 90.

208. Chávez 2007b.

209. Chávez 2005j: 461–462.

210. Chávez 2005l: 721–722; 2009.

211. De la Vega [1609] 1995.

212. De la Vega's writings have served as inspiration for millenarian longings for a second Inca empire. See Montoya Rojas 2005.

213. The indigenous movement in Bolivia is not monolithic. The minority Movimiento Indígena Pachacuti (Pachakuti Indigenous Movement, or MIP) led by the Aymara activist Felipe Quispe portrays itself to be the only "true" voice of the indigenous peoples in the country and is dismissive of the labor and socialist roots of the MAS and Evo Morales (Albro 2006; Mayorga 2005: 113–114).

214. On the importance of indigenous identity in Morales's victory, see Hall and Fenelon 2008: 5.

215. Van Cott 2007: 128.

216. Kolata 1993: 1–18.

217. Postero 2007: 1–2; Arze and Carranza 2006: 103–116.

218. *Conosur-Ñawpaqman* 2006.

219. Morales 2006e: 13.

220. Morales 2006e: 14–16. On the impact of this speech on the antiglobal left, see Hayden 2006.

221. Albro 2006: 411.

222. *La Razón* 2007b.

223. Postero 2007: 3.

224. Albro 2005: 443.

225. Dunkerley 2007: 24–25; Albro 2006: 412.

226. Gironda 2006: 79.

227. Flores Galindo 1988: 411; Postero 2007: 9–12.

228. Morales 2007f.

229. Morales 2006e: 21.

230. Agencia Boliviana de Información (ABI) 2005.

231. Thomson 2002.

232. On the *Katarista* movement, see Cusicanqui 1983.

233. While in captivity he was tortured (Sivak 2008: 307).

234. Morales 2006e: 108.

235. Morales 2006e: 95. On the continuing symbolic importance of Túpac Amaru, see Montoya Rojas 2005: 55.

236. Dunkerley 2007: 28–29.

237. García Linera 2004: 72

238. Varese 2006: 111; Albro 2006: 412; Colque Flores 2007: 46–47.

239. Holzer 2004.

240. *La Razón* 2007c. A 2008 documentary by Cuban director Jorge Fuentes Cruz about ascent of Evo Morales is titled *I Will Return, and I Will Be Millions.*

241. On Evolatria, see Sivak 2008: 310–312. On the strategy of taking power by leading grassroots social movements and not through the Leninist use of revolutionary vanguards, see García Linera 2006b: 26.

242. Morales 2006d.

243. Morales 2006e: 173; Cusicanqui 1991: 15.

244. Morales 2006e: 103–109.

245. Morales 2006c.

246. Morales 2007e.

247. Crabtree 2007.

248. Morales 2003.

249. Colque Flores 2008.

250. Crabtree 2007, 2008; Rochlin 2007; ABI 2008f.

251. Dangl 2009; Human Rights Watch (HRW) 2009. The most violent groups have been the Aymara group Ponchos Rojos (Red Ponchos) and the antigovernment Santa Cruz Youth Union.

252. Van Cott 2008; de la Torre 2009.

253. Morales 2007e.

254. Morales 2007d.

255. Morales 2006a.

256. Crabtree 2007.

257. Reel 2008; Crabtree 2007. The new charter was approved in January 2009 by 61 percent of the electorate. As with the recall referendum, it was rejected in all of the opposition-controlled eastern provinces.

258. García Linera 2006a.

259. A case in point is the former spokesperson of Evo Morales, Álex Contreras, who resigned and denounced a trend toward censorship, corruption, and lack of democracy. See La Razón 2008b.

260. (Cath News) CN 2009. On this issue see also, *La Razón*. 2007b.

261. ABN 2008f.

262. Landes 2006; Sivak 2008: 285. However, he has repeated this rallying cry less frequently since he took office.

263. Morales 2002.

264. Baspiniero 2005: 16.

265. Quoted in Arze and Carranza 2006: 88.

266. ABI 2008d. See also Morales 2008c and *La Razón*. 2007a

267. ABI 2008b.

268. Pinto and Navia 2007: 177.

269. Dirección de Prensa 2007.

270. As usual, support came mainly from the Western highlands. See *La Razón* 2008a.

271. ABI 2008l.
272. ABI 2008a.
273. Morales 2008d.
274. Morales 2007b; ABN 2008g.
275. Morales 2003.
276. Morales 2008b.
277. Moviemiento al Socialismo (MAS) 2001.
278. MAS 2001.
279. Varese 2006: 264–269.
280. Morales 2008a.
281. Morales 2002; Varese 2006: 276.
282. MAS 2001.
283. Pinto and Navia 2007: 83.
284. Sivak 2008: 21.
285. Like Chávez, Morales has been a regular presence in World Social Forums.
286. Morales 2007c; see also Morales 2007e.
287. MAS 2001.
288. *El Nacional* 2007.
289. See Morales 2006b.

Chapter 3

1. Bernanos 1950: 105.
2. Lasch 1981: 22.
3. The GRECE website is available at: www.grece-fr.net/accueil.php.
4. A parallel movement, elitist and aiming at cultural rejuvenation, commonly known as "New Confucianism" has been promoted since the 1980s by intellectuals in China, Taiwan, Hong Kong, and the United States; see Makeham 2003. On high-culture antiliberalism in general, see Webb 2006: 171–173.
5. De Benoist and Champetier 1999: 117.
6. De Benoist 1979: 62.
7. For twinship of liberalism and communism, see De Benoist and Champetier 1999: 121; Krebs 1997: 85; Sunic 2008: 35–65.
8. Krebs 1997: 94.
9. De Benoist and Champetier 1999: 117; Tarchi 2007b.
10. De Benoist 1994: 116.
11. Champetier 1999.
12. Identifying themselves with prophetic outsiders, ENR writings commonly praise heretics and nonconformists of the past (Krebs 1997: 47).
13. De Benoist 2004a.

14. R. Griffin 2007a: xiv.

15. De Benoist 1979: 258–259; 1994: 41.

16. De Benoist and Champetier 1999: 118.

17. De Benoist and Champetier 1999: 120.

18. De Benoist 2007c: 9; Krebs 1997: 76.

19. Krebs 1995.

20. Walker 1993: 5–6. For an opposing view, see Popper 1947: 363.

21. Proyecto Aurora 1993: 103–106.

22. Krebs 1997: 33.

23. For example, a major cultural reference for the ENR is Ernst Jünger (1939), whose popular writings testified both to the loss and disorientation caused by liberal, capitalist modernity and to the search for new foundations, new roots, and beginnings.

24. Moeller van den Bruck 1923: 23.

25. Moeller van den Bruck 1923: 23.

26. Stern 1974: xii.

27. De Benoist 1981: 199.

28. Walker 1993: 19.

29. Faye 1997.

30. Krebs 1997: 34.

31. De Benoist and Champetier 1999: 120.

32. Proyecto Aurora 1993.

33. Faye 1980: 5.

34. De Benoist 2004c: 79.

35. De Benoist 2004b: 4.

36. De Benoist 1981: 121.

37. De Benoist 2004c: 92.

38. De Benoist 2006d: 24; Esparza 1997: 19.

39. De Benoist 1981: 103.

40. But not all. See Sunic 1990: 153–55; Esparza 2008: 25.

41. O'Meara 2004: 99.

42. Faye 2001: 128.

43. An example is the Wicca movement. Wiccans have been present at many antiglobalization protests, reclaiming a new Earth-based spirituality (Sanders 2005: 145–161).

44. De Benoist 1981: 4.

45. Heidegger 1935: 40. Writing about the spiritual decline of human condition, Heidegger wrote, "For the darkening of the world, the flight of the gods, the destruction of the earth, the reduction of human beings to a mass, the hatred and mistrust

of everything creative and free has already reached such proportions throughout the whole earth that such childish categories as pessimism and optimism have long become laughable" (1935: 40–41).

46. De Benoist 1983: 11–61.

47. Faye 2001: 128.

48. Krebs 1997: 49.

49. The notion that the "real Europe" is different from the West is not exclusive to the ENR. See for example the scholarly work of Adam Webb, for whom, "The atomist West, the realm of superpower aggression and crass commercialism, sits atop the ruins of the real Europe—the Europe of Aquinas and Wagner, and of the cottagers and clansmen. The civilization of greater Europe is hardly the source of the plague. It has been its first and most pitiable victim" (Webb 2006: 142).

50. Tarchi 1987: 61.

51. Tarchi 2004: 143.

52. Krebs 1997: 47.

53. De Benoist 2006b: 104.

54. Faye 1986: 14.

55. Krebs 1997: 71.

56. During an early stage, the ENR and GRECE preached a radical critique of the "myth of equality." Gradually, the rejection of egalitarianism has given way to a more systematic rejection of individualism in their ideological evolution (Taguieff 1994: 250–254).

57. Tarchi 2007b: 27–28.

58. De Benoist 2004b: 4.

59. Faye 1981: 26–27.

60. Esparza 1985.

61. Faye 2001: 8.

62. De Benoist 1994: 158–59; Esparza 1998: 20–21.

63. In this, the ENR follows Werner Sombart's famous contrast between the ethics of the "trader" and the ethics of the "hero," originally published in 1915 (Sombart 2001: xxix). For ENR references to Sombart, see Faye 1981: 169 and de Benoist 1991: 13.

64. Guénon 1927: 126–127; O'Meara 2004: 57–60; Sombart 2001: 82–83.

65. De Benoist and Champetier 1999: 128.

66. De Herte 2005c; de Herte is a pseudonym occasionally used by de Benoist.

67. De Benoist, Giaccio, and Preve, 2005: 28.

68. De Benoist 2009b: 38.

69. Walker 1986a: 5.

70. Tarchi 2004: 142. For parallel views from mainstream thinkers, see Bauman 2005: 26 and Barber 2008: 74–76.

71. De Benoist 1982: 63; 2007d: 6.

72. Champetier 1994.

73. De Benoist 2007c: 4; de Herte 2005b.

74. Evola 1983: 24.

75. De Herte 2005a.

76. De Benoist 1992: 34–35.

77. Krebs 1997: 83.

78. Krebs 1997: 81–82.

79. Faye 1980: 5.

80. De Benoist 1992: 50.

81. Tarchi 1987: 61.

82. Esparza 1997. For an earlier attack on Western materialism, see Guénon 1927: 135.

83. Tarchi 1999a: 98.

84. Sunic 2008: 13.

85. Walker 1984: 2.

86. Cau 1992.

87. Southgate 2007: 256. Troy Southgate is a member of Britain's New Right, though his views are somewhat more esoteric and anarchist than other circles of the ENR. His website is available at: www.rosenoire.org. See also: www.new-right.org/.

88. Faye 2004: 198. It is not clear how the ENR faithful are able to resist American culture's irresistible appeal, nor is it clear why the feeble patriotism of Americans so easily corrodes the deeply rooted European conscience.

89. For an earlier critique of liberalism, see Moeller van den Bruck 1923: 90.

90. Krebs, 2008.

91. De Benoist 1996: 62 and 2001: 31.

92. De Herte 2005d.

93. Walker 2008.

94. Tarchi 2004: 143.

95. De Benoist 2004c.

96. Tarchi 2004: 25; Faye 1981, 36–37.

97. Loki 1997: 44.

98. De Benoist 2001: 132; Esparza 1997: 188. However, the line between conspiracy and nonconspiracy theories can be quite thin, as repeated references to "plans" and "designs" indicate.

99. Krebs 1997: 74.

100. De Benoist 2005: 14. Arnold Gehlen's view that humanity is living in a petrified posthistory—bland and devoid of surprises—is echoed in many of ENR writings (Niethammer 1992: 10–16).

101. Faye 1981: 177.

102. De Benoist 1982: 64–65.

103. De Benoist 1994: 115; italics in original.

104. Krebs 1997 (publisher's notes).

105. Krebs 2004; Tarchi 1987: 69.

106. Bar-On 2007: 91-93; Taguieff 1994.

107. De Benoist 1993b: 199.

108. See Herder 1968. Konrad Lorenz (1903–1989), the founder of ethology, won a Nobel Prize in Physiology and Medicine. He was part of the editorial board of *Nouvelle Ecole*, one of the main GRECE journals, and warned about the "waning of mankind's humaneness" (Lorenz 1987: 173).

109. O'Meara 2004: 50.

110. De Benoist and Champetier 1999: 124.

111. De Benoist 2004c: 113.

112. De Benoist 1993b: 181.

113. De Benoist and Champetier 1999: 134; Esparza 1985.

114. The reference is to Hardt and Negri 2004.

115. De Herte 2004; see also Tarchi 2004: 41. Freedom is understood not as a value but as a preexistent human necessity.

116. See, for instance, de Benoist 1993b. This argument is a reiteration of Herder's claim that ethnic mixtures are necessarily destructive of cultural essence.

117. Tarchi 1998: 92

118. De Benoist 1994: 149.

119. Faye 1980: 8.

120. De Benoist 1994: 111.

121. Southgate 2007: 322. For favorable views from the extreme right wing regarding Islam, see the work of George Michael, particularly 2006: 111–172. Latin American populists, such as Chávez, are also regularly praised (Michael 2008: 222–224).

122. De Herte 2005c.

123. De Benoist 2001: 31.

124. Faye 2000: 321.

125. For an example, see Arteault 2006.

126 De Benoist and Champetier 1999.

127. Proyecto Aurora 1994.

128. O'Meara 2004: 49–50; Fraquelli 2005: 139–155.

129. De Benoist 1985: 12.

130. De Herte 2007: 2. Anxiety about the evil consequences of the rise of a global technocratic "new class" pervades the ENR belief system. This notion appears also on the left. See Sassen 2007: 164–189.

131. De Benoist 2007b.

132. Walker 2006: 19.

133. De Herte 2001.

134. Benoist and Champetier 1999: 140.

135. De Benoist 1993b: 176.

136. De Benoist 2006b: 124–125.

137. De Herte 2003.

138. For an example from India, see Bahughuna 1997: 185.

139. De Herte 2001.

140. De Benoist 2006a: 210; 2009a.

141. De Benoist and Champetier 1999: 143. Environmental activist Edward Goldsmith (1928–2009) has been a major intellectual influence on the ENR (De Benoist 2006c; Bar-Tor 2007: 102).

142. De Herte 1980: 2.

143. De Benoist 1986: 219.

144. Walker 1986b: 9.

145. De Herte 2006.

146. De Herte 1991: 3.

147. De Herte 2006.

148. De Herte 2006.

149. Schmitt 1950: 243, 351–355; De Benoist 2007a; Ulmen 1993; Dean 2006.

150. De Benoist 2004b; Tarchi 1999a.

151. De Benoist 1993b: 204.

152. De Benoist, 1993a: 97.

153. De Benoist 2008: 7–15.

154. Tarchi 2007a: 4.

155. Hosking 2006: 83.

156. Dugin 1992b: 36.

157. Dugin 1992a: 2.

158. Ingram 2001. A dichotomy between sea and land was also one of the mainstays of Schmitt's geopolitical thinking (Schmitt 1954: 5).

159. De Benoist 2007a: 151.

160. Dugin, quoted in Umland 2006. De Benoist has denounced America as a modern-day Carthage (de Herte 1991: 30). For a recent statement on the "Carthaginian" geopolitical strategy of the United States see de Benoist 2007d: 152.

161. Eurasian Movement 2001. See also O'Meara 2004: 194.

162. Quoted in Laruelle 2006: 9.

163. Eurasianism has increasingly become an intellectual force in Russia's foreign policy circles. One of Putin's United Russia party chief ideologists, Ivan Demidov, is a "convinced Eurasian and an admirer of Dugin" (Umland 2009; *Christian Science Monitor* [CSM] 2008).

164. Graziani 2004; Ivanov 2008.

165. Southgate 2007: 256.

166. Brinkmann 2007. Many figures of the racial wing of the ENR support the foundation of Eurosiberia (Ravello 2005: 90).

167. Faye 2001: 8.

168. De Benoist 2007c: 12, 10.

169. Faye, 1997.

170. De Herte 2004.

171. R. Griffin 2007a: xv.

172. Scholars disagree on the best way to label modern political groups that base themselves on opposition to a myriad of "evil" threats to the nation. The most common approach is to associate such parties with right-wing "extremism," "radicalism," or "populism" (see Eatwell 2004: 1–15; for a discussion of the problems of applying a too simple categorization, see Mouffe 2005: 56–59).

173. Klandermans and Mayer 2006: 271–272; Mudde 2007: 12–23.

174. Barnes 2008a.

175. Le Pen 2007d.

176. Bossi 2003.

177. N. Griffin 2007a.

178. Le Pen 2009.

179. Mégret is a one-time Le Pen lieutenant who abandoned the National Front in 1999 to found his own nationalist party, the Mouvement National Républicain (Republican National Movement, or MNR). His party was unsuccessful, and Mégret withdrew from politics in June 2008.

180. Mégret 1992: 9.

181. *Identité* 1993: 4–20.

182. Bossi 1999d.

183. Pinto-Coelho 2007a.

184. Bossi 1990.

185. Taguieff (1994: 96–106) understands the "phobia of mixing" as a form of "cultural racism." Some sectors of the ENR accuse populist nationalists of fear mongering and demagoguery in their use of the notion of *difference*. According to de Benoist (2005: 23–24), the National Front is "a nationalist, antifederalist, antiregionalist, anti-European Jacobin party. On all these counts I oppose it." "The common ground between liberalism and nationalism," wrote de Benoist, "is their legitimization of selfishness—individual in the case of the first, collective in the case of the second" (2001: 50). However, the search for ethnic homogeneity and the need to roll back Islam in Europe is fully supported by many other ENR members.

186. Mégret 2003.

187. MNR 2008.

188. N. Griffin 2007b. On the BNP's "path to modernization," see Copsey 2004: 100–123.

189. Griffin 2004.
190. Le Pen 1994: 3.
191. Le Pen 1992b: 8.
192. Bossi 2003.
193. Poliakov 1980: 10–27.
194. Le Pen 2000.
195. Simmons 2003.
196. Partido Nacional Renovador (PNR) 2006; Milloz 1992: 82.
197. Bossi 1999b.
198. Direct references to Jewish conspiracies are not usually found in the parties' literature. When present, they appear mainly in the form of innuendo or allusions to a pervasive "Zionist" influence in public affairs.
199. Griffin 2004.
200. Lembo 1998: 41.
201. Bossi 1999a: 108.
202. Pinto-Coelho, 2006b.
203. Lefranc 1993: 5–9; Le Pen 1993: 3.
204. National Front (NF) 2002.
205. Bossi 1998.
206. DN 2008d.
207. Le Pen 2005; Holeindre 2003: 26.
208. Le Pen 2000.
209. Le Pen 1996a: 3.
210. Le Pen 1999a: 4.
211. Bossi 1999c.
212. MNR 2000: 8.
213. NF 1993: 16; Le Pen 1992b: 8.
214. Le Pen 1998.
215. Lembo 1999: 39.
216. Mégret 1997: 226–227.
217. DN 2008a.
218. Griffin 2004.
219. Pinto-Coelho 2007c.
220. Le Pen 2007d.
221. NL 2002: 21. The Northern League, the most anti-Islamic force in Italy, has toned down its criticisms of U.S. foreign policy since the Islamic question increased in importance. But its rejection of the American multicultural model has not subsided.
222. Bay 2007.
223. Mudde 2007: 23; Betz 2003: 77–80.
224. Le Pen 1992a: 6.

225. Canovan 2005: 124–130.
226. Maroni 2008.
227. *Identité* 1993: 20.
228. DN 2008c.
229. Pinto-Coelho 2007b.
230. DN 2008e.
231. Barnes 2008b.
232. Le Pen 1996b: 7.
233. Le Pen 2001b.
234. MNR 2000: 6.
235. BNP 2004.
236. NF 1993: 18; MNR 2008.
237. DN 2008a.
238. BNP 2004; MNR 2000: 149–151.
239. Some scholars see "crisis of representation" as "consubstantial" to democracy itself (Rosanvallon 2006: 91), while others see it as a dangerous trend that needs to be reversed (Mastropaolo 2005: 169–194). For our purposes, we merely point out that nationalist parties favor the latter perspective and offer a solution that is shared by many other aurora movements.
240. Le Pen 2006.
241. BNP 2007b.
242. On this issue see Zúquete 2007.
243. Mégret 2006: 204.
244. Le Pen 1992b: 6.
245. DN 2007.
246. Le Pen 2002.
247. *La Padania* 2005.
248. *National-Hebdo* 1996.
249. Le Pen 1991a: 25.
250. Le Pen 2007b.
251. DN 2007.
252. BNP 2008a.
253. See Bay 2007; Le Pen 1992b: 8.
254. Bossi 1999c: 119.
255. Le Pen 1991b: 7.
256. Barnes 2008b.
257. Mégret 1997: 51.
258. Bossi and Vimercati 1998: 45.
259. Le Pen 2001a.
260. Pinto-Coelho 2007c.

261. NF 2001.

262. Bossi 2000.

263. Le Pen 1992a: 9.

264. Le Pen 2007a.

265. Barnes 2008b. On the other end of the ideological spectrum there have been calls for an "Ecosocialism," so that a "new form of society may emerge no longer dependent upon accumulation and its progressive breakdown of ecosystems" (Kovel 2007: x).

266. MNR 2000: 46.

267. NF 1993: 356.

268. The development of transnational dynamics is not unprecedented in the history of European nationalism. See for example attempts to create a Fascist International (Sabatini 1997).

269. Le Pen 1996a: 3.

270. This development has been seen in myriad ways (Liang 2007; Mudde 2007: 172–183; Grumke 2003). However, from our point of view, even though still somewhat inchoate, the new transnationalism generally shares the same driving premises.

271. EuroNat 2005.

272. European National Front (ENF) 2008.

273 Quoted in Mudde 2007: 181.

274. On this issue see, for example, Bahl (2008).

275. *Deutsche Welle* (DW) 2008.

276. Griffin 2008.

277. Liang 2007: 28.

278. Le Pen 2007d; Martinez 2006: 6.

279. Valéry 1922: 307.

Chapter 4

1. 2003: 182. This book is a collective product that seeks to exemplify the virtues of new politics. The absence of a named general editor is a political statement.

2. Munck 2007: 127.

3. Acronyms are ubiquitous within the WSF and other global civil society movements. Taylor (2004) contains two pages of acronyms, fifty-eight in all. Shuman (2006: 8), for example, sees an "epochal struggle" in the world between the globalist/corporate forces of TINA "there is no alternative" and LOIS "local ownership and import substitution." The use of mind-numbing technical language characteristic of state bureaucracies is a symbolic instance of the truism that "groups that enter negotiations with the powerful become domesticated both in order to do so and as a result of so doing" (Rootes 2004: 60).

4. WSF 2002.

5. Monbiot 2003: 2.

6. Trevor Ngwane, quoted in Cock 2004: 181.

7. Jackie Smith, et al. 2008: xi. Like *We Are Everywhere*, *Global Democracy* is a collective product, assembled through Internet collaborations.

8. Chase-Dunn 2007: 15–19. See also Castells and Ince 2003: 65.

9. Other founders included Bernard Cassen, a founder of ATTAC and general director of *Le Monde Diplomatique*; Brazilians Oded Grajew, a former businessman; and Chico Whitaker, a Catholic activist; see Wintrebert (2007: 38) on the intellectual background of ATTAC.

10. Andretta and Mosca 2004: 47.

11. Ruggiero 2002: 54.

12. Nunes 2005: 281.

13. Harvey 2000: 13.

14. Klein: 81.

15. Cavanagh and Mander 2004: 29.

16. Quoted in *Los Angeles Times* 1999.

17. Amin 2007: 139–141. On the idea of a Fifth International of peoples against the world system of capitalism, see Amin 2008: 53–82.

18. Cavanagh and Mander: 29.

19. Smith 2008: 22.

20. For this term, see Young 1999: 252.

21. Murphy 2004: 35.

22. Notes from Nowhere: 286–287.

23. Other notable precursors include the movement to erase Third World Debt in the 1980s, the French strikes of 1995, and the mass protests against the London International Financial Futures Exchange in 1999 (Agrikoliansky, Fillieule, and Mayer 2005: 13–42; Wintrebert 2007: 45).

24. Munck 2004.

25. Notes from Nowhere 2003: 174.

26. See Clandestine Insurgent Rebel Clown Army (CIRCA) 2003.

27. The liberating role of the "carnivalesque" is documented by Bakhtin 1968.

28. Cook 2008: 39.

29. Lojowsky 2000: 14.

30. Melucci 1996: 13. For a dismissive view, see Wiarda 2007: 73.

31. Andretta and Mosca 2004.

32. Smith 2008: 67. See also Andretta and Mosca 2004.

33. Notes from Nowhere 2003: 508.

34. See Della Porta and Reiter 2006.

35. Notes from Nowhere 2003: 181.

36. Holloway 2005: 1.

37. McNally 2002: 92.

38. Lojowsky 2000: 12.

39. Fisher and Ponniah 2003: 7.

40. Smith 2008: 114.

41. Korten 1996: 26–27.

42. Fisher and Ponniah 2003: 10–11.

43. Cavanagh and Mander 2004: 55.

44. Cavanagh and Mander 2004: 22.

45. Susan George, quoted in Conway and Heynen 2006: 24–25.

46. Cavanagh and Mander 2004: 22.

47. For a similar view from a Christian standpoint, see Hopkins, for whom, "God in this religion [globalization] is the concentration of monopoly finance wealth, which functions both transcendentally and immanently. It gives faith to its believers that it is the one and only supreme god—a notion made even more plausible with the fall of the Berlin Wall. . . . To foster the aims of this god, the trinity of the World Trade Organization, international banks (including the IMF and World Bank), and monopoly capitalist corporations acts as messengers or 'angels' delivering this new gospel throughout the land" (2001: 28, 29).

48. Löwi and Betto 2003: 329, 330.

49. McNally 2002: 52.

50. Klein 2001: 82, 87, 89.

51. McNally 2002: 83, 192.

52. Reinsborough 2004: 177–178.

53. Wallerstein 2002: 37.

54. Monbiot 2003: 7, 9–10, 11, 15, 253, 261.

55. Monbiot 2003: 3.

56. WSF 2002.

57. Cavanagh and Mander 2004: 103, 149.

58. WSF 2002.

59. Taylor 2004: 4.

60. Quoted in Smith 2008: 72.

61. Santos 2007: 54.

62. Quoted in Santos 2007: 47.

63. Santos 2007: 68.

64. Nunes 2005: 287.

65. Santos 2007: 165.

66. Anderson and Reiff 2005: 32.

67. Santos 2007: 165.

68. There is a debate within the WSF as to whether the forum is a franchise or public domain. The first would mean groups wishing to use the WSF imprimatur must

apply for recognition, while the second would mean that anyone can organize anytime so long as they respect the WSF charter of principles. The same debate occurs in Slow Food.

69. For a skeptical evaluation of the political impact of the global civil society movement, see Rootes 2004.

70. Interviews and blogs were collected by Sarah Garton, March 2008.

71. Smith 2008; Andretta and Mosca 2004; Santos 2007.

72. Tarrow 2005a.

73. Munck 2004: 91.

74. Quoted in Smith 2008: 39.

75. For more, see the section on rave in this chapter.

76. Nunes 2005: 287.

77. Nunes 2005: 290, 296.

78. Juris 2008: 254–266.

79. Solomon 2005.

80. Notes from Nowhere 2003: 175, 181.

81. Smith 2008: 108, 133.

82. Whitaker 2004.

83. Smith 2008: 137–138.

84. McNally 2002: 256, 275.

85. WSF 2002.

86. Tormey 2005: 398.

87. Quoted in Smith 2008: 171.

88. Notes from Nowhere 2003: 183.

89. Negri 2003: 95; Hardt 2006: 14–15.

90. Klein 2001: 89.

91. Fisher and Ponniah: 3, 13, 14; Bello 2004: 69.

92. Couvrat 2007: 270. For ATTAC, see Wintrebert 2007: 63.

93. Hall and Fenelon 2008: 8.

94. Quoted in Cavanagh and Mander 2004: 129.

95. Reinsborough 2000; Solnit 2004.

96. Shrestha and Conway 2006: 205–206.

97. Cock 2004: 179.

98. John Gray 1998: 57.

99. Monbiot 2003: 8.

100. Chase-Dunn 2007: 23.

101. Monbiot 2003: 115.

102. Cavanagh and Mander 2004: xiii, 83, 84.

103. Notes from Nowhere 2003: 178.

104. Cavanagh and Mander 2004: 253.

105. Notes from Nowhere 2003: 183.

106. Monbiot 2003: 65–64; for similar sentiments from a different perspective, see Butler 1997.

107. Arendt 1958, quoted in Smith 2008: 14; Santos 2007; 15, 30.

108. Smith 2008: 24–25, 132.

109. Juris 2008: 9, 290, 296; Reinsborough 2004: 198.

110. Fougier 2008: 69, 119.

111. Notes from Nowhere 2003: 195, 511.

112. Reinsborough 2004: 203; Notes from Nowhere 2003: 177.

113. Monbiot 2003: 251, 252.

114. The following section is indebted to Siv Lie 2008.

115. Associazione ricreativa culturale italiana.

116. The Libera e benemerita associazone degli amici del Barolo.

117. Petrini and Padovani 2005: 4, 12.

118. Cooperativa I Tarocchi, or "Cooperative of the Tarots."

119. Hooper 2004.

120. Weiner 2005: 27.

121. Quoted in Katz 2006: 129.

122. Honoré 2004: 63.

123. National Public Radio 2004.

124. Petrini 2007a: 55–56.

125. Weiner 2005: 21.

126. Slow Food Foundation for Biodiversity 2003.

127. Slow Food Foundation for Biodiversity 2003.

128. Petrini 2007c.

129. Their website is available at: www.slowfood.com.

130. Petrini 2007c.

131. Petrini 2001: 38.

132. Freeman and Johnson 1999.

133. Petrini 2007b.

134. Petrini 2001: 12.

135. Chabrol 2004.

136. Petrini 2007b.

137. Petrini 2007a: 17, 18.

138. Petrini 2001: 58.

139. Ritzer 1998: 8.

140. Petrini 2007a: 26.

141. Petrini 2001: 102.

142. Musso Abbona, and Nano 2005.

143. Petrini 2001: xxiii.

144. Real Food Challenge 2007.

145. At the Second International Congress of Arcigola in 1991 in Perugia, Italy, Arcigola was renamed Arcigola Slow Food. As the movement gained international recognition, its name was shortened to Slow Food.

146. Petrini 2001: 69, 110.

147. Petrini 2007b; Leitch 2008.

148. Seremetakis 1994: 37.

149. Waters 2006: 13.

150. Lhéritier 2006.

151. Petrini 2001: 71.

152. Petrini 2001: 8.

153. The trope of terroir is not limited to France. According to Ivor Brown, the glory of Scotch whiskey evaporates when it leaves Scotland; "it will not travel" (quoted in Pacult 2005: 8).

154. Petrini 2001: 18–19, 39.

155. Laudan 2001.

156. Leitch 2008: 2008.

157. Veseth 2005: 201; see Weiner 2005 for a statistical breakdown of official Slow Food membership.

158. For a discussion of Italian food culture, see Castellanos and Bergstresser 2006. Convening the 2007 International Slow Food Congress in Puebla, Mexico, was an attempt to expand membership into the global south.

159. Quoted in Brooks 2000: 110.

160. *The Viand Zine #1* 2007.

161. Zelmanov 2003. The manifesto of the movement is available at: www.cittaslow .org.uk/images/Download/cittaslow_charter.pdf. See also Pink 2008.

162. Honoré 2004. On the Transition Movement, see Hopkins 2008; *NYT Magazine* 2009. The website of the Global Carfree Movement is available at: www.worldcarfree .net/about_us/global/

163. Petrini 2007b.

164. Katz 2006: xiv, xvi.

165. This movement was founded by the late philosopher and oenologist Luigi Veronelli. See Terra eLibertà/Critical Wine 2004: 5–40.

166. Andrews 2006: 10, 137, 203, 204, 217.

167. Honoré 2004: 14–15, 17, 279.

168. Petrini 2001: 86.

169. Weiner 2005: 3.

170. Petrini 2001: 73.

171. D'Andrea 2007: 176. For parallels between New Age religion and techno music, see D'Andrea 2007: 22.

172. Rietveld 2004; See also Fritz, 1999; Moore 1995.

173. Rietveld 2004: 55. By the time this book is released, rave will have evolved into new forms, called by new terms.

174. Rietveld 2004: 52.

175. For the effects of these drugs, see D'Andrea 2007: 212.

176. Rill 2006: 648.

177. D'Andrea 2007: 31.

178. Fritz 1999: 262. We do not have space to consider other global musical genres such as punk, indie rock, heavy metal, hip-hop, and reggae, which also promote anti-establishment values and promote countercultural moral codes.

179. Quoted in Partridge 2006: 54.

180. Grazian 2003: 21.

181. Rietveld 2004: 55.

182. Rietveld 2004: 55. See also D'Andrea 2007: 213.

183. Rietveld 2004: 212.

184. Ravers quoted in Goulding, Shankar, and Elliott 2002: 266, 273.

185. Quoted in St. John 2004a: 22.

186. Reynolds 1999: 5.

187. Quoted in St. John 2004a: 20.

188. Fritz 1999: 216–217.

189. D'Andrea 2007: 22.

190. D'Andrea 2007: 650.

191. Explaining the reasons that rave should appeal to certain populations and class positions is beyond the range of this book. But it would be well worth comparing the rave experience to other ecstatic "utopian" collective dance performances worldwide. For an example, see Sneed 2008.

192. Bey 1991. The concept of TAZ has become prominent in many alter-globalization circles as a way of describing "alternative spaces" against the repressive forces of "plutocratic globality." See Flusty 2004: 182, 193–196.

193. Quoted in Olaveson 2004: 96.

194. Bey 1991.

195. McKenna 1991: 157.

196. Paul Heelas quoted in St. John 2004a: 20.

197. McKenna 1992. McKenna (1946–2000) predicted that the end of time will occur on December 21, 2012. For other prophesies derived from the Mayan "dream-spell" calendar, see Argüelles and Argüelles 2002; Argüelles 2002.

198. Fritz 1999: 206.

199. M. Collin 1998: 191.

200. McKenna, quoted in St. John 2004b: 216.

201. McKenna 1991: 225.

202. Fraser Clark, quoted in St. John 2004b: 220; Clark 1995.

203. St. John 2004b.

204. Quoted in Fatone 2004: 198, 204–205.

205. The Spiral Tribe, quoted in Collin 1998: 203–204.

206. Chris Decker, the founder of Earthdance, quoted in St. John 2004a: 27.

207. Quoted in Partridge 2006: 48.

208. D'Andrea 2007: 12. This is usually a gradual process—beginning in occasional ecstatic nightclub experiences, then progressing to a "psychedelic tourist" searching out rave sites, and ending with a new identity as an "expressive cosmopolitan."

209. D'Andrea 2007: 208.

210. Braidotti 1994: 22.

211. These terms are from D'Andrea (2007: 6), who defines the former as "a stabilized form of self-cultivation" and the latter as "a temporary condition of acute self-derailment."

212. D'Andrea 2007: 55.

213. MacIntyre 1981.

214. Maffesoli 1996: 96; Gauthier 2004.

215. Goulding, Shankar, and Elliott 2002: 273.

216. Goulding, Shankar, and Elliott 2002: 274.

217. The term is from D'Andrea 2007; 224.

218. Other transformative pilgrimage sites included the Amazon (McKenna's favorite location, where ayahuasca was the transformative drug of choice), Bali in Indonesia, and Phuket in Thailand. These sites continually change, as the vanguard travelers seek to avoid the onslaught of tourists who are looking for the authentic ecstatic experience the psychedelic guerillas exemplify. The quest for authenticity in tourism is discussed at greater length in Lindholm 2008 and MacCannell 1999.

219. A "global nomad" quoted in D'Andrea 2007: 193.

220. Quoted in Partridge 2006: 47.

221. D'Andrea 2004: 242.

222. D'Andrea 2007: 76, 189.

223. Quoted in D'Andrea 2007: 203.

224. Bey 1991.

Chapter 5

1. Al-Mawdudi in Bukay 2008: 185.

2. Roy 2004: 49.

3. Our focus will be mostly on al-Qaeda and its predecessors in the Middle East, as well as their affiliates in Europe. We will not discuss the Palestine Liberation Organization (PLO) or other organizations, which are primarily political and so not com-

parable to millennial jihadist groups. For more on these distinctions, see Sageman 2004.

4. Johnson 2000.

5. For comparisons between al-Qaeda and other antimodernist groups, see Gray 2003: 3; Fukuyama 2006: 11; Charters 2007: 83; Mazarr 2007. But an emphasis on the contemporary character of the jihad would not do justice to the way jihadis themselves see their movement, nor would it permit a deeper understanding of the specific historical, ideological, and cultural framework within which they operate.

6. Abdullah Azzam, quoted in Cook 2005b: 129.

7. Azzam, together with his two sons, was assassinated in Peshawar in 1989. Rumors have long connected bin Laden with Azzam's death but without proof. Bin Laden always refers to Azzam with respect as his mentor.

8. An example of the latter is the Egyptian Islam Group.

9. For the continued salience of this aspiration, see Azzam 2008: 343.

10. This apocalyptic vision derives more from Western texts than from the traditional Islamic canon. See Cook 2005a. For a general history of Islam in the Middle East, see Lindholm 2002.

11. Quoted in Aaron 2008: 115.

12. Bin Laden says the clash of civilizations is "a very clear matter, proven in the Qur'an and the tradition of the Prophet" (2005: 124). Huntington's book is very popular in the Islamic world (Kepel 2002: 74).

13. Harris 2006. Insofar as radical Islam seeks a return to an idealized past, it is technically classed as a revitalization movement, as first defined by Wallace 1956.

14. Bin Laden's "Declaration of Jihad" from August 23, 1996 (2005: 26).

15. As noted in Fouda and Fielding 2003.

16. Cited in Cook 2005a: 179; Devji 2005: 43.

17. Roy 1994: 69.

18. Devji 2005: 126, 42, 43. Some of the instructions for the last night of the hijackers included: "1. Vow to accept death, renew admonition, shave the extra hair on the body, perfume yourself, and ritually wash yourself . . . 7. Purify your heart and cleanse it of stains. Forget and be oblivious to that thing called the world. For, the time for playing has passed, and the time has arrived for the rendezvous with the eternal truth! How much of our lives we have wasted! Shall we not take advantage of these hours to offer up acts of nearness [to God] and obedience?" (McDermott 2005: 249–251).

19. As discussed by Roy 2004: 170.

20. As documented in Cook 2005a: 153–154.

21. Atwan 2008: 35.

22. Quoted in Gerges 2006: 111.

23. Jihadis generally adhere to the Hanbalite school of law.

24. Jihadis do make use of findings by trained scholars who agree with them, such as Sheikh Omar Abdul Rahman.

25. Azzam 2008: 349.

26. A. B. el-Mehri "Introduction." In Qutb 2006: 11.

27. Al-Mawdudi 1932: 40. Mawdudi (1903–1979) was the first to revive and popularize the notion of jahiliyya. For more on Mawdudi's influence on Arab jihadists, see Devji 2005.

28. Qutb 2006: 51, 58.

29. Gerges 2006: 34.

30. For more on Qutb, see Choueiri 1990.

31. Al-Zawahiri 2006.

32. Bin Laden 2005: 70.

33. Faraj 1981: 40–41. Muhammad al-Salam Faraj was the founder of Jama'at Al-Jihad, which was responsible for the assassination of Anwar Sadat in 1981. Faraj was executed in 1982.

34. Faraj 1981: 61.

35. Qutb 2006: 161.

36. Azzam 1987: 34.

37. Quoted in Gerges 2006: 34–35.

38. Bin Laden 2005: 87.

39. For more on Saddam's practices, see al-Khalil 1989: 20.

40. Al-Zawahiri, 2006: 73. The torture he suffered—and the fact that he broke under torture—had a deep impact on him. According to a fellow Islamist close to al-Zawahiri at the time, "Despite all that he had suffered physically, what was really painful to Zawahiri was that, under the pain of torture, he was forced to testify against his fellow members . . . He was forced to confess against his friends, followers and disciples. He even tipped the police off about the whereabouts of one of his best friends" (al Zayyat 2002: 31–49).

41. Gerges 2005: 9.

42. Qutb 2006: 23–24.

43. Bin Laden: 2005: 18.

44. Quoted in Lia 2008: 95.

45. Faraj 1981: 24–26.

46. Azzam, quoted in Cook 2005b: 130.

47. Bin Laden 2005: 208–209.

48. Bin Laden 2007: 42–43.

49. Bin Laden 2005: n 46.

50. For accounts of the influence of al-Qaeda in Chechnya, see Hughes 2007. For Algeria, see Atwan 2008; Lav 2007.

51. It is worth noting that a firm belief in the *defensive dimension* of their actions is characteristic not only of Islamist terrorists, but also of other terrorist organizations. As Konrad Kellen has written, "Psychologically . . . by far the most important key to understanding terrorists is that they feel they are defending themselves against an aggressive, evil, intrusive, and murderous world" (Kellen 1990: 54–55).

52. Al-Muhajiroun, quoted in Baxter 2008: 63–66. Al-Muhajiroun was an organization initially founded in Saudi Arabia and then "exported" to Great Britain in the 1990's. Its founder and leader, Omar Bakri Muhammad, come first to public attention by calling a conference in London dedicated to September 11th as "A Towering Day in History." In 2005 Bakri was barred from entering the country and anti-terror legislation effectively ended his Islamist organization and its affiliated splinter groups.

53. Al-Muhajiroun, quoted in Baxter 2007: 63.

54. Quoted in al-Zawahiri 2008.

55. Quoted in Devji 2005: 34. The argument here is indebted to Devji's analysis.

56. For example, see the recantation by Shaikh Abu Mohammad al-Maqdisi, an early supporter of al-Qaeda who has criticized the organization for acting contrary to Islamic law. His opponents say his change in attitude is due to his unexpected release from prison in Jordan. Abu Yahya al-Libi, an al-Qaeda member who escaped from an American prison in Afghanistan in 2005, explained why militants disavow their past: "Tell me . . . what do you expect from someone who sees the sword above him, the rug in front of him and the sheik dictating to him the proof and evidence for the obligation of obeying the ruler?" (*NYT* 2008b). In contrast, jihadi narratives praise Qutb for his steadfastness and unwillingness to recant despite torture and the threat of death. The account of his last moments has acquired a mythical status (Maktabah 2008).

57. Bin Laden 2005: 40, 96, 141, 148.

58. Quoted in Lia 2008: 383.

59. Quoted in Lia 2008: 387.

60. Quoted in Bukay 2008: 275.

61. Al-Yazid 2008.

62. Quoted in Habeck 2006: 31.

63. Euben 1999: 121.

64. Al-Maqdisi 2008: 5, 6, 12, 27.

65. Al-Zawahiri 2008.

66. Al-Zawahiri "Sharia and Democracy," in Ibrahim 2007: 133.

67. Bin Laden 2005: 70, 167.

68. Bin Laden 2005: 70.

69. Bin Laden 2007: 40.

70. Bin Laden 2005: 125.

71. M. 'Arif quoted in Cook 2005a.

72. Qutb 2006: 92, 303.

73. Quoted in Kepel and Milelli 2005: 141.

74. Bin Laden 2005: 137. Conspiracy theories are not solely the property of jihadi extremists. See, for example, 'Ishq 2005.

75. Quoted in Devji 2005: 76–77.

76. Al-Yazid 2008.

77. Bin Laden 2005: 137–138, 217.

78. Bin Laden 2005: 108.

79. Habeck 2006: 51 citing Azhar *The Virtues of Jihad*.

80. Bin Laden 2007: 43.

81. Mazarr 2007: 31.

82. Bin Laden 2005: 39, 51.

83. Bin Laden 2005: 214.

84. Quoted in Gerges 2006: 155.

85. Lia 2008: 99.

86. Lia 2008: 352.

87. Quoted in el-Mehri 2006, "Introduction." In Qutb 2006: 8.

88. Qutb, quoted in Gerges 2006: 150–151.

89. Qutb, quoted in Gerges 2006: 163.

90. Bin Laden 2005: 168.

91. Qutb, quoted in Choueiri 1990: 124.

92. Al-Muhajiroun, quoted in Baxter 2007: 66.

93. Al-Zawahiri: 311.

94. Quoted in Lia 2008: 406.

95. Ayatollah Khomeini, quoted in Algar 1988: 276.

96. Bin Laden 2005: 168, 113.

97. Quoted in Cook 2005a: 27. Cook argues that the prevalent notion of a monstrous Jewish conspiracy is a novel aspect of Muslim apocalyptic thought, correlating with the increasing power of Israel.

98. Cook 2005a: 20.

99. Bin Laden 2005: 190.

100. Quoted in Cook 2005a: 227.

101. Often passages from the Quran about Jews are quoted to justify their damnation. For example: "They try to spread corruption in the land, but God does not love those who corrupt" (5: 64).

102. Bin Laden 2005: 87.

103. Qutb 2006: 26.

104. Bin Laden 2005: 166.

105. Qutb 2006: 70.

106. Al-Zawahiri 2006: 240–241.

107. Qutb 2006: 70, 101, 102.

108. Qutb 2006: 59.

109. Quoted in Gerges 2006: 39.

110. Quoted in Gerges 2006: 87.

111. Beinin 1988: 218.

112. Sayyid Abul Maududi, quoted in Cook 2005a: 100.

113. Qutb 2006: 82.

114. Qutb 2006: 123.

115. Euben 1999: 81.

116. Qutb 2006: 83.

117. Quoted in Cook 2005b: 105.

118. Euben 1999: 15.

119. Sageman 2004: 85.

120. Atwan 2008: 35.

121. Sageman 2004: 97.

122. Sageman 2004: 115, 131; see also the "seven-step theory of conversion" proposed by Lofland and Stark 1965. For a comparative theory of charismatic leaders and their organizations, see Lindholm 1990.

123. Roy 1994: 70.

124. For more, see Eickelman and Piscatori 2004.

125. Roy 2004: 23–24.

126. Sageman 2004: 151.

127. Marvasti 2008: 81–85.

128. Higher education is not exclusive to al-Qaeda. According to Russell and Miller (1983: 55), "two-thirds of those identified terrorists are persons with some university training, university graduates, or postgraduate students."

129. Quoted in Lia 2008: 435.

130. Ousman, quoted in Rosenthal: 48, 52

131. Hassan, quoted in Rosenthal: 50.

132. Quoted in Devji 2005: 98–99.

133. Quoted in Kepel and Milelli 2005: 58–59. On the relationship between the modern marginalization of ancient concepts and practices, such as honor, and jihad martyrdom, see Beit-Hallahmi 2003: 26.

134. Charters 2007: 85.

135. Quoted in Lia 2008: 374.

136. The supreme holy leader is usually called "amir" by Pakistanis, Tunisians, Afghans, and Soviet Muslims, "murshid" by Muslim brothers, "imam" in Iran. Unlike the Caliph, who had to be a member of Muhammad's lineage, in these modern movements the leader is selected solely on the basis of his personal virtue. See Roy 1994, 2004.

137. Roy 1994: 43.

138. Cited in Roy 1994.

139. Quoted in Gerges 2006: 133.

140. Quoted in Gerges 2006: 133–134.

141. A dominant moral model of religious charisma in the Middle East is based on modesty, indirect influence, and personal piety.

142. Quoted in Kepel and Milelli 2005: 141.

143. See *Washington Post* 2008.

144. Al-Salim 2003, "39 Ways to Serve and Participate in Jihad," quoted in Aaron 2008: 116.

145. Quoted in Gerges 2006: 87.

146. Bin Laden 2005: 194.

147. Al-Zawahiri 2006: 349–350.

148. Quoted in Rosenthal 2006: 44.

Chapter 6

1. Cioran 1960: 81.

2. Chesterton 1927: 234.

3. Wiarda 2007: 69.

4. Žižek 2008: 421.

5. Saramago 2007.

6. Jaspers, 1953: 51.

7. Associated Press (AP) 2008; MSNBC 2008.

8. Bin Laden, quoted in Atwan 2008: 34.

9. Price 2009.

10. For more on this topic, see Lindholm 1990; Durkheim 1965.

11. Seligman, Weller, Puett, and Simon 2008.

12. Hoffer (1951) argued that disenchanted intellectuals are the precursors of the "men of action" who actually undertake revolution and that intellectual radicals are often among the first to be eliminated if the revolution succeeds.

13. Brinton 1965.

14. Chesterton 1930: 235.

15. Polak 1966: 281.

16. Marin 1993: 419.

17. Manuel and Manuel 1979: 8.

18. Melucci 1996: 97–106.

19. Wallerstein 1998; Holloway 2002: 244–245; Hayden and El-Ojeili 2009.

20. There are parallels between the drastic transformation pursued by aurora movements and the great revolutions of the modern world. See Eisenstadt 2006: 3–35.

21. Castel 2009.

22. Solnit 2004: xxiv.

23. In this, they are orthodox. Islam is a religion favoring commerce, so long as believers are just in their dealings and pay *zakat* (tax) to support the poor.

24. This is the view of the anthropologist and alter-globalization activist David Graeber (2009).

25. Munck (2004, 2007) denounces this tendency as "presentism."

26. Aron 1955: 1.

27. Noël and Thérien (2008).

28. Steger 2008: 217.

29. William James 1982.

30. Alcanzar 2009: 13.

31. Kagan 2008; Oppenheimer 2008; Khanna 2008; Anderson, Ikenberry, and Risse 2008. For a critique of current prophecies of doom, see Lieber 2008, Herman 2009.

32. On the left turn in Latin America, see de la Torre (2007); Arditi (2008); and de la Barra and Della Buono (2009).

33. David Hume 1956 [1757].

34. Price et al. 2008.

35. In the nineteenth century, for example, Victor Hugo berated "the vulgar caprice of calumniating and dishonoring the age in which we live" (Hugo 1890: 434).

36. Winter 2006.

37. On this epochal change and visions of a new paradigm, see the work of the French sociologist Michel Maffesoli (for example, 2009). See also, Morin 2006: 143 and Touraine 2007.

38. Yeats 1994 (1920): 158–159.

BIBLIOGRAPHY

Aaron, David, ed. 2008. *In Their Own Words: Voices of Jihad*. Santa Monica, CA: RAND Corporation.

Adorno, Theodor. 1951. *Minima Moralia: Reflections from Damaged Life*. Reprinted 1978. Translated by E. F. N. Jephcott. London: Verso.

Agence France-Presse (AFP). 2007 (December 6). "Chávez Says He Will Govern until 2013 after Losing Referendum."

Agencia Bolivariana de Noticias (ABN). 2005 (February 15). "Obra de Alí Primera declarada patrimonio artístico de Venezuela."

Agencia Bolivariana de Noticias (ABN). 2006 (August 31). "Lorena Almarza: La Villa del Cine persigue la soberania audiovisual del país."

Agencia Bolivariana de Noticias (ABN). 2007a (December 12). "América Latina en Tiempos de Revolución inaugura Centro Nacional de Historia."

Agencia Bolivariana de Noticias (ABN). 2007b (December 10). "Chávez instó a pueblos de América a sembrar conciencia de patriotas verdaderos."

Agencia Bolivariana de Noticias (ABN). 2007c (July 28). "Chávez propuso cinco componentes para el socialismo Bolivariano."

Agencia Bolivariana de Noticias (ABN). 2007d (December 6). "Chávez qualificó de necesidad impostergable la transformación del modelo económico."

Agencia Bolivariana de Noticias (ABN). 2007e (November 28). "Lo que me quede de vida lo pasaré batallando por el futuro del pueblo."

Agencia Bolivariana de Noticias (ABN). 2007f (December 6). "Presidente Chávez instó a cuidar rumo de la Revolución Bolivariana."

Agencia Bolivariana de Noticias (ABN). 2007g (October 14). " Presidente Chávez rinde tributo a Ernesto 'Che' Guevara."

Agencia Bolivariana de Noticias (ABN). 2007h (November 12). "Si yo me callara gritarían las piedras de los pueblos de América Latina."

Agencia Bolivariana de Noticias (ABN). 2008a (January 11). "Alejar al país de la Guerra es uno de los más grandes logros de la Revolución."

Agencia Bolivariana de Noticias (ABN). 2008b (August 4). "Chávez espera que próximo Presidente de EEUU respete revolución democrática del Sur."

Agencia Bolivariana de Noticias (ABN). 2008c (January 6). "Chávez inauguró en Charallave Centro de Formación Socialista Ezequiel Zamora."

Agencia Bolivariana de Noticias (ABN). 2008d (July 4). "Chávez plantea crear cadena mundial de medios alternatives."

Agencia Bolivariana de Noticias (ABN). 2008e (April 10). "El imperio ya no controla este continente."

Agencia Bolivariana de Noticias (ABN). 2008f (April 22). "Morales afirmó creer en la consciencia de su pueblo para derrotar movimientos separatistas."

Agencia Bolivariana de Noticias (ABN). 2008g (May 22). "Morales invitó a todos los mandatarios sudamericanos a la Cumbre de Unasur."

Agencia Bolivariana de Noticias (ABN). 2008h (March 30). "Presidente Chávez: Encuentro contra Terrorismo Mediatico ha sido todo un exito."

Agencia Bolivariana de Noticias (ABN). 2008i (May 29). "Presidente Chávez invitó al pueblo a desmontar plan del impero de dividir el pais."

Agencia Bolivariana de Noticias (ABN). 2008j (July 5). "Presidente Chávez llamo a la union para hacer Patria."

Agencia Bolivariana de Noticias (ABN). 2008k (January 12). "PSUV es la escuela forjaadora de voluntad socialista revolucionaria."

Agencia Bolivariana de Noticias (ABN). 2008l (March 24). "Terrorismo mediatico es una vieja practica imperial para sequestrar las mentes."

Agencia Bolivariana de Noticias (ABN). 2008m (May 23). "Unasur es un passo importante para la unidad suramericana."

Agencia Bolivariana de Noticias (ABN). 2009a (February 15). "Esta Victoria es de todos los pueblos de América Latina."

Agencia Bolivariana de Noticias (ABN). 2009b (February 15). "¡Hoy 15 de febrero! Ser o no ser."

Agencia Boliviana de Información (ABI). 2005 (July 4). "Tupac Katari y Bartolina Sisa fueron declarados héroes nacionales."

Agencia Boliviana de Información (ABI). 2008a (August 4). "Evo asegura que en referendo el pueblo elegirá entre la patria y la antipatria."

Agencia Boliviana de Información (ABI). 2008b (January 5). "Evo lamenta que oposición use algunos medios para enfrentar a los bolivianos."

Agencia Boliviana de Información (ABI). 2008c (June 8). "Gobierno afirma que son irreversibles los cambios, así como la rebellión indigena."

Agencia Boliviana de Información (ABI). 2008d (July 6). "Gobierno evidencia que la Embajada de EEUU gobernaba Bolivia, hoy conspira."

Agencia Boliviana de Información (ABI). 2008e (July 24). "Proclama de Tupac Katari 'volveré y seré millones,' fue levada al cine."

Agencia Boliviana de Información (ABI). 2008f (February 10). "Unionistas piden independencia, queman la tricolor y Policía detiene a 7 de ellos."

Agencia EFE. 2006 (June 5). "Chávez abre una Villa del Cine contra la 'dictadura de Hollywood."

Agrikoliansky, Éric, Olivier Fillieule, and Nonna Mayer. 2005. *L'Altermondialisme en France: La longue histoire d'une nouvelle cause.* Paris: Éditions Flammarion.

Albro, Robert. 2005. "The Indigenous in the Plural in Bolivian Oppositional Politics." *Bulletin of Latin America Research,* 24 (4), 433–453.

Albro, Robert. 2006. "Bolivia's 'Evo Phenomenon': From Identity to What?" *Journal of Latin America Anthropology,* 11(2), 408–428.

Albrow, Martin. 1996. *The Global Age: State and Society beyond Modernity.* Stanford, CA: Stanford University Press.

Alcanzar, Alonso. 2009. "On Radical-Leftist Strategy." *Left Curve,* 33, 4–15.

Algar, Hamid. 1988. "Imam Khomeini, 1902–1962: The Pre-Revolutionary Years." In Edmund Burke III and Ira Lapidus, eds., *Islam, Politics and Social Movements,* 263–288. Berkeley: University of California Press.

Al-Khalil, Samir. 1989. *Republic of Fear: The Politics of Modern Iraq.* Berkeley: University of California Press.

Al-Maqdisi, Abu Mohammad. "Democracy: A Religion." Available at: www.maktabah .net/store/images/35/DemocracyReligion.pdf

Al-Mawdudi, Abu. 1932. *Towards understanding Islam.* Reprinted 1983. Khushid Ahmad, ed. and trans. Indianapolis: Islamic Teaching Center.

Almeyra, Guillermo, and Emiliano Thibaut. 2006. *Zapatistas: Un Nuevo Mundo en Construcción.* Buenos Aires: Editorial Maipue.

Al-Yazid, Mustafa Abu. 2008 (July 24). "Al-Qaeda Commander: Islam Doesn't Distinguish between American People, American Gov't—Both Are Infidels and at War with Islam." Available at: www.memri.org/bin/latestnews.cgi?ID=SD200008

Al-Zawahiri, Ayman. 2006. *His Own Words: A Translation of the Writings of Dr. Ayman al Zawahiri.* Laura Mansfield, trans. Old Tappan, NJ: TLG Publications.

Al-Zawahiri, Ayman. 2008 (April 23). "Open Meeting with Sheikh Ayman Al-Zawahiri—Part II." Available at: www.memri.org/bin/articles.cgi?Page= archives&Area=sd&ID=SP190708

Al-Zayyat, Montasser. 2002. *The Road to Al-Qaeda: The Story of Bin Laden's Right-Hand Man.* Reprinted 2004. Ahmed Fekry, trans. Sterling, VA: Pluto Press.

Amin, Samir. 2007. "Towards the Fifth International?" In Katarina Sehm Patomäki and Marko Ulvila, eds., *Global Political Parties,* 123–143. London: Zed Books.

Amin, Samir. 2008. *The World We Wish to See: Revolutionary Objectives in the Twenty-First Century.* New York: Monthly Review Press.

Analítica—Venezuela Analítica. 2000 (February 2). "En el Panteón Nacional Chávez inició la celebración de su primer año de gobierno." Available at: www.analitica .com/va/politica/noticias/6516339.asp

Anderson, Jeffrey, G. John Ikenberry, and Thomas Risse, eds. 2008. *The End of the West? Crisis and Change in the Atlantic Order.* Ithaca, NY: Cornell University Press.

Anderson, K., and B. Reiff. 2005. "Global Civil Society: A Skeptical View." In H. Anheier, M. Glasius, and M. Kaldor, eds., *Global Civil Society Yearbook 2004–05.* New York: Oxford University Press.

Andretta, Massimiliano, and Lorenzo Mosca. 2004. "Understanding the Genoa Protest." In Rupert Taylor, ed., *Creating a Better World: Interpreting Global Civil Society,* 43–63. Bloomfield CT: Kumarian Press.

Andrews, Cecile. 2006. *Slow Is Beautiful: New Visions of Community, Leisure and Joie de Vivre.* Gabriola Island, BC: New Society Publishers.

Angell, Norman. 1933. *The Great Illusion.* New York: G. P. Putnam's Sons.

Aporrea. 2007 (January 10). "Nace la República Socialista de Venezuela." Available at: www.aporrea.org/ideologia/a29278.html

Arditi, Benjamin. 2008. "Arguments about the Left Turns In Latin America: A Post-Liberal Politics?" *Latin America Research Review,* 43 (3), 59–81.

Arenas, Nelly, and Luis Gómez Calcaño. 2006. "Los Círculos Bolivarianos. El mito de la unidad del pueblo." In Germán Carrera Damas et al., eds., *Mitos Políticos en las Sociedades Andinas: Orígenes, invenciones y ficciones,* 363–388. Caracas: Editorial Equinoccio.

Arendt, Hannah. 1958. *The Human Condition.* Chicago: University of Chicago Press.

Argüelles, José. 2002 (November–December). "Visionary of the New Time: Michael Moynihan Speaks with José Argüelles." *New Dawn: A Journal of Alternative News & Information,* 75. Available at: www.newdawnmagazine.com.au/articles/ Interview%20With%20Jose%20Arguelles.html

Argüelles, José, and Lloydine Argüelles. 2002. *Time and the Technosphere: The Law of Time in Human Affairs.* Rochester, NY: Bear and Co.

Aron, Raymond. 1955. *The Opium of the Intellectuals.* Reprinted 1977. Terence Kilmartin, trans. Westport, CT: Greenwood Press.

Arteault, Jean-Patrick. 2006. "Etre Gaulois a l'ere de la mondialisation." *Terre et Peuple: La Revue,* 29 (Fall), 11–20.

Arthur, Anthony. 1999. *The Tailor-King: The Rise and Fall of the Anabaptist Kingdom of Muenster.* New York: St. Martin's Press.

Arze, Reginaldo Ustariz, and Alejandria Carranza. 2006. *Evo Morales: Um indígena Presidente.* São Paulo: Editora Brasbol.

Associated Press (AP). 2008 (May 24). "Energy Fears Looming, New Survivalists Prepare."

Atwan, Abdel Bari. 2008. *The Secret History of al Qaeda*. Updated edition (originally published 2006). Berkeley and Los Angeles: University of California Press.

Azzam, Abdullah. 1987. *Join the Caravan*. Reprinted, 2001. London: Azzam Publications.

Azzam, Maha. 2008 (September). "Understanding Al Qa'eda." *Political Studies Review*, 6 (3), 340–353.

Babeuf, Gracchus. 1795. "Le Manifeste des Plébéiens." Reprinted, 1965, in Claude Mazauric, ed., *Babeuf: Textes Choisis*. Paris: Éditions Sociales.

Báez, René. 1996. *Conversaciones con Marcos*. Quito: Eskeletra Editorial.

Bakhtin, Mikhail. 1968. *Rabelais and His World*. Reprinted 1984. Hélène Iswolsky, trans. Bloomington: Indiana University Press.

Bahl, Claudia. 2008. "Europeanized Nationalism? European Right-Wing Populist Parties and the Notion of European Identity," Available at www.euroculturemaster .org/docs/2-Bahl_Claudia-D-SE.pdf

Bahughuna, Sunderlal. 1997. In Tinzin Rigzin, ed., *Fire in the Heart, Firewood on the Back: Writings on and by Himalayan Crusader Sunderlal Bahughuna*. Tehri, India: Parvatiya Navjeevan Mandal.

Barber, Benjamin R. 1993 (March). "Jihad vs. McWorld." *The Atlantic*, 269 (3), 53–63.

Barber, Benjamin R. 2008. "Shrunken Sovereign: Consumerism, Globalization, and American Emptiness." *World Affairs*, 170, 4 (Spring), 73–81.

Barnes, John Lee. 2008a (February 3). "The Rebirth of the Sun," Available at: http:// leejohnbarnes.blogspot.com/2008/02/rebirth-of-sun.html

Barnes, John Lee. 2008b (May 17). E-mail communication.

Bar-On, Tamir. 2007. *Where Have All the Fascists Gone?* Hampshire, U.K.: Ashgate.

Baronnet, Bruno. 2008 (July). "Rebel Youth and Zapatista Autonomous Education." *Latin American Perspectives*. 35, 161 (4), 112–124.

Baspineiro, Alex Contreras. 2005. *Evo: Una Historia de Dignidad*. La Paz: U.P.S. Editorial.

Bauman, Zygmunt. 1999. *In Search of Politics*. Cambridge, U.K.: Polity Press.

Bauman, Zygmunt. *Work, Consumerism and the New Poor*, 2nd ed. New York: Open University Press, 2005.

Baxter, Kylie. 2007. *British Muslims and the Call to Global Jihad*. Victoria, Australia: Monash University Press.

Bay, Nicolas. 2007 (October 27). "Défendons notre identité." Discours de Nicolas Bay au colloque "Synthèse nationale." Paris.

Beinin, Joel. 1988. "Islam, Marxism and the Shubra al-Khayma Textile Workers: Muslim Brothers and Communists in the Egyptian Trade Union Movement." In Edmund Burke III and Ira Lapidus, eds., *Islam, Politics and Social Movements*, 207–227. Berkeley: University of California Press.

Beit-Hallahmi, Benjamin. 2003. "The Return of Martyrdom: Honour, Death and Immortality." *Totalitarian Movements & Political Religions*, 4 (3, Winter), 11–34.

Bell, Daniel. 2000. *The End of Ideology: On the Exhaustion of Political Ideas in the Fifties.* (Originally published1960.) Cambridge, MA: Harvard University Press.

Bello, Walden. 2004. "The Global South." In Tom Mertes, ed., *A Movement of Movements: Is Another World Really Possible?* 49–69. New York: Verso.

Benjamin, Thomas. 2001 (April). "A Time of Reconquest: History, the Maya Revival, and the Zapatista Rebellion in Chiapas," *The American Historical Review*, 105 (2), 417–450.

Berlin, Isaiah. 1978. "The Decline of Utopian Ideas in the West." Reprinted 1997. In Henry Hardy, ed., *The Crooked Timber of Humanity: Chapters in the History of Ideas*, 20–48. Princeton, NJ: Princeton University Press.

Bernanos, Georges. 1950. *Tradition of Freedom.* Original French publication 1947. London: Dennis Dobson.

Betz, Hans-Georg. 2003. "The Growing Threat of the Radical Right." In Peter H. Merkl and Leonard Weinberg, eds., *Right-Wing Extremism in the Twenty-First Century*, 74–93. Portland, OR; Frank Cass Publishers.

Bey, Hakim. 1991. *T.A.Z; The Temporary Autonomous Zone, Ontological Anarchy, Poetic Terrorism.* Brooklyn, NY: Autonomedia. Available at: www.hermetic .com/bey/taz3.html#labelTAZ

Billington, James H. 1980. *Fire in the Minds of Men: Origins of the Revolutionary Faith.* Reprinted 1999. New Brunswick, NJ: Transaction Publishers.

Bin Laden, Osama. 2005. *Messages to the World: The Statements of Osama bin Laden*, Bruce Lawrence, ed., James Howarth, trans. London: Verso.

Bin Laden, Osama. 2007. "Moderate Islam Is a Prostration to the West." In Raymond Ibrahim, ed. and trans., *The Al Qaeda Reader*, with an introduction by Victor Davis Hanson, 17–62. New York: Random House.

Bloch, Ernst. 1986. *The Principle of Hope.* Neville Plaice, Stephen Plaice, and Paul Knight, trans. Oxford, U.K.: Basil Blackwell.

Bolivarian Congress of People (CBP) 2004. Available online at www .congresobolivariano.org

Bonnett, Alastair. 2004. *The Idea of the West: Culture, Politics and History.* New York: Palgrave Macmillan.

Bossi, Fernando Ramón. 2005. *10 puntos para conocer el ALBA: Construendo el ALBA desde los pueblos.* Mar del Plata, Argentina: Congresso Bolivariano de los Pueblos.

Bossi, Umberto. 1990 (May 20). "Discorso di Pontida." Pontida. Available at: www .leganord.org

Bossi, Umberto. 1998 (July 19). *La Padania.*

Bossi, Umberto. 1999a. *La Lega: 1979–1989*. Milan: Editoriale Nord.

Bossi, Umberto. 1999b (February 6). *La Padania*.

Bossi, Umberto. 1999c (April 7). *La Padania*.

Bossi, Umberto. 1999d (November 14). *La Padania*.

Bossi, Umberto. 2000 (September 17). *La Padania*.

Bossi, Umberto. 2003 (September 21). "Intervento del Segretario Federale." Available at: www.leganord.org/segretariofederale/discorsi_venezia/2003_21settembre.pdf

Bossi, Umberto, and Daniele Vimercati. 1998. *Processo alla Lega*. Milan: Sperling & Kupfer.

Braidotti, Rosi. 1994. *Nomadic Subjects: Embodiment and Sexual Difference in Contemporary Feminist Theory*. New York: Columbia University Press.

Brinkmann, Patrick. 2007. "Entretien avec Patrick Brinkmann Continent Europe." *Terre et Peuple: La Revue*, 32 (Summer), 20–21.

Brinton, Crane. 1965. *The Anatomy of Revolution*. New York: Vintage Books.

British Broadcasting Corporation (BBC). 2003 (August 9). "Zapatistas Party for the Cause." Available at: http://news.bbc.co.uk/2/hi/americas/3137061.stm

British National Party (BNP). 2004. "Britain First!—Party Program." Retrieved February 2004 from: www.bnp.org.uk

British National Party (BNP). 2007b. "British National Party: Summary Manifesto." Available online at http://bnp.org.uk/Mini-Manifesto.pdf

British Nationalist Party (BNP). 2008 (May 1). "As a People, Where Are We, and Where We Are Going." Available at: http://bnp.org.uk/2008/05/as-a-people-where-are-we-and-where-we-are-going

Brooks, David. 2000. *Bobos in Paradise: The New Upper Class and How They Got There*. New York: Simon and Schuster.

Bukay, David. 2008. *From Muhammad to Bin Laden: Religious and Ideological Sources of the Homicide Bombers Phenomenon*. New Brunswick, NJ: Transaction Publishers.

Butler, Judith. 1997. "Sovereign Performatives in the Contemporary Scene of Utterance." *Critical Inquiry*, 23: 350–377.

Canovan, Margaret. 2005. *The People*. Malden, MA: Polity Press.

Carlyle, Thomas. 1853. "The Present Time." In Thomas Carlyle, ed. *Later-Day Pamphlets*. Reprinted 1972. New York: Books for Libraries Press.

Carrera Damas, Germán. 2006. "Mitología Política e Ideologías Alternativas; El Bolivarianismo-Militarismo." In Germán Carrera Damas et al., eds., *Mitos Políticos en las Sociedades Andinas: Orígenes, invenciones y ficciones*. Caracas: Editorial Equinoccio, 391–420.

Castel, Robert. 2009 (February 28). "Le glas a sonné pour le libéralisme sauvage." *Le Monde*.

Castellanos, Erick, and Sara M. Bergstresser. 2006. "Food Fights at the EU Table: The Gastronomic Assertion of Italian Distinctiveness." *European Studies: An Interdisciplinary Series in European Culture, History and Politics*, 22 (1), 179–202.

Castells, Manuel, and Martin Ince. 2003. *Conversations with Manuel Castells*. Cambridge, U.K.: Polity Press.

CathNews (CN). 2009 (February 5). "Church leaders main enemy: Bolivia's Morales." Available at: www.cathnews.com/article.aspx?aeid=11516

Cau, Jean. 1992. "Le triomphe de Mickey." In *Etats-Unis: Danger*, Actes du XXV colloque national du GRECE. Paris: Éditions du Labyrinthe, 7–19.

Cavanagh, John, and Jerry Mander, eds. 2004. *Alternatives to Economic Globalization: A Better World Is Possible*. San Francisco: Berrett-Koehler Publishers.

Chabrol, Didier 2004. "Slow Food, un mouvement qui crée le chemin en marchant . . ." Unpublished article.

Champetier, Charles. 1994. *Homo consumans: Archéologie du don et de la dépense*. Paris: Éditions du Labyrinthe.

Champetier, Charles. 1999. "Porquoi la Nouvelle Droite?" Available at: http://grecefr .celeonet.fr/textes/_txtWeb.php?idArt=246

Chanda, Nayan. 2007. *Bound Together: How Traders, Preachers, Adventurers, and Warriors Shaped Globalization*. New Haven, CT: Yale University Press.

Charters, David A. 2007. "Something Old, Something New . . . ? Al Qaeda, Jihadism, and Fascism." *Terrorism and Political Violence*, 19 (1, Spring), 65–93.

Chase-Dunn, Christopher. 2007. "The World Revolution of 20xx*." In Jerry Harris, ed., *Contested Terrains of Globalization: Conference Documents*, 6–26. Chicago: Global Studies Association.

Chase-Dunn, Christopher, and Ellen Reese. 2007. "The World Social Forum—A Global Party in the Making?" In Katarina Sehm Patomäki and Marko Ulvila, eds., *Global Political Parties*, 53–91. London: Zed Books.

Chávez, Hugo. 1999a (May 23). "Discurso del Presidente de la República Bolivariana de Venezuela, Hugo Chávez Frías, con Motivo del Acto Conmemorativo de los 100 Años de la Revolución Restauradora." In *Selección de Discursos del Presidente de la República Bolivariana de Venezuela, Hugo Chávez Frías: 1999, 'Año de la Refundación de la Republica. Gobierno Bolivariano, Año 1, Tomo 1*. 2005. Caracas: Ediciones de la Presidencia de la República, 189–213.

Chávez, Hugo. 1999b (July 24). "Discurso del Presidente de la República Bolivariana de Venezuela, Hugo Chávez Frías, con Motivo de la Celebración del 216 Aniversario del Natalicio del Libertador Simón Bolívar." In *Selección de Discursos del Presidente de la República Bolivariana de Venezuela, Hugo Chávez Frías: 1999, 'Año de la Refundación de la Republica. Gobierno Bolivariano, Año 1, Tomo 1*. 2005. Caracas: Ediciones de la Presidencia de la República, 253–260.

Chávez, Hugo. 1999c (December 4). "Discurso del Presidente de la República Bolivariana de Venezuela, Hugo Chávez *Frías*, con Motivo del Encuentro Nacional de la Constituyente Educativa. In *Selección de Discursos del Presidente de la República Bolivariana de Venezuela, Hugo Chávez Frías: 1999, 'Año de la Refundación de la Republica. Gobierno Bolivariano, Año 1, Tomo 1.* 2005. Caracas: Ediciones de la Presidencia de la República, 481–496.

Chávez, Hugo. 1999d (August 5). "Discurso del Presidente de la República Bolivariana de Venezuela, Hugo Chávez *Frías*, con Motivo de la Instalación de la Asamblea Nacional Constituyente." In *Selección de Discursos del Presidente de la República Bolivariana de Venezuela, Hugo Chávez Frías: 1999, Año de la Refundación de la Republica. Gobierno Bolivariano, Año 1, Tomo 1.* 2005. Caracas: Ediciones de la Presidencia de la República, 273–310.

Chávez, Hugo. 1999e (October 30). "Discurso del Presidente de la República Bolivariana de Venezuela, Hugo Chávez *Frías*, con Motivo de la Presentacion al Pais de los Resultados de su Viaje por asia y Europa." In *Selección de Discursos del Presidente de la República Bolivariana de Venezuela, Hugo Chávez Frías: 1999, Año de la Refundación de la Republica. Gobierno Bolivariano, Año 1, Tomo 1.* 2005. Caracas: Ediciones de la Presidencia de la República, 397–436.

Chávez, Hugo. 1999f (May 13). "Discurso del Presidente de la República Bolivariana de Venezuela, Hugo Chávez *Frías*, con Motivo de los Primeros 100 Días de Gobierno," In *Selección de Discursos del Presidente de la República Bolivariana de Venezuela, Hugo Chávez Frías: 1999, Año de la Refundación de la Republica. Gobierno Bolivariano, Año 1, Tomo 1.* 2005. Caracas: Ediciones de la Presidencia de la República, 139–187.

Chávez, Hugo. 1999g (September 22). "Discurso del Presidente de la República Bolivariana de Venezuela, Hugo Chávez *Frías*, con Motivo de la Sesión Protocolar del Consejo Permanente de la OEA." In *Selección de Discursos del Presidente de la República Bolivariana de Venezuela, Hugo Chávez Frías: 1999, Año de la Refundación de la Republica. Gobierno Bolivariano, Año 1, Tomo 1.* 2005. Caracas: Ediciones de la Presidencia de la República, 333–342.

Chávez, Hugo. 1999h (May 26). "Discurso del Presidente de la República Bolivariana de Venezuela, Hugo Chávez *Frías*, en el Acto de Inauguración de la XI Cumbre Presidencial Andina." In *Selección de Discursos del Presidente de la República Bolivariana de Venezuela, Hugo Chávez Frías: 1999, Año de la Refundación de la Republica. Gobierno Bolivariano, Año 1, Tomo 1.* 2005. Caracas: Ediciones de la Presidencia de la República, 215–222

Chávez, Hugo. 2001a (November 13). "Discurso del Presidente de la República Bolivariana de Venezuela, Hugo Chávez *Frías*, con Motivo del Encuentro Latinoamericano y Caribeño sobre el Dialogo de Civilizaciones." In *Selección de Discursos del Presidente de la República Bolivariana de Venezuela, Hugo Chávez Frías: 2001, Año de las Leys Habilitantes: La Revolución Avanza a Paso de Vencedores. Gobierno Bolivariano, Año 3, Tomo III.* 2005. Caracas: Ediciones de la Presidencia de la República, 589–604.

Chávez, Hugo. 2001b (December 11). "Discurso del Presidente de la República Bolivariana de Venezuela, Hugo Chávez Frías, con Motivo de la Inauguración de la Cumbre del Caribe." In *Selección de Discursos del Presidente de la República Bolivariana de Venezuela, Hugo Chávez Frías: 2001, Año de las Leys Habilitantes: La Revolución Avanza a Paso de Vencedores. Gobierno Bolivariano, Año 3, Tomo III.* 2005. Caracas: Ediciones de la Presidencia de la República, 683–693.

Chávez, Hugo. 2001c (December 5). "Discurso del Presidente de la República Bolivariana de Venezuela, Hugo Chávez Frías, con Motivo del Lanzamiento de la Ley de la Pequeña y Mediana Industria," December 5. In *Selección de Discursos del Presidente de la República Bolivariana de Venezuela, Hugo Chávez Frías: 2001, Año de las Leys Habilitantes: La Revolución Avanza a Paso de Vencedores. Gobierno Bolivariano, Año 3, Tomo III.* 2005. Caracas: Ediciones de la Presidencia de la República, 615–640.

Chávez, Hugo. 2001d (October 29). "Discurso del Presidente de la República Bolivariana de Venezuela, Hugo Chávez Frías, con Motivo del Primer Encuentro Nacional de Voceros y Comunicadores Populares." In *Selección de Discursos del Presidente de la República Bolivariana de Venezuela, Hugo Chávez Frías: 2001, Año de las Leys Habilitantes: La Revolución Avanza a Paso de Vencedores. Gobierno Bolivariano, Año 3, Tomo III.* 2005. Caracas: Ediciones de la Presidencia de la República, 509–526.

Chávez, Hugo. 2001e (December 10). "Discurso del Presidente de la República Bolivariana de Venezuela, Hugo Chávez Frías, con Motivo de la Promulgación de la Ley de Tierras y Desarrollo Agrario." In *Selección de Discursos del Presidente de la República Bolivariana de Venezuela, Hugo Chávez Frías: 2001, Año de las Leys Habilitantes: La Revolución Avanza a Paso de Vencedores. Gobierno Bolivariano, Año 3, Tomo III.* 2005. Caracas: Ediciones de la Presidencia de la República, 673–682.

Chávez, Hugo. 2001f (May 4). "Discurso del Presidente de la República Bolivariana de Venezuela, Hugo Chávez Frías, con Motivo de su Visita al Congreso de Colombia." In *Selección de Discursos del Presidente de la República Bolivariana de Venezuela, Hugo Chávez Frías: 2001, Año de las Leys Habilitantes: La Revolución Avanza a Paso de Vencedores. Gobierno Bolivariano, Año 3, Tomo III.* 2005. Caracas: Ediciones de la Presidencia de la República, 157–171.

Chávez, Hugo. 2001g (February 1). "Discurso del Presidente de la República Bolivariana de Venezuela, Hugo Chávez Frías, frente al Sarcófago del General Ezequiel Zamora," In *Selección de Discursos del Presidente de la República Bolivariana de Venezuela, Hugo Chávez Frías: 2001, Año de las Leys Habilitantes: La Revolución*

Avanza a Paso de Vencedores. Gobierno Bolivariano, Año 3, Tomo III. 2005. Caracas: Ediciones de la Presidencia de la República, 89–97.

Chávez, Hugo. 2002a (January 24). "Discurso del Presidente de la República Bolivariana de Venezuela, Hugo Chávez *Frías*, con Motivo del Saludo al Cuerpo Diplomatico Acreditado ante el Gobierno de Venezuela." In *Selección de Discursos del Presidente de la República Bolivariana de Venezuela, Hugo Chávez Frías: 2002, 'Año de la Resistencia Antiimperialista', Año 4, Tomo IV*. 2005. Caracas: Ediciones de la Presidencia de la República, 129–149.

Chávez, Hugo. 2002b (December 31). "Mensage del Presidente de la República Bolivariana de Venezuela Hugo Chávez *Frías*, con motivo del fin de año." In *Selección de Discursos del Presidente de la República Bolivariana de Venezuela, Hugo Chávez Frías: 2002, 'Año de la Resistencia Antiimperialista', Año 4, Tomo IV*. 2005. Caracas: Ediciones de la Presidencia de la República,. 537–544.

Chávez, Hugo. 2003a (October 16). "Discurso del Presidente de la República Bolivariana de Venezuela, Hugo Chávez *Frías*, con Motivo del Acto de Juramentación de la Comisión Presidencial Misión Ribas." In *Selección de Discursos del Presidente de la República Bolivariana de Venezuela, Hugo Chávez Frías: 2003, 'Año de la Contraofensiva Revolucionaria y la Victoria Imperialista. Gobierno Bolivariano, Año 5, Tomo V*. 2005. Caracas: Ediciones de la Presidencia de la República, 591–604.

Chávez, Hugo. 2003b (July 17). "Discurso del Presidente de la República Bolivariana de Venezuela, Hugo Chávez *Frías*, con Motivo del Acto de Solidaridad en Apoyo a la Misión Barrio Adentro." In *Selección de Discursos del Presidente de la República Bolivariana de Venezuela, Hugo Chávez Frías: 2003, 'Año de la Contraofensiva Revolucionaria y la Victoria Imperialista. Gobierno Bolivariano, Año 5, Tomo V*. 2005. Caracas: Ediciones de la Presidencia de la República, 389–408.

Chávez, Hugo. 2003c (January 23). "Discurso del Presidente de la República Bolivariana de Venezuela, Hugo Chávez *Frías*, con Motivo de la Celebración del Aniversario del 23 de Enero de 1958," In *Selección de Discursos del Presidente de la República Bolivariana de Venezuela, Hugo Chávez Frías: 2003, 'Año de la Contraofensiva Revolucionaria y la Victoria Imperialista. Gobierno Bolivariano, Año 5, Tomo V*. 2005. Caracas: Ediciones de la Presidencia de la República, 73–101.

Chávez, Hugo. 2003d (February 4). "Discurso del Presidente de la República Bolivariana de Venezuela, Hugo Chávez *Frías*, con Motivo de la Conmemoración del 4 de Febrero de 1992," In *Selección de Discursos del Presidente de la República Bolivariana de Venezuela, Hugo Chávez Frías: 2003, 'Año de la Contraofensiva Revolucionaria y la Victoria Imperialista. Gobierno Bolivariano, Año 5, Tomo V*. 2005. Caracas: Ediciones de la Presidencia de la República, 133–152.

Chávez, Hugo. 2003e (January 26). "Discurso del Presidente de la República Bolivariana de Venezuela, Hugo Chávez *Frías*, con Motivo del Encuentro de Solidaridad con la Revolución Bolivariana, en el Marco del Foro Social Mundial." In *Selección de Discursos del Presidente de la República Bolivariana de Venezuela, Hugo Chávez Frías: 2003, 'Año de la Contraofensiva Revolucionaria y la Victoria Imperialista. Gobierno Bolivariano, Año 5, Tomo V.* 2005. Caracas: Ediciones de la Presidencia de la República, 103–132.

Chávez, Hugo. 2003f (July 22). "Discurso del Presidente de la República Bolivariana de Venezuela, Hugo Chávez Frías, con Motivo de explicar el Desarrollo Endógeno del Pais." In *Selección de Discursos del Presidente de la República Bolivariana de Venezuela, Hugo Chávez Frías: 2003, 'Año de la Contraofensiva Revolucionaria y la Victoria Imperialista. Gobierno Bolivariano, Año 5, Tomo V.* 2005. Caracas: Ediciones de la Presidencia de la República, 409–433.

Chávez, Hugo. 2003g (December 27). "Discurso del Presidente de la República Bolivariana de Venezuela, Hugo Chávez Frías, con Motivo de la Graduación de Un Millón de Alfabetizados, en la Quinta Oleada de la Misión Robinson." In *Selección de Discursos del Presidente de la República Bolivariana de Venezuela, Hugo Chávez Frías: 2003, 'Año de la Contraofensiva Revolucionaria y la Victoria Imperialista. Gobierno Bolivariano, Año 5, Tomo V.* 2005. Caracas: Ediciones de la Presidencia de la República, 649–658.

Chávez, Hugo. 2003h (April 13). "Discurso del Presidente de la República Bolivariana de Venezuela, Hugo Chávez Frías, con Motivo de la Gran Concentración 'Dia del Pueblo Soberano.'" In *Selección de Discursos del Presidente de la República Bolivariana de Venezuela, Hugo Chávez Frías: 2003, 'Año de la Contraofensiva Revolucionaria y la Victoria Imperialista. Gobierno Bolivariano, Año 5, Tomo V.* 2005. Caracas: Ediciones de la Presidencia de la República, 259–289.

Chávez, Hugo. 2003i (August 19). "Discurso del Presidente de la República Bolivariana de Venezuela, Hugo Chávez Frías, con Motivo de la Inauguración de la Cátedra Bolivariana en la Universidad Popular Madres de Plaza de Mayo," In *Selección de Discursos del Presidente de la República Bolivariana de Venezuela, Hugo Chávez Frías: 2003, Año de la Contraofensiva Revolucionaria y la Victoria Imperialista. Gobierno Bolivariano, Año 5, Tomo V.* 2005. Caracas: Ediciones de la Presidencia de la República, 521–538.

Chávez, Hugo. 2003j (November 11). "Discurso del Presidente de la República Bolivariana de Venezuela, Hugo Chávez Frías, con Motivo de la Inauguración de Vive Television." In *Selección de Discursos del Presidente de la República Bolivariana de Venezuela, Hugo Chávez Frías: 2003, 'Año de la Contraofensiva Revolucionaria y la Victoria Imperialista. Gobierno Bolivariano, Año 5, Tomo V.* 2005. Caracas: Ediciones de la Presidencia de la República, 623–630.

Chávez, Hugo. 2003k (February 20). "Discurso del Presidente de la República Bolivariana de Venezuela, Hugo Chávez Frías, con Motivo de la Juramentación de la Comisión Presidencial del Área de Libre Comercio de las Américas ALCA." In *Selección de Discursos del Presidente de la República Bolivariana de Venezuela, Hugo*

Chávez Frías: 2003, Año de la Contraofensiva Revolucionaria y la Victoria Imperialista. Gobierno Bolivariano, Año 5, Tomo V. 2005. Caracas: Ediciones de la Presidencia de la República, 199–214.

Chávez, Hugo. 2003l (August 16). "Discurso del Presidente de la República Bolivariana de Venezuela, Hugo Chávez *Frías*, con Motivo de la Sesión Extraordinaria de la asociación Latinoamericana de Integración ALADI." In *Selección de Discursos del Presidente de la República Bolivariana de Venezuela, Hugo Chávez Frías: 2003, Año de la Contraofensiva Revolucionaria y la Victoria Imperialista. Gobierno Bolivariano, Año 5, Tomo V.* 2005. Caracas: Ediciones de la Presidencia de la República, 493–519.

Chávez, Hugo. 2003m (June 19). "Discurso del Presidente de la República Bolivariana de Venezuela, Hugo Chávez *Frías*, con Motivo de la XXIV Cumbre del Mercado Comun del Sur Mercosur." In *Selección de Discursos del Presidente de la República Bolivariana de Venezuela, Hugo Chávez Frías: 2003, Año de la Contraofensiva Revolucionaria y la Victoria Imperialista. Gobierno Bolivariano, Año 5, Tomo V.* 2005. Caracas: Ediciones de la Presidencia de la República, 355–364.

Chávez, Hugo. 2004a. *Acto de Concentración contra la intervención: Venezuela se Respeta! Caracas, 29 de Febrero de 2004.* Caracas: República Bolivariana de Venezuela, Ministerio de Energia y Minas.

Chávez, Hugo. 2004b (December 5). "Discurso del Presidente de la República Bolivariana de Venezuela, Hugo Chávez *Frías*, con Motivo de la Clausura del Primer Encuentro Mundial de Intelectuales y Artistas por la Defensa de la Humanidad." In *Selección de Discursos del Presidente de la República Bolivariana de Venezuela, Hugo Chávez Frías: 2004, Año de la Gran Victoria Popular y Revolucionaria. Gobierno Bolivariano, Año 6, Tomo VI.* 2005. Caracas: Ediciones de la Presidencia de la República, 659–675.

Chávez, Hugo. 2004c (August 8). "Discurso del Presidente de la República Bolivariana de Venezuela, Hugo Chávez *Frías*, con Motivo de la Marcha por la Victoria." In *Selección de Discursos del Presidente de la República Bolivariana de Venezuela, Hugo Chávez Frías: 2004, 'Año de la Gran Victoria Popular y Revolucionaria. Gobierno Bolivariano, Año 6, Tomo VI.* 2005. Caracas: Ediciones de la Presidencia de la República, 439–484.

Chávez, Hugo. 2005a (September 25). "Aló Presidente no. 234. Desde el Estado Barinas, Hacienda La Marqueseña." Available at: www.gobiernoenlinea.ve/docMgr/sharedfiles/Alo_Presidente_234.pdf

Chávez, Hugo. 2005b (March 5). "Discurso del Presidente de la República Bolivariana de Venezuela, Hugo Chávez *Frías*, con Motivo del Acto de Masas en Calcuta." In *Selección de Discursos del Presidente de la República Bolivariana de Venezuela, Hugo Chávez Frías: 2005, 'Año del Salto Adelante': Hacia la Construcción del*

Socialismo del Siglo XXI. Gobierno Bolivariano, Año 7, Tomo VII. 2005. Caracas: Ediciones de la Presidencia de la República, 197–203.

Chávez, Hugo. 2005c (November 4). "Discurso del Presidente de la República Bolivariana de Venezuela, Hugo Chávez *Frías*, con Motivo de la Clausura de la III Cumbre de los Pueblos de América. In *Selección de Discursos del Presidente de la República Bolivariana de Venezuela, Hugo Chávez Frías: 2005, 'Año del Salto Adelante': Hacia la Construcción del Socialismo del Siglo XXI. Gobierno Bolivariano, Año 7, Tomo VII.* 2005. Caracas: Ediciones de la Presidencia de la República, 593–619.

Chávez, Hugo. 2005d (May 1). "Discurso del Presidente de la República Bolivariana de Venezuela, Hugo Chávez *Frías*, con Motivo de la Conmemoración del Día Internacional del Trabajador." In *Selección de Discursos del Presidente de la República Bolivariana de Venezuela, Hugo Chávez Frías: 2005, 'Año del Salto Adelante': Hacia la Construcción del Socialismo del Siglo XXI. Gobierno Bolivariano, Año 7, Tomo VII.* 2005. Caracas: Ediciones de la Presidencia de la República, 305–335.

Chávez, Hugo. 2005e (October 28). "Discurso del Presidente de la República Bolivariana de Venezuela, Hugo Chávez *Frías*, con Motivo de la Declaratoria de Venezuela como Territorio Libre de Analfabetismo y Conmemoración del 234 Aniversario del Nacimiento de Simón Rodríguez." In *Selección de Discursos del Presidente de la República Bolivariana de Venezuela, Hugo Chávez Frías: 2005, 'Año del Salto Adelante': Hacia la Construcción del Socialismo del Siglo XXI. Gobierno Bolivariano, Año 7, Tomo VII.* 2005. Caracas: Ediciones de la Presidencia de la República, 567–591.

Chávez, Hugo. 2005f (January 30). "Discurso del Presidente de la República Bolivariana de Venezuela, Hugo Chávez *Frías*, con Motivo del Foro Social Mundial 'El Sur, Norte de Nuestros Pueblos.'" In *Selección de Discursos del Presidente de la República Bolivariana de Venezuela, Hugo Chávez Frías: 2005, 'Año del Salto Adelante': Hacia la Construcción del Socialismo del Siglo XXI. Gobierno Bolivariano, Año 7, Tomo VII.* 2005. Caracas: Ediciones de la Presidencia de la República, 75–98.

Chávez, Hugo. 2005g (August 8). "Discurso del Presidente de la República Bolivariana de Venezuela, Hugo Chávez *Frías*, con Motivo de la Inaugración del XVI Festival de la Juventud y los Estudiantes." In *Selección de Discursos del Presidente de la República Bolivariana de Venezuela, Hugo Chávez Frías: 2005, 'Año del Salto Adelante': Hacia la Construcción del Socialismo del Siglo XXI. Gobierno Bolivariano, Año 7, Tomo VII.* 2005. Caracas: Ediciones de la Presidencia de la República, 413–424.

Chávez, Hugo. 2005h (September 6). "Discurso del Presidente de la República Bolivariana de Venezuela, Hugo Chávez *Frías*, con Motivo de la Instalación de la II Cumbre de Jefes de Estado y de Gobierno sobre Petróleos del Caribe Petrocaribe." In *Selección de Discursos del Presidente de la República Bolivariana de Venezuela,*

Hugo Chávez Frías: 2005, 'Año del Salto Adelante': Hacia la Construcción del So-cialismo del Siglo XXI. Gobierno Bolivariano, Año 7, Tomo VII. 2005. Caracas: Edi-ciones de la Presidencia de la República, 463–478.

Chávez, Hugo. 2005i (January 23). "Discurso del Presidente de la República Bolivari-ana de Venezuela, Hugo Chávez *Frías*, con Motivo de la Marcha en Defensa de la Soberanía Nacional." In *Selección de Discursos del Presidente de la República Boli-variana de Venezuela, Hugo Chávez Frías: 2005, 'Año del Salto Adelante': Hacia la Construcción del Socialismo del Siglo XXI. Gobierno Bolivariano, Año 7, Tomo VII.* 2005. Caracas: Ediciones de la Presidencia de la República, 55–73.

Chávez, Hugo. 2005j (August 14). "Discurso del Presidente de la República Bolivari-ana de Venezuela, Hugo Chávez *Frías*, con Motivo del Tribunal Internacional An-tiimperialista en el Marco del XVI Festival Mundial de la Juventud y los Estu-diantes." In *Selección de Discursos del Presidente de la República Bolivariana de Venezuela, Hugo Chávez Frías: 2005, 'Año del Salto Adelante': Hacia la Construc-ción del Socialismo del Siglo XXI. Gobierno Bolivariano, Año 7, Tomo VII.* 2005. Caracas: Ediciones de la Presidencia de la República, 425–462.

Chávez, Hugo. 2005k (October 16). "Discurso del Presidente de la República Bolivari-ana de Venezuela, Hugo Chávez *Frías*, con Motivo de su Visita al Monte Sacro." In *Selección de Discursos del Presidente de la República Bolivariana de Venezuela, Hugo Chávez Frías: 2005, 'Año del Salto Adelante': Hacia la Construcción del So-cialismo del Siglo XXI. Gobierno Bolivariano, Año 7, Tomo VII.* 2005. Caracas: Edi-ciones de la Presidencia de la República, 521–536.

Chávez, Hugo. 2005l (December 24). "Discurso del Presidente de la República Boli-variana de Venezuela, Hugo Chávez Frías, con Motivo de su Visita al Centro de Desarrollo Endogeno Integral Humano 'Manantial de los Suenos.'" In *Selección de Discursos del Presidente de la República Bolivariana de Venezuela, Hugo Chávez Frías: 2005, 'Año del Salto Adelante': Hacia la Construcción del Socialismo del Siglo XXI. Gobierno Bolivariano, Año 7, Tomo VII.* 2005. Caracas: Ediciones de la Presi-dencia de la República, 715–733.

Chávez, Hugo. 2006a (January 8). "Aló Presidente no. 243. Núcleo de Desarrollo Endógeno José Félix Ribas." Available at: http://alopresidente.gob.ve/component/option,com_docman/Itemid,0/task,doc_view/gid,81/

Chávez, Hugo. 2006b (December 16). "Chávez llama a conformar el Partido So-cialista: Al socialismo no vamos a llegar por arte de magia . . . necessitamos un partido, no una sopa de letras." Available at: www.aporrea.org/ideologia/n87995.html

Chávez, Hugo. 2006c (Dec. 3). "Discurso luego del primer boletin del CNE Balcón del Pueblo—Palacio de Miraflores."

Chávez, Hugo. 2006d (January 27). "President Chavez's Speech to the 6th World Social Forum—Americas." Available at: www.venezuelanalysis.com/analysis/1728

Chávez, Hugo. 2006e (June 29). "Sólo el socialismo salvará a la especie humana; Fragmentos del discurso pronunciado con motivo del Tercer Aniversario del Frente Francisco de Miranda." Caracas.

Chávez, Hugo. 2007a (March 27). "Aló Presidente No. 279. Graduación Misión Robinson II Sala Rios Reyna, Teatro Teresa Carreño."

Chávez, Hugo. 2007b (August 19). "Aló Presidente No. 290. Teatro Teresa Carreño."

Chávez, Hugo. 2007c (January 8). "Palabras del presidente reelecto Hugo Chávez Frías, durante acto de juramentación en el Teatro Teresa Carreño."

Chávez, Hugo. 2009. YouTube link. Retrieved on January 30, 2009, from www .youtube.com/watch?v=EB3N4OrcTd8

Chesterton, G. K. 1927. *The Outline of Sanity*. New York: Dodd, Mead & Company.

Chesterton, G. K. 1930. "The Spirit of Europe." In Lawrence J. Clipper, ed., *The Collected Works of G. K. Chesterton XXXV: The Illustrated London News 1929–1931*, 234–238. Reprinted 1991. San Francisco: Ignatius Press.

Chin, Christine B. N., and James H. Mittelman. 2000. "Conceptualizing Resistance to Globalization." in Barry K. Gills, ed., *Globalization and the Politics of Resistance*, 29–45. New York: St. Martin's Press.

Choueiri, Youssef M. 1990. *Islamic Fundamentalism*. Boston: Twayne Publishers.

Christian, David. 2004. *Maps of Time: An Introduction to Big History*. Berkeley: University of California Press.

Christian Science Monitor (CSM). 2008 (September 19). "Moscow's Moves in Georgia Track a Script by Right-Wing Prophet." Available at: www.csmonitor .com/2008/0920/p01s01-woeu.html

Cioran, E. M. 1960. *History and Utopia*. Reprinted 1996. Richard Howard, trans. London: Quartet Books.

Cittaslow UK. "Charter." Retrieved on September 20, 2009, from www.cittaslow.org .uk/images/Download/cittaslow_charter.pdf

Clandestine Insurgent Rebel Clown Army (CIRCA). 2003. "About the Army." Available at: www.clownarmy.org/about/about.html

Clark, Fraser. 1995. "Zippy Pronoia Tour to US '94." Available at: athttp://www .pronoia.net/tour/essays/fraser.html

Cleaver, Harry. 1998. "The Zapatistas and the Electronic Fabric of Struggle." In John Holloway and Eloína Peláez, eds., *Zapatista!: Reinventing Revolution in Mexico*. Sterling, VA: Pluto Press, 81–103.

Cock, Jacklyn. 2004. "The World Social Forum and New Forms of Social Activism." In Rupert Taylor, ed., *Creating a Better World: Interpreting Global Civil Society*, 170–183. Bloomfield CT: Kumarian Press.

Cohen, Daniel. 2006. *Globalization and its Enemies*. Original French edition, 2004; Jessica B. Baker, trans. Cambridge, MA: MIT Press.

Cohn, Norman. 1984. *The Pursuit of the Millennium: Revolutionary Millenarians and Mystical Anarchists of the Middle Ages.* Rev. ed. London: Paladin Books.

Collin, Matthew. 1998. *Altered State: The Story of Ecstasy Culture and Acid House.* London: Serpent's Tail.

Colque Flores, Cristóbal. 2007. *Con Evo Morales Ayma empieza a escribirse la verdadera Historia de Bolivia sin k'aras ni t'aras.* El Alto: MAS.

Colque Flores, Cristóbal. 2008. *Los enemigos de la patria quieren dividir Bolivia.* El Alto: MAS.

Conosur-Ñawpaqman—Rivista rural Bilingue para la Nacion Quechua. 2006 (February–March). "Desde Tiwanaku plantean la revolucion latinoamericana atraves de los indigenas," 117.

Conway, Dennis, and Nik Heynen. 2006. "The Ascendancy of Neoliberalism and Emergence of Contemporary Globalization." In Dennis Conway and Nik Heynen, eds., *Globalization's Contradictions: Geographies of Discipline, Destruction and Transformation,* 17–34. New York: Routledge.

Cook, Brian. 2008 (October). "Sleepwalking through Seattle." *In These Times,* 32 (10), 38–39. Available at: www.inthesetimes.com/article/3912/sleepwalking_through _seattle

Cook, David. 2005a. *Contemporary Muslim Apocalyptic Literature.* Syracuse, NY: Syracuse University Press.

Cook, David. 2005b. *Understanding Jihad.* Berkeley: University of California Press.

Copsey, Nigel. 2004. *Contemporary British Fascism: The British National Party and the Quest for Legitimacy.* New York: Palgrave Macmillan.

Couvrat, Christine. 2007. *L'essor de l'altermondialisme: Expression de la montée en Occident d'une culture "démocrate-radicale."* Paris: L'Harmattan.

Crabtree, John. 2007 (December 10). "Bolivia's controversial constitution." Available at www.opendemocracy.net

Crabtree, John. 2008 (July 2). "Bolivia's Democratic Tides." Available at: www .opendemocracy.net

Cusicanqui, Silvia Rivera. 1983. "Luchas Campesinas Contemporáneas en Bolivia; El Movimiento 'Katarista': 1970–1980." In René Zavaleta Mercado, ed., *Bolivia, Hoy,* 129–168. Mexico: Siglo Veintiuno Editores.

Cusicanqui, Silvia Rivera. 1991. *Pachakuti: los aymara de Bolivia frente a medio milenio de colonialismo.* La Paz–Chukiyawu: Ediciones del Taller de Historia Oral.

D'Andrea, Anthony. 2004. "Global Nomads: Techno and New Age as Transnational Countercultures in Ibiza and Goa." In Graham St. John, ed., *Rave Culture and Religion,* 236–255. London: Routledge.

D'Andrea, Anthony. 2007. *Global Nomads: Techno and New Age as Transnational Countercultures in Ibiza and Goa.* New York: Routledge.

Dangl, Benjamin. 2009 (March 14). "Decolonization's rocky road: corruption, expropriation and justice in Bolivia." Available at: http://upsidedownworld.org/main/content/view/1764/1

Dean, Mitchell. 2006. "A Political Mythology of World Order: Carl Schmitt's Nomos." *Theory, Culture & Society*, 23 (5). 1–22.

De Benoist, Alain. 1979. *Les idées à l'endroit*. Paris: Éditions Libres/Hallier.

De Benoist, Alain. 1981. *On Being a Pagan*. Reprinted 2004. Jon Graham, trans.; Greg Johnson, ed. Atlanta, GA: Ultra.

De Benoist, Alain. 1982. "Pour une declaration du droit des peoples." In *La Cause Des Peuples*, Actes du XV colloque national du G.R.E.C.E. Paris: Éditions du Labyrinthe.

De Benoist, Alain. 1983. "Ernst Jünger: La figure du travailleur entre les Dieux et les Titans," *Nouvelle Ecole*, 40 (Autumn), 11–61.

De Benoist, Alain. 1985. *Démocracie: Le Problème*. Paris: Éditions du Labyrinthe.

De Benoist, Alain. 1986. *Europe, Tiers Monde, Même Combat*. Paris: Éditions Robert Lafont.

De Benoist, Alain. 1991. "Le Bourgeois: figure et domination." *Éléments pour la culture européenne*, 72 (Winter), 11–16.

De Benoist, Alain. 1992. "C'est encore loin, l'Amerique?" In *Etats-Unis: Danger*. Actes du XXV colloque national du GRECE. Paris: Éditions du Labyrinthe.

De Benoist, Alain. 1993a. "The Idea of Empire." *Telos*, 98–99 (December 1993–May 1994), 81–98.

De Benoist, Alain. 1993b. "Three Interviews with Alain de Benoist." *Telos*, 98–99 (December 1993–May 1994), 173–207.

De Benoist, Alain. 1994. *Le grain de sable: Jalons pour une fin de siècle*. Paris: Éditions du Labyrinthe.

De Benoist, Alain. 1996 (May–August). "Gli Orizzonti Della Mondializzazione." In *Trasgressioni: Rivista Quadrimestrale di Cultura Politica*, 11 (2), 47–68.

De Benoist, Alain. 2001 (December). "C'est le 11 septembre 2001 que le XXe siècle s'est terminé." *Éléments pour la civilization européenne*, 103, 20–31.

De Benoist, Alain. 2001. *Dernière année: Notes pour conclure le siècle*. Lausanne, Switzerland: L'Age D'Homme.

De Benoist, Alain. 2004a. "Entrevue," *Le Félin Identitaire*, 4.

De Benoist, Alain. 2004b (October/December). "Entretien." *Italicum*, 4–5.

De Benoist, Alain. 2004c. "On Being a Pagan: Ten Years Later: An Interview with Alain de Benoist," *TYR: Myth-Culture-Tradition*, 2 (2003–2004). Atlanta, GA: Ultra, 77–109.

De Benoist, Alain. 2005. "European Son: An Interview with Alain de Benoist." *The Occidental Quarterly*, 5, 3 (Fall), 7–27.

De Benoist, Alain. 2006a. *Critica della Ragion Mercantile. Dal sistema dei consumu globali alla civiltà dell'economia locale.* Bologna: Arianna Editrice.

De Benoist, Alain. 2006b. *Nous et les autres—Problématique de l'identité.* Paris: Krisis.

De Benoist, Alain. 2006c. "Objectif décroissance." *Éléments pour la civilization européenne,* 119 (Winter), 28–40.

De Benoist, Alain. 2006d. "Reply to Milbank," *Telos,* 134 (Spring), 22–30.

De Benoist, Alain. 2007a. *Carl Schmitt Actuel: Guerre Juste, Terrorisme, État d'Urgence, Nomos de La Terre.* Paris: Éditions Krisis.

De Benoist, Alain. 2007b (April). "La gouvernance: L'OPA des oligarchies sur la démocracie." *Éléments pour la civilization européenne,* 124, 38–43.

De Benoist, Alain. 2007c (November–December). "Il Pensiero Ribelle di Alain de Benoist," *Diorama Letterario,* 286, 5–12.

De Benoist, Alain. 2007d (September–October). "La Politica del Populismo." *Diorama Letterario,* 285, 5–7.

De Benoist, Alain. 2008 (January-February). "L'Europa tra delusione e speranza." *Diorama Letterario,* 287, 1–15.

De Benoist, Alain. 2009a. "La crise: Ça ne fait que commencer!" *Éléments pour la civilization européenne,* 130 (Winter), 5.

De Benoist, Alain. 2009b. "L'empire du Bien ou le degré zéro de la vie sociale." *Éléments pour la civilization européenne,* 130 (Winter), 36–43.

De Benoist, Alain, and Charles Champetier. 1999 (February). "Manifeste: la Nouvelle Droite de l'an 2000." *Eléments,* 94.

De Benoist, Alain, Giuseppe Giaccio, and Costanzo Preve. 2005. *Dialoghi sul presente. Alienazione, globalizzazione, Destra/Sinistra, atei devoti. Per un pensiero ribelle.* Naples: Controcorrente Edizioni.

De Blij, Harm. 2008. *The Power of Place: Geography, Destiny, and Globalization's Rough Landscape.* New York: Oxford University Press.

De Herte, Robert. 1980 (April). "Ni des esclaves, ni des robots." *Éléments pour la civilization européenne,* 34, 2.

De Herte, Robert. 1991. "L'Amérique c'est Carthage." *Éléments pour la culture européenne,* 70 (Spring), 3.

De Herte, Robert. 2001 (March). "L'heure de la micropolitique." *Éléments pour la civilization européenne,* 100.

De Herte, Robert. 2003 (June). "Pour une humanité plurielle." *Éléments pour la civilization européenne,* 109.

De Herte, Robert. 2004 (January). "L'altermonde." *Éléments pour la civilization européenne,* 111.

De Herte, Robert. 2005a. "L'Amérique qu'on aime." *Éléments pour la civilization européenne,* 116 (Spring).

De Herte, Robert. 2005b. "De Marx a Heidegger." *Éléments pour la civilization européenne*, 115 (Winter).

De Herte, Robert. 2005c. "Panoptique." *Éléments pour la civilization européenne*, 118 (Fall).

De Herte, Robert. 2005d. "Peut-on vivre sans un au-dela de soi?" *Éléments pour la civilization européenne*, 117 (Summer).

De Herte, Robert. 2006. "Vers un nouveau Nomos de la Terre." *Éléments pour la civilization européenne*, 122 (Fall).

De Herte, Robert. 2007 (April 2). "Le capitalisme libéral contre la souveraineté du people." *Éléments pour la civilization européenne*, 124.

De La Barra, Ximena, and Richard A. Dello Buono. 2009. *Latin America after the Neoliberal Debacle: Another Region Is Possible*. Lanham, MD: Rowman and Littlefield Publishers.

De La Torre, Carlos. 2007. "The Resurgence of Radical Populism in Latin America." *Constellations*, 14 (3,) 384–397.

De La Torre, Carlos. Forthcoming. "The contested meanings of democratic and populist revolutions in the Andes."

De la Vega, Garcilaso Inca. 1995. "The origins of the Incas" (Original publication 1609). In Orin Star, Carlos Iván Degregori, and Robin Kirk, eds., *The Peru Reader: History, Culture, Politics*, 49–54. Durham, NC: Duke University Press.

Della Porta, Donatella, and Herbert Reiter, eds. 2006. *Organizational Ideology and Visions of Democracy in the Global Justice Movement*. Brussels: Report to *European Commission*, WP3 Integrated Report for the Demos Project.

Democracia Nacional (DN). 2007. "El homenaje a El Cid en MD." Available at: www .democracianacional.org/dn/modules.php?name=News&file=article&sid=944

Democracia Nacional (DN). 2008a. "Nuestro Decálogo." Available at: www .democracianacional.org/dn

Democracia Nacional (DN). 2008b. "Preguntas: Si creo que el Euro no es la solución a nuestros problemas." Available at: www.democracianacional.org/dn

Democracia Nacional (DN). 2008c. "Preguntas: Si estoy contra de la globalisacion y el mundialismo." Available at: www.democracianacional.org/dn

Democracia Nacional (DN). 2008d. "Preguntas: Si estoy contra el NEO-IMPERIALISMO Yankee." Available at: www.democracianacional.org/dn

Democracia Nacional (DN). 2008e. "Preguntas: Si soy ecologista." Available at www .democracianacional.org/dn

Deutsche Welle (DW). 2008 (January 26). "Right-Wing leaders to Form a European 'Patriotic' Party."

Devji, Faisal. 2005. *Landscapes of the Jihad: Militancy, Morality, Modernity*. Ithaca, NY: Cornell University Press.

Dirección de Prensa d Palacio de Gobierno. 2007 (November 7). "Presidente acusa a algunos comités cívicos de ser instrumentos del neoliberalismo y de la Embajada de EEUU."

Dostoyevsky, Fyodor. 1872. *The Possessed.* Reprinted 1936. Constance Garnett, trans. New York: The Modern Library.

Dugin, Alexander. 1992a. "Ideology of the World Government." *Elementy*, 2. 1–2. Victor Olevich, trans.

Dugin, Alexander. 1992b. "La Russie, L'Europe, Le Monde." *Éléments pour la civilization européenne*, 73, 36.

Dunkerley, James. 2007. *Bolivia: Revolution and the Power of History in the Present: Essays.* London: Institute for the Study of Americas.

Durán, Marta. 2001. *El Tejido del Pasamontañas: Entrevista con el Subcomandante Marcos.* Mexico City: Rizoma.

Durkheim, Emile. 1965. *The Elementary Forms of the Religious Life.* Original publication 1912. New York: Free Press.

Eastwood, Jonathan. 2007. "Contextualizando a Chávez: el nacionalismo venezolano contemporáneo desde una perspectiva histórica." *Revista Mexicana de Sociología*, 69, 4 (Oct–Dec), 605–639. Available at www.ejournal.unam.mx/rms/2007-4/RMS007000402.pdf

Eatwell, Roger. 2004. "Introduction: The New Extreme Right Challenge." In Roger Eatwell and Cas Mudde, eds., *Western Democracies and the New Extreme Right Challenge*, 1–15. New York: Routledge.

Eickelman, Dale F., and James Piscatori. 2004, *Muslim Politics.* Princeton, NJ: Princeton University Press.

Eisenstadt, S. N. 2006. *The Great Revolutions and the Civilizations of Modernity.* Boston: Brill.

Ejército Zapatista de Liberación Nacional (EZLN). 1994 (April 19). "Communiqué, from the Revolutionary Indigenous Clandestine Committee." Chiapas, Mexico: EZLN.

Ejército Zapatista de Liberación Nacional (EZLN). 1995 (October 12). "Communiqué, from the Revolutionary Indigenous Clandestine Committee—General Command of the Zapatista Army for National Liberation." Available at: http://nativenet.uthscsa.edu/archive/nl/9510/0237.html

Ejército Zapatista de Liberación Nacional (EZLN). 2001 (February 24). "Communiqué, Clandestine Revolutionary Indigenous Committee-General Command of the Zapatista Army of National Liberation," Available at: http://flag.blackened.net/revolt/mexico/ezln/2001/ccri/san_chris_feb.html

Ejército Zapatista de Liberación Nacional (EZLN). 2003 (August 12). "Comandanta Esther's Words in Oventik." Available at: www.ainfos.ca/03/aug/ainfos00376.html

Ejército Zapatista de Liberación Nacional (EZLN). 2008 (September 16). "*Communiqué from the Indigenous Revolutionary Clandestine Committee.*" Available at: www.indymedia.org.uk/en/2008/09/408975.html

Ellner, Steve. 2008. *Rethinking Venezuelan Politics: Class, Conflict, and the Chávez Phenomenon.* Boulder, CO: Lynne Rienner Publishers.

Ellwood, Wayne. 2001. *The No-Nonsense Guide to Globalization.* Reprinted 2004. London: Verso.

el-Mehri, A. B. 2006. "Introduction." In Sayyid Qutb, *Milestones.* Birmingham, U.K.: Makrabah Booksellers.

Esparza, José Javier. 1985. "El etnocidio contra los pueblos," *Punto y Coma,* 4. Available at: http://foster.20megsfree.com/101.htm

Esparza, José Javier. 1997. *Curso General de Disidencia: Apuntes para una visión del mundo alternativa.* Ediciones Madrid: El Emboscado.

Esparza, José Javier. 1998. "Hispanidad y Globalización. Reflexiones a proposito del 98 y su centenario." *Disenso,* 18, 7–28.

Esparza, José Javier. 2008 (January–March). "La Nueva Derecha y la cuestión religiosa." *El Manifiesto: contra la muerte del espiritu y la tierra,* 5, (9), 9–31.

Euben, Roxanne L. 1999. *Enemy in the Mirror: Islamic Fundamentalism and the Limits of Modern Rationalism—A Work of Comparative Political Theory.* Princeton, NJ: Princeton University Press.

Eurasian Movement. 2001. Manifesto of the Eurasianist Movement. Available at: www.evrazia.info/modules.php?name=News&file=article&sid=454

EuroNat. 2005. Available at: http://euronat.org

European National Front (ENF). 2008. Available at: www.europeannationalfront.org

Evola, Julius. 1983. "*Civiltà*" *Americana.* Rome: Fondazione Julius Evola.

Fanon, Frantz. 1961. *The Wretched of the Earth.* Reprinted 2004. Richard Philcox, trans. New York: Grove Press.

Faraj, Mohammad Abdus Salaam. 1981. *Jihad: The Absent Obligation.* Reprinted 2000. Birmingham, U.K.: Maktabah Al Ansaar Publications.

Fatone, Gina Andrea. 2004. "*Gamelan,* Techno-Primitivism, and the San Francisco Rave Scene." In Graham St. John, ed., *Rave Culture and Religion,* 197–210. New York: Routledge.

Faye, Guillaume. 1980 (April). "Pour en finir avec la civilisation occidentale," *Éléments pour la culture européenne,* 34, 5–11.

Faye, Guillaume. 1981. *Le Système à tuer les peoples.* Paris: Copernic.

Faye, Guillaume. 1986. "Panem et Circenses: A Critique of 'The West.'" *The Scorpion,* 9 (Spring).

Faye, Guillaume. 1998. *L'Archéofuturisme,* Paris: L'Aencre.

Faye, Guillaume. 2000. *La colonization de l'Europe: Discours vrai sur l'immigration et l'Islam.* Paris: Aencre.

Faye, Guillaume. 2001a. "La guerre necessaire." *Terre et Peuple: La Revue*, 10 (Winter), 7–8.

Faye, Guillaume. 2001. "Les Titans et les Dieux: Entretien avec Guillaume Faye." *Antaios*, printemps, 111-129

Faye, Guillaume. 2004. *Le coup d'Etat mondial: Essai sur le Nouvel Impérialisme Américain.* Paris: Aencre.

Fehrer, Kendra. 2007/2008 (Dec./Jan.). "Reconfiguring Democracy: Venezuela's New Communal Councils Confront Bureaucracy." *PeaceWork*, 8–29.

Fisher, William, and Thomas Ponniah, eds. 2003. "Introduction: The World Social Forum and the Reinvention of Democracy." In William Fisher and Thomas Ponniah, eds. *Another World Is Possible: Popular Alternatives to Globalization at the World Social Forum*, 1–20. New York: Zed Books.

Flanagan, Thomas. 2000. "Modernity and the Millennium: From Robespierre to Radical Feminism." In Martha F. Lee, ed., *Essays on Twentieth-Century Millenarianism.* Westport, CT: Praeger.

Flores, Rafael Correa. 2005. *Construyendo El Alba: "Nuestro Norte es el Sur."* Caracas: Republica Bolivariana de Venezuela.

Flores Galindo, Alberto. 1988. *Buscando un Inca: Identidad y Utopia en los Andes*, 3rd ed. Lima: Editorial Horizonte.

Flusty, Steven. 2004. *De-Coca-Colonization: Making the Globe from the Inside Out.* New York: Routledge.

Foran, John. 2000. "The Future of Revolutions at the *Fin de Siècle.*" In Rosemary H. T. O'Kane, ed., *Revolution: Critical Concepts in Political Science*, Volume IV, 417–450. New York: Routledge.

Fouda, Yosri, and Fielding, Nick. 2003 *Masterminds of Terror: The Truth behind the Most Devastating Terrorist Attack the World Has Ever Seen.* New York: Arcade Publishing.

Fougier, Eddy. 2008. *L'Altermondialisme.* Paris: Le Cavalier Bleu Editions.

Fraquelli, Marco. 2005. *A destra di Porto Alegre. Perchè la Destra è più noglobal della Sinistra.* Soveria Mannelli, Italy: Rubbettino Editore.

Freeden, Michael. 2006. "Confronting the Chimera of a 'Post-Ideological' Age." In Gayil Talshir, Mathew Humphrey, and Michael Freeden, eds., *Taking Ideology Seriously: 21st Century Reconfigurations.* New York: Routledge, 141–156.

Freeman, Jo, and Victoria Johnson. 1999. "Introduction." In Jo Freeman and Victoria Johnson, eds., *Waves of Protest: Social Movements Since the Sixties*, 1–6. Lanham, MD: Rowman & Littlefield.

Frente Francisco de Miranda (FFM). 2008. Available at: www.frentefrancisco demiranda.org.ve/quienes.htm

Friedman, Jonathan. 1994. *Cultural Identity and Global Process.* London: Sage Publications.

Friedman, Jonathan. 2005. "Plus Ça Change? On Not Learning from History." In Jonathan Friedman and Christopher Chase-Dunn, eds., *Hegemonic Decline: Present and Past*, 89–114. Boulder, CO: Paradigm Publishers.

Friedman, Thomas L. 2007. *The World Is Flat 3.0: A Brief History of the Twenty-first Century*. New York: Picador.

Fritz, J. 1999. *Rave Culture: An Insider's Overview*. Victoria, BC: Smallfry Press.

Fukuyama, Francis. 1989. "The End of History?" *The National Interest*, No. 16 (Summer), 3–18.

Fukuyama, Francis. 2006. *The End of History and the Last Man*. (Originally published 1992.) New York: Free Press.

Furet, François. 1995. *The Passing of an Illusion: The Idea of Communism in the Twentieth Century*. Reprinted 1999. Deborah Furet, trans. Chicago: University of Chicago Press.

Gaceta Oficial. 2006 (April 10). "Ley de los Consejos Comunales," Asamblea Nacional de la República Bolivariana de Venezuela.

Galeano, Eduardo. 2000. *Upside Down: A Primer for the Looking-Glass World*. (Originally published 1998). Mark Fried, trans. New York: Metropolitan Books.

García Linera, Álvaro. 2004 (April). "La sublevación indígeno-popular en Bolivia." *Artículo Primero: Revista de debate social y juridico*, 71–87.

García Linera, Álvaro. 2006a (January). "El capitalismo andino-amazónico." *Le Monde Diplomatique*.

García Linera, Álvaro. 2006b (July). "El evismo: lo nacional popular en acción," *Observatorio Social de America Latina*, VI (19), 25–32.

García Márquez, Gabriel. 1992. *Elogio de la Utopia: Una entrevista de Nahuel Maciel*. Buenos Aires: El Cronista Ediciones.

Garrido, Alberto. 2007. *Chávez con uniforme: Antibiografia, únicamente para Chavólogos*. Venezuela: Author's Edition.

Gauchet, Marcel. 2006 (March 12). "L'Occident est aveugle sur les effets de la mondialisation de l'économie et des moeurs." *Le Monde*.

Gauthier, François. 2004. "Rapturous Ruptures: The 'Instituant' Religious Experience of Rave." in Graham St. John, ed., *Rave Culture and Religion*, 64–84. New York: Routledge.

Gerges, Fawaz A. 2005. *The Far Enemy: Why Jihad Went Global*. New York: Cambridge University Press.

Gerges, Fawaz A. 2006. *Journey of the Jihadist: Inside Muslim Militancy*. Orlando, FL: Harcourt Books.

Gill, Stephen. 2008. *Power and Resistance in the New World Order*, 2nd ed. New York: Palgrave Macmillan.

Gills, Barry K. 2000. "Introduction: Globalization and the Politics of Resistance." In Barry K. Gills, ed., *Globalization and the Politics of Resistance*, 3–11. New York: St. Martin's Press.

Gilman-Opalsky, Richard. 2008. *Unbounded Publics: Transgressive Public Spheres, Zapatismo, and Political Theory*. Lanham, MD: Lexington Books.

Giordani, Lourdes, and Villalón, María Eugenia. 2002. "An Expansion of Citizenship in Venezuela." *NACLA Report on the Americas*, 35, 6 (May/June), 44–45.

Gironda, Eusebio. 2006. *El Pachakuti Andino: 'Trascendencia Historica de Evo Morales.'* La Paz: Edobol.

Giugni, Marco G. 2002. "Explaining Cross-National Similarities among Social Movements." In Jackie Smith and Hank Johnston, eds., *Globalization and Resistance: Transnational Dimensions of Social Movements*, 13–29. Lanham, MD: Rowman & Littlefield Publishers.

Gollnisch, Bruno. 2008 (February 14). "L'Union europpenne aux orders des Etats-Unis?" Available at www.frontnational.com

Goodwin, Jeff. *No Other Way Out: States and Revolutionary Movements, 1945–1991*. Cambridge, U.K.: Cambridge University Press, 2001.

Gott, Richard. 2000. *In the Shadow of the Liberator: The Impact of Hugo Chávez on Venezuela and Latin America*. New York: Verso.

Goulding, Christina, Avi Shankar, and Richard Elliott. 2002. "Working Weeks, Rave Weekends: Identity Fragmentation and the Emergence of New Communities." *Consumption, Markets and Culture*, 5 (4), 261–284.

Graeber, David. 2009 (May–June). "[Tactical Briefing]." *Adbusters: Journal of the Mental Environemnt*, 83, 17 (3).

Gray, John. 1998. *False Dawn: The Delusions of Global Capitalism*. London: Granta.

Gray, John. 2003. *Al Qaeda and What It Means to Be Modern*. London: Faber & Faber.

Grazian, David. 2003. *Blue Chicago: The Search for Authenticity in Urban Blues Clubs*. Chicago: University of Chicago Press.

Graziani, Tiberio. 2004 (October 6). "Carta da Visita." *Eurasia: Rivista di studi Geopolitici*.

Greider, William. 1997. *One World, Ready or Not: The Manic Logic of Global Capitalism*. New York: Simon & Schuster.

Griffin, Nick. 2004. "Cults, Jets and Greed—the Frantic Rush to 'One World.'" Retrieved October 2004 from: http://bnp.org.uk

Griffin, Nick. 2007a (December). "The crisis of globalism." *Identity: Magazine of the British National Party*.

Griffin, Nick. 2007b (December 31). "New Year's Message." Available at: www.bnp .org.uk

Griffin, Nick. 2008 (February 4). "Nick Griffin Interviewed by Austria's Freedom Party Newspaper." Available at: www.bnp.org.uk

Griffin, Roger. 2007a. "Another Face? Another Mazeway? Reflections on the Newness and Rightness of the European New Right," in Tamir Bar-On, ed., *Where Have All the Fascists Gone?* Hampshire, U.K.: Ashgate, vii–xvii.

Griffin, Roger. 2007b. *Modernism and Fascism: The Sense of a Beginning under Mussolini and Hitler.* New York: Palgrave Macmillan.

Grumke, Thomas. 2003 (July–September). "The Transatlantic Dimension of Right-Wing Extremism." *Human Rights Review*, 4, 4, 56–72.

Guénon, René. 1927. *The Crisis of the Modern World.* Reprinted, 1942. Arthur Osborne, trans. London: Luzac & Co.

Guevara, Ernesto "Che." 1977. "El Socialismo y el Hombre en Cuba." (Original publication 1965). In *Ernesto Che Guevara: Escritos y Discursos 8*, 253–272. Havana: Editorial de Ciencias Sociales.

Habeck, Mary R. 2006. *Knowing the Enemy: Jihadist Ideology and the War on Terror.* New Haven, CT: Yale University Press.

Hall, Thomas D., and James V. Fenelon. 2008 (March). "Indigenous Movements and Globalization: What Is Different? What Is the Same?" *Globalizations*, 5, 1, 1–11.

Hands Off Venezuela (HOV). 2002. "Constitution of the Hands Off Venezuela Campaign." Available at: www.handsoffvenezuela.org/constitution_hands _off_venezuela_campaign

Hardt, Michael. 2006. "Welcoming the Multitude." *The Brown Journal of World Affairs*, 13 (1), 11–18.

Hardt, Michael, and Antonio Negri. 2004. *Multitude: War and Democracy in the Age of Empire.* New York: Penguin.

Hardy, Thomas. 1901. *Poems of the Past and the Present.* New York: Harper & Brothers.

Harris, Lee. 2006 (October–November). "Jihad Then and Now." *Policy Review* 139, 74–82.

Harvey, David. 2000. *Spaces of Hope.* Edinburgh, U.K.: Edinburgh University Press.

Hayden, Patrick, and Chamsy El-Ojeili. 2009. "Introduction: Reflections on the Demise and Renewal of Utopia in a Global Age." In Patrick Hayden and Chamsy El-Ojeili, eds., *Globalization and Utopia: Critical Essays*, 1–12. New York: Palgrave Macmillan.

Hayden, Tom. 2006 (January 27). "New Day for Bolivia." *The Nation: Online edition.* Available at: www.thenation.com/doc/20060213/hayden/3

Heidegger, Martin. 1935. *Introduction to Metaphysics.* Reprinted 2000. Gregory Fried and Richard Polt, trans. New Haven, CT: Yale University Press.

Held, David. 2000. "Introduction." In David Held, ed., *A Globalizing World? Culture, Economics, Politics*, 1–4. New York: Routledge.

Hellinger, Daniel. 2001. *Nationalism, Globalization, and Chavismo*. Paper delivered at the 2001 meeting of the Latin American Studies Association, Washington, DC, XXIII, September 6–8.

Henck, Nick. 2007. *Subcommander Marcos: The Man and the Mask*. Durham, NC: Duke University Press

Herder, Johann Gottfried von. 1968. *Reflections on the Philosophy of the History of Mankind*. (Originally published 1791). Chicago: University of Chicago Press.

Herman, Arthur. 2009. "The Pessimist Persuasion," *The Wilson Quarterly*, 33 (2, Spring): 59–66.

Hernáiz, Hugo Antonio Pérez. 2008 (October). "The Uses of Conspiracy Theories for the Construction of a Political Religion in Venezuela," *World Academy of Science, Engineering, and Technology*, 34, 709–720.

Hill, Christopher. 1972. *The World Turned Upside Down: Radical Ideas during the English Revolution*. Reprinted 1991. New York: Penguin Books.

Hobsbawm, E. J. 1990. *Nations and Nationalism since 1870: Programme, Myth, Reality*, 2nd ed. Reprinted 1992. New York: Cambridge University Press.

Hoffer, Eric. 1951. *The True Believer: Thoughts on the Nature of Mass Movements*. New York: Harper and Row.

Holeindre, Roger. 2003. *SOS Hystérie II*. Paris: Godefroy de Bouillon.

Holloway, John. 2002. *Change the World without Taking Power*. Reprinted 2005. Ann Arbor, MI: Pluto Press.

Holzer, Jessica. 2004 (February 4). "Dispatches from Bolivia: Coca Is Not Cocaine." *Slate*.

Honoré, Carl. 2004. *In Praise of Slowness: How a Worldwide Movement Is Challenging the Cult of Speed*. San Francisco: HarperSanFrancisco.

Hooper, John. 2004 (October 20). "Peasant Farmers of the World Unite!" *The Guardian*.

Hopkins, Dwight N. 2001. "The Religion of Globalization." In Dwight N. Hopkins, Lois Ann Lorentzen, Eduardo Mendieta, and David Batstone, eds., *Religions/Globalizations: Theories and Cases*, 7–32. Durham, NC: Duke University Press.

Hopkins, Rob. 2008. *The Transition Handbook: From Oil Dependency to Local Resilience*. White River Junction, VT: Chelsea Green Publishing.

Hosking, Geoffrey. 2006. *Rulers and Victims: The Russians in the Soviet Union*. Cambridge, MA: Harvard University Press.

Hughes, James. 2007. *Chechnya: From Nationalism to Jihad*. Philadelphia: University of Pennsylvania Press.

Hugo, Victor. 1900. *History of a Crime*. Volume II, Boston: Dana Estes & Company.

Human Rights Watch (HRW). 2009 (March 12). "Bolivia: Unequivocally Condemn Mob Violence," Available at: www.hrw.org/en/news/2009/03/12/bolivia-unequivocally-condemn-mob-violence

Hume, David. 1956. *Natural History of Religion*. (Original publication 1757.) Stanford, CA: Stanford University Press.

Huntington, Samuel P. 1989. "No Exit: The Errors of Endism." *The National Interest*, 17 (Fall), 3–10.

Huntington, Samuel P. 1993. "The Clash of Civilizations?" *Foreign Affairs*, 73 (3, Summer), 22–49.

Huntington, Samuel P. 2007. "The Clash of Civilizations Revisited." *New Perspectives Quarterly*, 24, (1, Winter), 53–59.

Ibrahim, Raymond, ed. and trans. *The Al Qaeda Reader*, with an introduction by Victor Davis Hanson. New York: Random House.

Identité: revue d'études nationals. 1993. "Le Front National," 21.

Ingram, A. 2001 (November). "Alexander Dugin: Geopolitics and Neo-Fascism in Post-Soviet Russia." *Political Geography*, 20 (8), 1029–1051.

'Ishq, Anwar. 2005 (September 9). "Anwar 'Ishqi, Director of the Middle East Center for Strategic Studies in Jeddah, Saudi Arabia, Al-Jazeera TV, February 16," in Memri, *Special Report No. 38*. Available at: www.memri.org/bin/articles .cgi?Page=archives&Area=sr&ID=SR3805

Ivanov, Evgueni. 2008. "Rencontre avec Evgueni Ivanov, rédacteur en chef de la revue Eurasia et member de l'association 'Les Notres.'" In Christian Bouchet, ed., *Jeunes Nationalistes d'Aujourd'Hui: Qui sont-ils, que veulent-ils?*, 87–97. Paris; Éditions Déterna.

Jacoby, Russell. 1999. *The End of Utopia: Politics and Culture in an Age of Apathy*. New York: Basic Books.

James, William. 1982. *Varieties of Religious Experience*. (Originally published 1902.) New York: Viking Press.

Jaspers, Karl. 1953. *The Origin and Goal of History*. New York: Routledge.

Johnson, Chalmers. 2000. *Blowback*. New York: Henry Holt.

Jung, Courtney. 2008. *The Moral Force of Indigenous Politics: Critical Liberalism and the Zapatistas*. New York: Cambridge University Press.

Jünger, Ernst. 1939. *On the Marble Cliffs*. Reprinted 1947. Stuart Hood, trans. London: A New Directions Book.

Juris, Jeffrey S. 2008. *Networking Futures: The Movements against Corporate Globalization*. Durham, NC: Duke University Press.

Kagan, Robert. 2008 (April 23). "The End of the End of History: Why the Twenty-First Century Will Look Like the Nineteenth." *The New Republic, A Journal of Politics and the Arts*, 238 (4, 834), 40–47.

Kahn, Richard, and Douglas Kellner. 2007. "Resisting Globalization." In George Ritzer, ed., *The Blackwell Companion to Globalization*, 662–674. Malden, MA: Blackwell Publishing.

Kaplan, Robert D. 2000. *The Coming Anarchy: Shattering the Dreams of the Post Cold War*. New York: Vintage Books.

Katz, Sandor Ellix. 2006. *The Revolution Will Not Be Microwaved: Inside America's Underground Food Movements*. White River Junction, VT: Chelsea Green Publishing.

Katzenberger, Elaine. 1995. "Introduction." In Elaine Katzenberger, ed., *First World, Ha Ha Ha! The Zapatista Challenge*, i–vii. San Francisco: City Lights.

Kellen, Konrad. 1990. "Ideology and Rebellion: Terrorism in West Germany." In Walter Reich, ed., *Origins of Terrorism: Psychologies, Ideologies, Theologies, States of Mind*, 43–58. New York: Cambridge University Press.

Kepel, Gilles. 2002. *Bad Moon Rising: A Chronicle of the Middle East Today*. Reprinted 2003. Pascale Ghazaleh, trans. London: Saqi Books.

Kepel, Gilles, and Jean-Pierre Milelli, eds. 2005. *Al Qaeda in Its Own Words*. Reprinted 2008. Cambridge, MA: Harvard University Press.

Khanna, Parag. 2008 (January 27). "Waving Goodbye to Hegemony." *The New York Times Magazine*, 34–41, 62.

Kiely, Ray. 2005. *The Clash of Globalisations: Neo-Liberalism, the Third Way and Anti-Globalisation*. Leiden, Netherlands: Brill.

Kirchheimer, Otto. 1966. "The Transformation of the Western European Party Systems." In Joseph LaPalombara and Myron Weiner, eds., *Political Parties and Political Development*, 177–200. Princeton, NJ: Princeton University Press.

Klandermans, Bert, and Nonna Mayer. 2006. "Through the Magnifying Glass: The World of Extreme Right Activists." In Bert Klandermans and Nonna Mayer, eds., *Extreme Right Activists in Europe: Through the Magnifying Glass*, 269–276. New York: Routledge.

Klein, Naomi. 2001 (May–June). "Reclaiming the Commons." *New Left Review*, 9, 81–89.

Kolakowski, Leszek. 1983. "The Death of Utopia Reconsidered." In Sterling M. McMurrin, ed., *The Tanner Lectures on Human Values* IV, 227–247. Salt Lake City: University of Utah Press.

Kolata, Alan. 1993. *The Tiwanaku: Portrait of an Andean Civilization*. Cambridge, MA: Blackwell.

Korten, David C. 1996. "The Failures of Bretton Woods." In Jerry Mander and Edward Goldsmith, eds., *The Case against the Global Economy and for a Turn toward the Local*, 20–30. San Francisco: Sierra Club Books.

Kovel, Joel. 2007. *The Enemy of Nature: The End of Capitalism or the End of the World*, 2nd ed. New York: Zed Books.

Krebs, Pierre. 1995. "The Metapolitical Rebirth of Europe," in Roger Griffin, ed., *Fascism*, 348–349. New York; Oxford University Press.

Krebs, Pierre. 1997. *La lucha por lo esencial.* 1997. Reprinted 2006. Olegario de las Eras, trans. Valencia: Publicaciones Kontinent Europa.

Krebs, Pierre. 2004 (April). "La Resistencia por los derechos de los pueblos: Entrevista con el Dr. Pierre Krebs sobre la ideología mundialista, la Guerra de Irak, el mestizaje y el Judeocristianismo." *Deutsche Stimme.*

Krebs, Pierre. 2008 (April 29). E-mail communication.

Lacey, Jim (Ed). 2008. *The Canons of Jihad: Terrorists' Strategy for Defeating America,* Annapolis, MD: Naval Institute Press.

Lang, Michael. 2006, Dec. "Globalization and Its History." *The Journal of Modern History,* Vol. 78, 899–931.

Landes, Alexandro. 2006. *Cocalero.* Bolivia: Morocha Films. Available on DVD.

Laruelle, Marlene. 2006. "Aleksander Dugin: A Russian Version of the European Radical Right?" Occasional Paper 294. Washington, DC: Kennan Institute, Woodrow Wilson International Center for Scholars, 1–25.

Lasch, Christopher. 1981. "Mass Culture Reconsidered." *Democracy: A Journal of Political Renewal and Radical Change,* 1 (4, October), 7–22.

Laudan, Rachel. 2001 "A Plea for Culinary Modernism: Why We Should Love New, Fast, Processed Food." *Gastronomica: The Journal of Food and Culture,* charter issue, 36–44.

Lav, Daniel. 2007 (March 7). "The Al-Qaeda Organization in the Islamic Maghreb: The Evolving Terrorist Presence in North Africa." Available at: http://memri .org/bin/articles.cgi?Page=archives&Area=ia&ID=IA33207

Lefranc, Didier. 1993. "L'ordre mondial: une imposture." *Identité: revue d'études nationales,* 18 (Spring–Summer), 5–9.

Leitch, Alison. 2008. "Slow Food and the Politics of Pork Fat." In Carole Counihan, ed., *Food and Culture: A Reader,* 387–388. New York: Routledge.

Lembo, Alberto. 1998. *Mondialismo e resistenza etnica,* Padova: Edizioni di Ar.

Le Pen, Jean-Marie. 1991a. *Le Pen 90: Analyses et propositions.* Maule: Éditions de Présent.

Le Pen, Jean-Marie. 1991b (August 30–September 2). "Le discours de la Trinité: démarxiser la France." *Présent.*

Le Pen, Jean-Marie. 1992a (September 2–3). "Le discours de Jean-Marie Le Pen à la Trinité," *Présent.*

Le Pen, Jean-Marie. 1992b (September 12–13). "Le discours du serment de Reims." *Présent.*

Le Pen, Jean-Marie. 1993. "Agir pour rester libre," *Identité: revue d'études nationales,* 18 (Spring–Summer), 3.

Le Pen, Jean-Marie. 1994. "Le sinistre mea culpa de l'homme blanc." *Identité: revue d'études nationales,* 22 (Spring–Summer), 3.

Le Pen, Jean-Marie. 1996a. "Le bras armé du Nouvel Ordre mondial." *Identité: revue d'études nationales*, 23.

Le Pen, Jean-Marie. 1996b (September 5–6). "Entendez le chant du people Francais." *Présent*.

Le Pen, Jean-Marie. 1998 (May 1). "Fête de Jeanne d'Arc." Available at: www .frontnational.com/doc_interventions_detail.php?id_inter=7

Le Pen, Jean-Marie. 1999a (June 10–16). "Jean-Marie Le Pen: Il n'y a qu'une seule liste qui defende la souverainete francaise: la notre," *National-Hebdo*, 3–4.

Le Pen, Jean-Marie. 1999b (September 3). Université d'été 1999 du Front National à l'Orange."

Le Pen, Jean-Marie. 2000 (May 1). "Fête de Jeanne d'Arc." Available at: www .frontnational.com/doc_interventions_detail.php?id_inter=12

Le Pen, Jean-Marie. 2001a (August 23–29). "Le Pen à la Trinité: Une grande journée entre symboles et espoirs," *National-Hebdo*.

Le Pen, Jean-Marie. 2001b (September 23). "21ème Fête des Bleau-Blanc-Rouge." Available at: www.frontnational.com/doc_interventions_detail.php?id_inter=15

Le Pen, Jean-Marie. 2002 (May 1). "Fête de Jeanne d'Arc," Available at: www .frontnational.com

Le Pen, Jean-Marie. 2005 (October 9). "22ème Fête des Bleu-Blanc-Rouge au Bourget," Available at: www.frontnational.com/doc_interventions_detail .php?id_inter=3

Le Pen, Jean-Marie. 2006 (September 20). "Discours de Jean-Marie Le Pen à Valmy." Available at: www.frontnational.com/doc_interventions_detail.php?id_inter=43

Le Pen, Jean-Marie. 2007a (February 11). "Discours à Nantes sur le thème de l'environnement." Available at: www.frontnational.com/doc_interventions _detail.php?id_inter=59

Le Pen, Jean-Marie. 2007b (May 1). "Discours à l'occasion du défilé du 1er mai." Available at: www.frontnational.com/doc_interventions_detail.php?id_inter=79

Le Pen, Jean-Marie. 2007d (November 18). "Discours de clôture du XIIIe Congrès du Front National." Available at: www.frontnational.com/doc_interventions_detail .php?id_inter=92

Le Pen, Jean-Marie. 2009 (March 15). "Discours à Arras." Available at: www .frontnational.com/doc_interventions_detail.php?id_inter=135

Lhéritier, Jean. 2006 (November 24). Personal interview by Siv Lie. Tours, France.

Lia, Brynjar. 2008. *Architect of Global Jihad: The Life of Al Qaeda Strategist Abu Mus'ab Al-Suri*. New York: Columbia University Press.

Liang, Christina Schori. 2007. "Europe for the Europeans: The Foreign and Security Policy of the Populist Radical Right." In Christina Schori Liang, ed., *Europe for the Europeans: The Foreign and Security Policy of the Populist Radical Right*, 1–32. Burlington, VT: Ashgate.

Libcom.org. 2008. "Slogans of 68." Accessed September 19, 2009, at: http://libcom .org/history/slogans-68.

Lie, Siv. 2008. *Gastrorevolution! The Age of Slow Food.* University Professors' Program: Boston University, undergraduate honors thesis.

Lieber, Robert J. 2008. "Falling Upwards. Declinism: The Box Set." *World Affairs,* Summer, 48–56.

Lindholm, Charles. 1990. *Charisma.* Cambridge, MA: Basil Blackwell.

Lindholm, Charles. 2002. *The Islamic Middle East: Tradition and Change* (revised edition). Malden, MA: Blackwell.

Lindholm, Charles. 2008. *Culture and Authenticity.* Malden, MA: Blackwell.

Lofland, J., and R. Stark (1965) "Becoming a World-Saver: A Theory of Conversion to a Deviant Perspective." *American Sociological Review,* 30: 862–874.

Lojowsky, M. 2000. "Comes a Time." In Stephanie Guilloud, ed., *Voices from the WTO: An Anthology of Writings from the People Who Shut Down the World Trade Organization,* 12–16. Olympia, WA: Evergreen State College Bookstore.

Loki. 1997. "In the Grape Vine." *The Scorpion,* 18 (Spring), 43–44.

Lorenz, Konrad. 1983. *The Waning of Humaneness.* Reprinted 1987. Robert Warren Kickert, trans. Boston: Little, Brown and Company.

Los Angeles Times. 1999 (December 2). "400 Jailed as Police Occupy Seattle Streets."

Löwi, Michael, and Frei Betto. 2003. "Values of a New Civilization." In William F. Fisher and Thomas Ponniah, eds., *Another World Is Possible: Popular Alternatives to Globalization at the World Social Forum,* 329–337. New York: Zed Books.

Luttwak, Edward. 1999. *Turbo-Capitalism: Winners and Losers in the Global Economy.* New York: Harper Collins Publishers.

Maaga, Mary McCormick. 1998. *Hearing the Voices of Jonestown.* Syracuse, NY: Syracuse University Press.

MacCannell, Dean. 1999. *The Tourist: A New Theory of the Leisure Class.* Berkeley: University of California Press.

Maffesoli, Michel. 1996. *The Time of the Tribes: The Decline of Individualism in Mass Society.* London: Sage.

Maffesoli, Michel. 2009. *Apocalypse.* Paris: CNRS.

Magallanes-Blanco, Claudia. 2008. *The Use of Video for Political Consciousness-Raising in Mexico: An Analysis of Independent Videos about the Zapatistas.* Lewiston, NY: The Edwin Mellen Press.

Makeham, John, ed. 2003. *New Confucianism: A Critical Examination.* New York: Palgrave Macmillan.

Maktabah. 2008. "Two Witnesses of Sayyid Qutbs Hanging." Available at: www .maktabah.net/store/Products/ViewProductDetails.aspx?ProductID=28817&ID= 0#ProductArticles

Mannheim, Karl. 1949. *Ideology and Utopia: An Introduction to the sociology of Knowledge*. (Originally published 1936). London: Routledge & Kegan Paul.

Manuel, Frank E., and Fritzie P. Manuel. 1979. *Utopian Thought in the Western World*. Cambridge, MA: Harvard University Press.

Marcos, Subcomandante. 2000a. *Detrás de nosotros estamos ustedes*. Barcelona: Plaza & Janés Editores.

Marcos, Subcomandante. 2000b. "To Señor Ernesto Zedillo Ponce de Leon." In Ziga Vodovnik, ed., *Ya Basta! Ten Years of the Zapatistas Uprising*, 505–508. Oakland, CA: AK Press, 2004.

Marcos, Subcomandante. 2001a. "The Fourth World War." Irlandesa, trans. Available at: www.inmotionmagazine.com/auto/fourth.html

Marcos, Subcomandante. 2001b. In Juana Ponce de Leon, ed., *Our Word Is Our Weapon: Selected Writings*. New York: Seven Stories Press.

Marcos, Subcomandante. 2004a. "I Shit on All the Revolutionary Vanguards of This Planet." Original 2003 article reprinted in Ziga Vodovnik, ed., *Ya Basta! Ten Years of the Zapatistas Uprising*, 583–588. Oakland, CA: AK Press.

Marcos, Subcomandante. 2004b. "The Seven Loose Pieces of the Global Jigsaw Puzzle: Neoliberalism as a Puzzle." Original 1997 article reprinted in Ziga Vodovnik, ed., *Ya Basta! Ten Years of the Zapatistas Uprising*, pp. 257–278. Oakland, CA: AK Press.

Marcos, Subcomandante. 2005a. In Acción Zapatista Editorial Collective, eds., *Conversations with Durito: Stories of the Zapatistas and Neoliberalism*. New York: Autonomedia.

Marcos, Subcomandante. 2005b (July 1). *EZLN: Sixth Declaration of the Selva Lacandona*. Irlandesa, trans. Available at http://chiapas.indymedia.org/display .php3?article_id=114072

Marcos, Subcomandante. 2007a (October 11). *Palabras del EZLN en la inauguración del Encuentro de Pueblos Indígenas de América*. Available at: www.encuentroindigena .org/?p=39

Marcos, Subcomandante Insurgente. 2007b. In Canek Peña-Vargas and Greg Ruggiero, eds., *The Speed of Dreams: Selected Writings: 2001–2007*. San Francisco: City Lights.

Mariátegui, José Carlos. 2005. *Invitación a la vida heróica. José Carlos Mariátegui. Textos esenciales*. Lima: Fondo Editorial del Congresso del Perú.

Marin, Louis. 1993. "Frontiers of Utopia: Past and Present." *Critical Inquiry*, 19 (3, Spring), 397–420.

Maroni, Roberto. 2008 (April 11). "Lega, garanzia di democrazia." Available at: www.leganord.org

Martinez, Jean-Claude. 2006 (August 11). "Sarkozy et Royal, c'est le même classicisme." *Le Figaro*.

Marvasti, Jamshid A. 2008. "Homegrown 'Worrier' and 'Warrior': Muslims in Europe and the United States." In Jamshid A. Marvasti, ed., *Psycho-Political Aspects of Suicide Warriors, Terrorism and Martyrdom: A Critical View from "Both Sides" in Regard to Cause and Cure*, 78–104. Springfield, IL: Charles C. Thomas.

Mastropaolo, Alfio. 2005. *La mucca pazza della democrazia; Nuove destre, populismo, antipolitica*. Torino: Bollati Boringhieri editore.

Mayorga, Fernando. 2005 (July–December). "La izquierda campesina e indígena en Bolivia: El Movimiento Al Socialismo MAS." *Revista Venezolana de Ciencia Política*, 28, 91–119.

Mazarr, Michael J. 2007. *Unmodern Men in the Modern World: Radical Islam, Terrorism and the War on Modernity*. New York: Cambridge University Press.

McDermott, Terry. 2005. *Perfect Soldiers. The Hijackers: Who They Were, Why They Did It*. New York: HarperCollins Publishers.

McKenna, Terence. 1991. *The Archaic Revival: Speculations on Psychedelic Mushrooms, the Amazon, Virtual Reality, UFOs, Evolution, Shamanism, the Rebirth of the Goddess, and the End of History*. New York: Harper Collins.

McKenna, Terence. 1992. "Re: Evolution." Available at: http://deoxy.org/t_re-evo.htm (words); www.youtube.com/watch?v=xvsZMSni7Ts (audio and visual).

McNally, David. 2002. *Another World Is Possible: Globalization and Anti-Capitalism*. Winnipeg, MB: Arbeiter Ring Publishing.

Mégret, Bruno. 1992. "Preface: Reflections sur le mondialisme." In Jacques Robichez, ed., *Le Mondialisme: Mythe et réalité*, 2nd ed., 7–9. Paris: Éditions Nationales.

Mégret, Bruno. 1997. *L'Alternative Nationale: Les priorités du Front National*. Collection Idées en poche, Paris: Éditions Nationales.

Mégret, Bruno. 2003 (November 15). "Les lignes de fracture: Intervention au Conseil national du MNR." Available at: www.m-n-r.fr/

Mégret, Bruno. 2006. *L'autre scénario: Pour la France et l'Europe*. Paris: Éditions Cité Liberté.

Melucci, Alberto. 1989. In John Keane and Paul Mier, eds., *Nomads of the Present: Social Movements and Individual Needs in Contemporary Society*. London: Hutchinson Radius.

Melucci, Alberto. 1996. *Challenging Codes: Collective Action in the Information Age*. New York: Cambridge University Press.

Mentinis, Mihalis. 2006. *Zapatistas: The Chiapas Revolt and What It Means for Radical Politics*. Ann Arbor, MI: Pluto Press.

Michael, George. 2006. *The Enemy of My Enemy: The Alarming Convergence of Militant Islam and the Extreme Right*. Lawrence: University Press of Kansas.

Michael, George. 2008. *Willis Carto and the American Far Right*, Gainesville: University Press of Florida.

Michelet, Jules. 1953. *History of the French Revolution*. Partially reprinted 1967; originally published 1847–1853. Charles Cocks, trans; Gordon Wright, ed. Chicago: University of Chicago Press.

Milloz, Pierre. 1992. "Le mondialisme: un mot qui cache une réalité." In Jacques Robichez, ed., *Le Mondialisme: Mythe et réalité*, 2nd ed., 81–106. Paris: Éditions Nationales.

Ministerio del Poder Popular para la Participación y Protección Social (MPS). 2008 (April 13). "Anunciado el lanzamiento de la misión 13 de abril."

Mittelman, James H. 2004. *Whither Globalization? The Vortex of Knowledge and Ideology*. New York: Routledge.

Moeller van den Bruck, Arthur. 1923. *Germany's Third Empire*. Reprinted 1934. E. O. Lorimer, ed. London: George Allen & Unwin.

Monbiot, George. 2003. *Manifesto for a New World Order*. New York: The New Press.

Montoya Rojas, Rodrigo. 2005. *De la utopía andina al socialismo mágico Antropología, Historia y Política: en el Perú*. Cusco, Perú: Instituto Nacional de Cultura.

Moore, D. 1995. "Raves and the Bohemian Search for Self and Community. A Contribution to the Anthropology of Public Events." *Anthropological Forum*, 7 (2), 193–214.

Morales, Evo. 2002 (August 25). "El neoliberalismo es la reedición del capitalismo salvaje." Interview by Pablo Stefanoni, *La Arena/La Insignia*. Available at: www .lainsignia.org/2002/agosto/ibe_117.htm

Morales, Evo. 2003 (November 26). "Legalizing the Colonization of the Americas," Interview by Ben Dangl. *ZNet*. Available at: www.zmag.org/content/showarticle .cfm?ItemID=4569

Morales, Evo. 2006a (May 27). "Palabras del Presidente de la Republica, Evo Morales Ayma, en la firma de los acuerdos de cooperacion y solidaridad." La Paz: Presidencia de la Republica de Bolivia, Discursos e Intervenciones.

Morales, Evo. 2006b (October 24). "Palabras del Presidente de la República, Evo Morales Ayma en la inauguracion del seminario internacional de derechos humanos." Santa Cruz: Presidencia de la Republica de Bolivia, Discursos e Intervenciones.

Morales, Evo. 2006c (August 6). "Palabras del Presidente de la Republica, Evo Morales Ayma, en la instalacion de la Asamblea Constituyente." Sucre: Agencia Boliviana de Información.

Morales, Evo. 2006d (October 12). "Palabras del Presidente de la República, Evo Morales Ayma, en la movilización por los 514 años de colonialismo." La Paz: Agencia Boliviana de Información.

Morales, Evo. 2006e. *La Revolución Democrática y cultural: Diez discursos de Evo Morales*. La Paz: Editorial Malatesta.

Morales, Evo. 2007a (August 6). "Mensaje-Informe del Presidente Evo Morales Ayma, en el 182 aniversario de fundación de la República de Bolivia," Sucre: Agencia Boliviana de Información (ABI).

Morales, Evo. 2007b (October 8). "Palabras del Presidente de la República, Evo Morales Ayma, en el acto por los 40 años de la muerte de Ernesto Che Guevara." Vallegrande, Santa Cruz: Agencia Boliviana de Información (ABI).

Morales, Evo. 2007c (October 10). "Palabras del Presidente de la República, Evo Morales Ayma, en el acto de homenaje a las personas que lucharon por la democracia en Bolivia, realizado en Palacio Quemado." La Paz: Agencia Boliviana de Información (ABI).

Morales, Evo. 2007d (October 10). "Palabras del Presidente de la República, Evo Morales Ayma, en el Congreso Nacional durante el homenaje a los 25 años de la democracia." La Paz: Agencia Boliviana de Información (ABI).

Morales, Evo. 2007e (November 7). "Palabras del Presidente de la República, Evo Morales Ayma, en la promulgación de la Ley de Declaración de las Naciones Unidas sobre los derechos de los pueblos indigenas." La Paz: Agencia Boliviana de Información (ABI).

Morales, Evo. 2007f (September 24). "Palabras del Presidente de la Republica, Evo Morales Ayma, en la 62 sesion de la Asamblea General de las Naciones Unidas ONU, sobre el medio ambiente." New York: Agencia Boliviana de Información (ABI).

Morales, Evo. 2008a (July 18). "Carta del Presidente Evo Morales a la Organización Mundial del Comercio."

Morales, Evo. 2008b (January 26). "Palabras del Presidente de la República, Evo Morales Ayma, en la VI Cumbre de la Alternativa Bolivariana para los Pueblos de America y el Caribe ALBA." Caracas: Agencia Boliviana de Información (ABI).

Morales, Evo. 2008c (March 7). "Palabras del Presidente de la Republica, Evo Morales Ayma, en su intervencion durante la XX Cumbre del grupo de Rio." Santo Domingo, Dominican Republic: Agencia Boliviana de Información (ABI).

Morales, Evo. 2008d (August 10). "Palabras del Presidente de la Republica, Evo Morales Ayma, en su mensaje al pais luego de ser ratificado con el 63 por ciento en el referendo revocatorio realizado este 10 de Agosto." Agencia Boliviana de Información.

Morin, Edgar. 2006 (February). "Realism and Utopia." Diogenes, 53 (1), 135–144.

Mouffe, Chantal. 2005. "The 'End of Politics' and the Challenge of Right-wing Populism." In Francisco Panizza, ed., Populism and the Mirror of Democracy, 50–71. New York: Verso.

Mouvement National Républicain (MNR). 2000. Pour que vive la France: Programme du MNR, Paris: Éditions Cité Liberté.

Mouvement National Républicain (MNR). 2008. "Démocratie." Available at: www.m-n-r.net/aaz39.htm

Movimiento al Socialismo (MAS). 2001. "Nuestros Principios Ideologicos." Available at: www.masbolivia.org/mas/programa/principios.htm

MSNBC. 2008 (October 21). "In Hard Times, Some Flirt with Survivalism."

Mudde, Cas. 2007. *Populist Radical Right Parties in Europe*. New York: Cambridge University Press.

Mueller, John. 1989. *Retreat from Doomsday: The Obsolescence of Major War*. Reprinted 1996. Rochester, NY: University of Rochester Press.

Munck, Ronaldo. 2004. "Global Civil Society: Myths and Prospects." In Rupert Taylor, ed., *Creating a Better World: Interpreting Global Civil Society*, 13–26. Bloomfield CT: Kumarian Press.

Munck, Ronaldo. 2007. *Globalization and Contestation: The New Great Counter-Movement*. New York: Routledge.

Muñoz, Agustin Blanco. 1998. *Habla El Comandante Hugo Chávez Frias*. Caracas: Universidad Central de Venezuela.

Murphy, Gillian Hughes. 2004. "The Seattle WTO Protests: Building a Global Movement." In Rupert Taylor, ed., *Creating a Better World: Interpreting Global Civil Society*, 27–42. Bloomfield CT: Kumarian Press.

Musso, Valter, Alessandra Abbona, and Paola Nano. 2005 (November 5). "4th Slow Food International Congress." *Slow Food International*. Available at: http://press.slowfood.com/press/eng/leggi.lasso?cod=527&ln=en

El Nacional. 2006 (September 9). "Chávez creará partido único de la revolución a mediados de 2007."

El Nacional. 2007 (November 5). "Evo Morales dice que permanecerá mucho tiempo en el poder en Bolivia."

El Nacional. 2009. "Chávez llama a Obama 'pobre ignorante,'" March 23.

National Front (NF). 1993. *300 Mesures Pour la Renaissance de la France: Front National, Programme de Gouvernement*. Paris; Éditions Nationales.

National Front (NF). 2001. "L' Universalité, la Mémoire et le Sacré," Available at: www.frontnational.com/doc_id_france.php

National Front (NF). 2002. "Les mythes de la mondialisation," Available at www.frontnational.com/argumentaires/mythesdelamondialisation.php

National-Hebdo. 1996 (April 18–24). "Clovis—Joan of Arc—Le Pen: The Same Struggle."

National Public Radio. 2004 (November 24). "Report from the Salone del Gusto," *Morning Edition*.

Negri, Antonio. 2003. *Reflections on Empire*. Reprinted 2008. Ed Emery, trans. Malden, MA: Polity Press.

New York Times (NYT). 2002, April 16. "Bush Officials Met with Venezuelans Who Ousted Leader,"

New York Times (NYT). 2008a (November 14). "Frugal Mexico—Frugal Traveler Blog."

New York Times (NYT). 2008b (April 4). "Rising Leader for Next Phase of Al Qaeda's War."

New Tork Times Magazine. 2009 (April 19). "The End Is Near! Yay," 28–35.

Niethammer, Lutz. 1992. *Posthistoire: Has History Come to an End?* Translated from the original 1989 German edition by Patrick Camiller. London: Verso.

Nietzsche, Friedrich. 1891. *Thus Spoke Zarathustra: A Book for All and None.* Reprinted 2006. Adrian del Caro, trans. New York: Cambridge University Press.

Niezen, Ronald. 2004. *A World beyond Difference: Cultural Identity in the Age of Globalization.* Malden, MA: Blackwell Publishing.

Noël, Alain, and Jean-Philippe Thérien. 2008. *Left and Right in Global Politics.* New York: Cambridge University Press.

Northern League (NL). 2002 (September). "Ragionare sull' Immigrazione: La Nuova Legge Bossi." Segreteria Politica Federale. Available at: www.padaniaoffice.org/pdf/scuola_politica_federale/baveno4_5_10_03/baveno_marelli.pdf

Notes from Nowhere. 2003. *We Are Everywhere: The Irresistible Rise of Global Anticapitalism.* New York: Verso.

Nunes, Rodrigo. 2005. "The Intercontinental Youth Camp as the Unthought of the World Social Forum." *Ephemera*, 5 (2), 277–296.

Olaveson, Tim. 2004. "'Connectedness' and the Rave Experience: Rave as New Religious Movement?" In Graham St. John, ed., *Rave Culture and Religion*, 85–106. New York: Routledge.

Olesen, Thomas. 2005. *International Zapatismo: The Construction of Solidarity in the Age of Globalization.* New York: Zed Books.

Olesen, Thomas. 2006. "Global Democratic Protest: The Chiapas Connection," In Ingo K. Richter, Sabine Berking, and Ralf Muller-Schmid, eds., *Building a Transnational Civil Society; Global Issues and Global Actors.* New York: Palgrave Macmillan, 135–155.

O'Meara, Michael. 2004. *New Culture, New Right: Anti-Liberalism in Postmodern Europe.* Bloomington, IN: 1st Books.

Oppenheimer, Michael F. 2008. "The End of Liberal Globalization." *World Policy Journal*, 24 (4, Winter), 1–9.

Ortiz, Pedro, Marco Brige, and Rogério Ferrari. 2007. *Zapatistas: A Velocidade do Sonho*, Brasília: Thesaurus Editora.

Pacult, Paul F. 2005. *A Double Scotch: How Chivas Regal and The Glenlivet Became Global Icons.* New York: John Wiley and Sons.

La Padania. 2005 (June 22). "Il ritorno di Umberto Bossi."

Partido Nacional Renovador (PNR). 2006 (July 3). "Liberdade, Igualdade, Fraternidade?"

Partridge, Christopher. 2006. "The Spiritual and the Revolutionary: Alternative Spirituality, British Free Festivals, and the Emergence of Rave Culture." *Culture and Religion* 7 (1), 42–60.

Petrini, Carlo. 2001. *Slow Food: The Case for Taste*, William McCuaig, trans. New York: Columbia University Press.

Petrini, Carlo. 2007a. *Slow Food Nation: Why Our Food Should Be Good, Clean and Fair*. New York: Penguin Books.

Petrini, Carlo. 2007b (9 Nov). Speech delivered at the Slow Food International Congress in Puebla, Mexico. Transcription by Siv Lie.

Petrini, Carlo. 2007c. *Taking Back Life*. Available at: http://content.slowfood.it/upload/3E6E345B143db18EA9jQk3D9FAE7/files/Terraeluna_EN.pdf

Petrini, Carlo, and Gigi Padovani. 2005. *Slow Food Revolution: A New Culture for Eating and Living*. Francesca Santovetti, trans. New York: Rizzoli.

Pink, Sarah. 2008 (June). "Re-thinking Contemporary Activism: From Community to Emplaced Sociality." *Ethnos: Journal of Anthropology*, 73 (2), 163–188.

Pinto, Darwin, and Roberto Navia. 2007. *Un Tal Evo: Biografía no Autorizada*. Santa Cruz de la Sierra, Bolivia: Editorial El País.

Pinto-Coelho, José. 2006 (June 14). E-mail communication.

Pinto-Coelho, José. 2007a (January 1). "Do Presidente aos Nacionalistas." Available at: www.pnr.pt

Pinto-Coelho, José. 2007b (June 10). "10 de Junho—Discurso." Available at: www.pnr.pt

Pinto-Coelho, José. 2007c (December 1). "1 de Dezembro—Discurso." Available at: www.pnr.pt

Polak, Frederik L. 1966. "Utopia and Cultural Renewal." In Frank E. Manuel, ed., *Utopias and Utopian Thought*, 281–295. Cambridge, MA: The Riverside Press.

Polanyi, Karl. 1944. *The Great Transformation: The Political and Economic Origins of Our Time*. Reprinted 2001. Boston: Beacon Press.

Poliakov, Leon. 1980. *La Causalité diabolique; essai sur l'origine des persécutions*. Paris: Calmann-Lévy.

Popol Vuh: The Mayan Book of the Dawn of Life. Reprinted 1986. Dennis Tedlock, trans. New York: Simon & Schuster.

Popper, Karl. 1947. "Utopia and Violence." Reprinted 1969 in *Conjectures and Refutations: The Growth of Scientific Knowledge*, 355–363. London: Routledge and Kegan Paul.

Postero, Nancy Grey. 2007 (April). "Andean Utopias in Evo Morales's Bolivia." *Latin American and Caribbean Ethnic Studies*, 2, 1, 1–28.

Price, Charles, Donald Nonini, and Erich Fox Tree. 2008. "Grounded Utopian Movements: Subjects of Neglect." *Anthropological Quarterly*, 81, (1, Winter), 127–159.

Price, Tony Curzon. 2009 (February 9). "The Liberty of the Networked (1)." Available at: www.opendemocracy.net/article/email/the-liberty-of-the-networked-part-1 "The liberty of the networked (pt 2)"; www.opendemocracy.net/article/email/the-liberty-of-the-networked-pt-2

Proyecto Aurora. 1993 (May). "Manifiesto del Proyecto Cultural Aurora," *Hespérides: Revista de Estudios del Proyecto Cultural Aurora*, 1, 103–106.

Proyecto Aurora. 1994. I. El Proyecto Aurora: una comunidad de reflexión por una nueva visión del mundo. Available at: http://es.geocities.com/proaurora_es/proyecto.htm

Qutb, Sayyid. 2006. *Milestones*. Birmingham, U.K.: Makrabah Booksellers.

Radio Nacional de Venezuela (RNV). 2007a (November 4). "Presidente Chávez envió pésame a familiars de estudiantes en el Zulia."

Radio Nacional de Venezuela (RNV). 2007b (November 28). "Video transmitido por CNN podría ser instigación al magnicidio."

Rajchenberger, Enrique, and Catherine Héau-Lambert. 1998. "History and Symbolism in the Zapatista Movement." In John Holloway and Eloína Peláez, eds., *Zapatista!: Reinventing Revolution in Mexico*. Sterling, VA: Pluto Press.

Ramírez, Gloria Muñoz. 2003. *EZLN: 20 y 10, el fuego y la palabra*. Mexico City: La Jornada Ediciones.

Ravello, Enrique. 2005. "Pedro I el Grande, el Zar que miró a Europa." *Nihil ObstAt: Revista de ideas, cultura y metapolítica*, 6 (Autumn/Winter), 83–92.

La Razón. 2007a (December 7). "Evo acusa a la Embajada de EEUU de liderar el complot."

La Razón. 2007b, October 12. "Evo asegura que la Iglesia se allió con la oligarquia para dominar."

La Razón. 2007c (October 25). "Evo Pueblo utiliza la ficción para enlazar toda una vida."

La Razón. 2008a (August 11). "El No a Morales supera el 50% en cuatro regiones opositoras."

La Razón. 2008b (April 2). "Se va el vocero de Evo y revela crisis interna."

Real Food Challenge (RFC). 2007. "What is Real Food?" Available at: http://realfoodchallenge.org/about/realfood

Reel, Monte. 2008 (February 2). "Bolivia's Burning Question: Who May Dispense Justice?" *The Washington Post*.

Reinsborough, Patrick. 2000 (July). "Victory for the U'wa." *Earth First! The Radical Environmental Journal*, 20 (6), 4.

Reinsborough, Patrick. 2004. "Decolonizing the Revolutionary Imagination: Values Crisis, the Politics of Reality, and Why There's Going to Be a Common-Sense Revolution in This Generation." In David Solnit, ed., *Globalize Liberation: How to*

Uproot the System and Build a Better World, 161–210. San Francisco: City Lights Books.

Reitan, Ruth. 2007. *Global Activism*. New York: Routledge.

Reynolds, Simon. 1999. *Generation Ecstasy: Into the World of Techno and Rave Culture*. London: Routledge.

Rietveld, Hillegonda C. 2004. "Ephemeral Spirit: Sacrificial Cyborg and Communal Soul." In Graham St. John, ed., *Rave Culture and Religion*, 46–62. London: Routledge.

Rill, Byran. 2006. "Rave, Communitas, and Embodied Idealism." *Music Therapy Today*, 7 (3), 648–660.

Ritzer, George. 1998. The McDonaldization Thesis: Explorations and Extensions. New York: Sage.

Rochlin, James. 2007. "Latin America's Left Turn and the New Strategic Landscape: The Case of Bolivia." *Third World Quarterly*, 28, 7, 1327–1342.

Rodríguez, Francisco. 2008. "Venezuela's Revolution in Decline," *World Policy Journal*, 25, 1 (Spring), 45–58.

Rohsenow, John S. 2002. *ABC Dictionary of Chinese Proverbs*. Honolulu: University of Hawaii Press.

Rootes, Christopher. 2004. "Global Civil Society and the Lessons of European Environmentalism." In Rupert Taylor, ed., *Creating a Better World: Interpreting Global Civil Society*, 147–169. Bloomfield, CT: Kumarian Press.

Rosanvallon, Pierre. 2006. In Samuel Moyn, ed., *Democracy Past and Future*. New York: Columbia University Press.

Rosen, Fred. 2005 (November 22). "Venezuela's New Popular Movements Grow from Above and from Below." *IRC Americas Program Special Report*, 1–5.

Rosenthal, John. 2006. "The French Path to Jihad." *Policy Review* 139 (October–November): 39–59.

Ross, John. 2000. *The War against Oblivion: Zapatista Chronicles, 1994–2000*. Monroe, ME: Common Courage Press.

Ross, John. 2006. *Zapatistas!* New York: Nation Books.

Ross, John. 2009 (February 18). "Zapatista Villages Become Hot Tourist Destinations." *CMI*. Available at: http://chiapas.indymedia.org/display.php3?article_id= 162317

Rovira, Guiomar. 2003. *EZLN: Documentos y comunicados 5. La Marcha del Color de la Tierra*. Mexico City: Ediciones Era.

Roy, Olivier. 1994. *The Failure of Political Islam*. Original French edition, 1992. Cambridge, MA: Harvard University Press.

Roy, Olivier. 2004. *Globalized Islam: The Search for a New Ummah*. New York: Columbia University Press.

Ruggiero, Vincenzo. 2002. "'ATTAC: A Global Social Movement?" *Social Justice*, 29 (1–2), 48–60.

Rupert, Mark. 2000. *Ideologies of Globalization: Contending Visions of a New World Order.* New York: Routledge.

Russell, Charles A., and Bowman H. Miller. 1983. "Profile of a Terrorist." In Lawrence Zelic Freedman and Yonah Alexander, eds., *Perspectives on Terrorism*, 45–60. Wilmington, DE: Scholarly Resources.

Sabatini, Davide. 1997. *L'internazionale di Mussolini: La diffusione del fascismo in Europa nel progetto politico di Asvero Gravelli.* Rome: Edizioni Tusculum.

Sageman, Marc. 2004. *Understanding Terror Networks.* Philadelphia: University of Pennsylvania Press.

St. John, Graham. 2004a. "The Difference Engine: Liberation and the Rave Imaginary." In Graham St. John, ed., *Rave Culture and Religion*, 19–45. New York: Routledge.

St. John, Graham. 2004b. "Techno Millennium: Dance, Ecology and Future Primitives." In Graham St. John, ed., *Rave Culture and Religion*, 213–235. New York: Routledge.

Sanders, Catherine Edwards. 2005. *Wicca's Charm: Understanding the Spiritual Hunger behind the Rise of Modern Witchcraft and Pagan Spirituality.* Colorado Springs, CO: Waterbrook Press.

Sanderson, Stephen K. 2005. *Revolutions: A Worldwide Introduction to Political and Social Change.* Boulder, CO: Paradigm Publishers.

Santos, Boaventura de Sousa. 2007. *The Rise of the Global Left: The World Social Forum and Beyond.* London: Zed Books.

Saramago, José. 2007 (June 13). "Escritor apela à insubmissão." *Público.*

Sassen, Saskia. 2007. *A Sociology of Globalization.* New York: W. W. Norton & Company.

Schmitt, Carl. 1950. *The Nomos of the Earth in the International Law of the Jus Publicum Europaeum.* Reprinted 2003. G. L. Ulmen, trans. New York: Telos Press.

Schmitt, Carl. 1942. *Land and Sea.* Reprinted 1954. Simona Draghici, trans. Washington DC: Plutarch Press.

Seligman, Adam, Robert Weller, Michael Puett, and Bennet Simon. 2008. *Ritual and Its Consequences: An Essay on the Limits of Sincerity.* New York: Oxford University Press.

Seremetakis, C. Nadia. 1994. "The Memory of the Senses, Part II: Still Acts." In C. Nadia Seremetakis, ed., *The Senses Still: Perception and Memory in the Material Culture of Modernity*, 23–44. Boulder, CO: Westview.

Shklar, Judith N. 1957. *After Utopia: The Decline of Political Faith.* Reprinted 1969. Princeton, NJ: Princeton University Press.

Shrestha, Nanda, and Dennis Conway. 2006. "Globalization Cultural Challenges: Homogenization, Hybridization and Heightened Identity." In Dennis Conway and

Nik Heynen, eds., *Globalization's Contradictions: Geographies of Discipline, Destruction and Transformation*, 196–211. New York: Routledge.

Shuman, Michael E. 2006. *The Small-Mart Revolution: How Local Businesses Are Beating the Global Competition*. San Francisco: Berrett-Koehler Publishers.

Simmons, Harvey G. 2003. "The French and European Extreme Right and Globalization." Unpublished paper.

Sivak, Martín. 2008. *Jefazo: Retrato íntimo de Evo Morales*. Buenos Aires: Editorial Sudamericana.

Slow Food Foundation for Biodiversity. 2003. Available at: www.slowfoodfoundation .com/eng/fondazione.lasso

Smith, Anthony D. 1995. *Nations and Nationalism in a Global Era*. Cambridge, U.K.: Polity Press.

Smith, Jackie, Marina Karides, Marc Becker, Dorval Brunelle, Christopher Chase-Dunn, Donatella della Porta, Rosalba Icaza Garza, Jeffrey S. Juris, Lorenzo Mosca, Ellen Reese, Peter (Jay) Smith, and Rolando Vazquez. 2008. *Global Democracy and the World Social Forums*. Boulder, CO: Paradigm Publishers.

Sneed, Paul. 2008. "Favela Utopias: The *Bailes Funk* in Rio's Crisis of Social Exclusion and Violence. " *Latin American Research Review*, 43 (2), 57–79.

Snyder, Robert S. 1999. "The End of Revolution." *The Review of Politics*. 61 (1, Winter), 5–28.

Solnit, David, ed. 2004. *Globalize Liberation: How to Uproot the System and Build a Better World*. San Francisco: City Lights Books.

Solomon, Alisa. 2005 (March 21). "Porto Alegre Postcard." *The Nation*. Available at www.thenation.com/doc/20050321/solomon

Solzhenitsyn, Aleksandr Isayevich. 1986. *The Gulag Archipelago: 1918–1956. An Experiment in Literary Investigation*. Thomas P. Whitney and Harry Willets, trans. London: Collins Harvill.

Solzhenitsyn, Aleksandr Isayevich. 1993, September 14. "We Have Ceased to See the Purpose." Address to the International Academy of Philosophy, Liechtenstein. Reprinted 2006 in Edward E. Ericson Jr. and Daniel F. Mahoney, eds., *The Solzhenitsyn Reader: New and Essential Writings. 1947–2005*, 591–601. Wilmington, DE: Intercollegiate Studies Institute.

Sombart, Werner. 2001. In Nico Stehr and Reiner Grundmann, eds., *Economic Life in the Modern Age*. New Brunswick, NJ: Transaction Publishers.

Sonntag, Heinz. 2006 (April 9). "El fascismo de los años treinta ha vuelto en una edición más moderna." *El Nacional*.

Southgate, Troy. 2007. *Tradition & Revolution: Collected Writings*. Aarhus, Denmark: Integral Tradition Publishing.

Stahler-Sholk, Richard. 2007. "Resisting Neoliberal Homogenization: The Zapatista Autonomy Movement." *Latin American Perspectives*, 34, 153 (2, March), 48–63.

Steger, Manfred. B. 2003. *Globalization: A Very Short Introduction*. Oxford, U.K.: Oxford University Press.

Steger, Manfred B. 2007. "Globalization and Ideology." In George Ritzer, ed., *The Blackwell Companion to Globalization*, 367–381. Malden, MA: Blackwell Publishing.

Steger, Manfred B. 2008. *The Rise of the Global Imaginary: Political Ideologies from the French Revolution to the Global War on Terror*. New York: Oxford University Press.

Stern, Fritz. 1974. "The Politics of Cultural Despair: A Study in the Rise of the Germanic Ideology. Reprinted from original 1961 publication. Berkeley: University of California Press, 1974.

Stiglitz, Joseph E. 2001. "Foreword." In Karl Polanyi, *The Great Transformation: The Political and Economic Origins of Our Time*, vii–xvii. Boston: Beacon Press.

Stoll, Steven. 2008. *The Great Delusion: A Mad Inventor, Death in the Tropics, and the Utopian Origins of Economic Growth*. New York: Hill and Wang.

Students for a Democratic Society (SDS). 1962. *The Port Huron Statement*. Reprinted 2004. Chicago: Charles H. Kerr Publishing Company.

Sunic, Tomislav. 1990. *Against Democracy and Equality: The European New Right*. New York: Peter Lang.

Sunic, Tomislav. 2008. *Homo Americanus: Hijo de la Era Posmoderna*. Marcellí Bellsolà, trans. Barcelona: Ediciones Nueva República.

Taguieff, Pierre-André. 1994. *Sur la Nouvelle Droite: Jalons d'une Analyse Critique*. Paris: Descartes & Cie.

Talmon, Jacob L. 1960. *Political Messianism: The Romantic Phase*. Reprinted 1968. New York: Frederick A. Praeger.

Tarchi, Marco. 1987 (January–April). "La Colonizzazione Sottile: 'American Way of Life' e dinamica sociale." *Trasgressioni: Rivista Quadrimestrale di Cultura Politica*, II, 1, 59–69.

Tarchi, Marco. 1998 (January–April). "Il 'crimine' etnopluralista," *Trasgressioni: Rivista Quadrimestrale di Cultura Politica*, 12 (1), 91–97.

Tarchi, Marco. 1999a (May–August). "Alternativa senza Barbarie: Una risposta a Sergio Benvenuto." *Trasgressioni: Rivista Quadrimestrale di Cultura Politica*, 14 (2), 97–102.

Tarchi, Marco. 1999b (February). "Italie, Europe et Nouvelle Droite." *Éléments pour la civilization européenne*, 94.

Tarchi, Marco. 2004. *Contro l'Americanismo*. Roma-Bari: Laterza.

Tarchi, Marco. 2007a (November–December). "A chi giova l'occidentalismo?" *Diorama Letterario*, 286, 1–4.

Tarchi, Marco. 2007b (November-December). "Il peso del passato e le immagini del futuro." *Diorama Letterario*, 286, 25–28.

Tarrow, Sidney. 2005a. "The Dualities of Transnational Contention: 'Two Activist Solitudes' or a New World Altogether?" *Mobilization* 101: 53–72.

Tarrow, Sidney. 2005b. *The New Transnational Activism*. New York: Cambridge University Press.

Taylor, Rupert. 2004. "Interpreting Global Civil Society." In Rupert Taylor, ed., *Creating a Better World: Interpreting Global Civil Society*, 1–12. Bloomfield, CT: Kumarian Press.

Televisora Venezolana Social (TVes). 2007. "Ideales de TVes." Available at: http://tves .org.ve/el-canal/3/21.

Terra e Libertà/Critical Wine. 2004. *Sensibilità planetarie, agricultura contadina e rivoluzione dei consumi*. Rome: DeriveApprodi.

Thomson, Sinclair. 2002. *We Alone Will Rule: Native Andean Politics in the Age of Insurgency*. Madison: University of Wisconsin Press.

Tilly, Charles. 2004. *Social Movements: 1768–2004*. Boulder, CO: Paradigm Publishers.

Tormey, Simon. 2005. "From Utopian Worlds to Utopian Spaces: Reflections on the Contemporary Radical Imaginary and the Social Forum Process." *Ephemera*, 5(2), 394–408.

Touraine, Alain. 1981. *The Voice and the Eye: An Analysis of Social Movements*. Alan Duff, trans. New York: Cambridge University Press.

Touraine, Alain. 2007. *A New Paradigm for Understanding Today's World*. Gregory Elliott, trans. Cambridge, U.K.: Polity Press.

Turner, Bryan S. 2007. "The Futures of Globalization." In George Ritzer, ed., *The Blackwell Companion to Globalization*, 675–692. Malden, MA: Blackwell Publishing.

Ulmen, Gary. 1993. "The concept of 'Nomos': Introduction to Schmitt's 'Appropriation/distribution/production,'" *Telos*, 95 (Spring), 39–52.

Ultimas Noticias. 2006 (November 27). "Chávez: No nos dejemos invadir por el triunfalismo."

Umland, Andreas. 2006 (June 1). "The Philosophy behind the Nationalism." *The Moscow Times*.

Umland, Andreas. 2009 (May 29). "Fascist Tendencies in Russia's Political Establishment," *History News Network*.

El Universal. 2008 (April 7). "ABP: Rechazamos utilizar aulas como laboratorios para implantar ideologización."

Valéry, Paul. 1922. "The European." In *History and Politics*. Reprinted 1962. Denise Folliot and Jackson Mathews, trans. Bollingen Series 45 (10), 307–323. New York: Pantheon Books.

Van Cott, Donna Lee. 2007. "Latin America's Indigenous Peoples." *Journal of Democracy*, 18 (4, October), 127–141.

Van Cott, Donna Lee. 2008. *Radical Democracy in the Andes*. New York: Cambridge University Press.

Varese, Stefano. 2006. *Witness to Sovereignty: Essays on the Indian Movement in Latin America*. Copenhagen: International Work Group for Indigenous Affairs.

Veseth, Michael. 2005. *Globaloney: Unraveling the Myths of Globalization*. Boston, MA: Rowman & Littlefield Publishers.

The Viand Zine #1. 2007 (April). Available at: www.viand.net/zines/zine1.html.

Walker, Michael. 1984. "Editorial." *The Scorpion*, 7 (Summer), 2.

Walker, Michael. 1986a. "Against All Totalitarianisms." *The Scorpion*, 10 (Autumn), 3–6.

Walker, Michael. 1986b. "We, the Other Europeans." *The Scorpion*, 9 (Spring), 9–12.

Walker, Michael. 1993. "Running the Time Machine," *The Scorpion*, 16 (Summer), 3–20.

Walker, Michael. 2006. "Democracy We Presume? Michael Walker Asks Himself What Democracy Really Is in Theory and in Practice." *The Scorpion*, 24, 3–19.

Walker, Michael. 2008 (April 13). E-mail communication.

Wallace, A. F. C. 1956. "Revitalization Movements." *American Anthropologist* 58, 264–281.

Wallerstein, Immanuel. 1998. *Utopistics: Or Historical Choices of the Twenty-First Century*. New York: The New Press.

Wallerstein, Immanuel. 2002 (Nov/Dec). *New Left Review*, 18, 29–39.

Washington Post. 2008 (May 1). "Bounties a Bust in Hunt for Al-Qaeda."

Waters, Alice. 2006 (September 11). "Slow Food Nation." *The Nation*, 283 (7), 13.

Webb, Adam, K. 2006. *Beyond the Global Culture War*. New York: Routledge.

Weber, Max. 2001. *The Protestant Ethic and the Spirit of Capitalism*. Stephen Kalberg, trans. London: Taylor and Francis.

Weiner, Sarah. 2005. *The Slow Food Companion*. Bra (Cn), Italy: Slow Food. Available at: www.slowfoodgtc.com/pdf/COMPANION_ENG.PDF

Whitaker, Chico. 2004. "The WSF as Open Space." In Jai Sen, Anita Anand, Arturo Escobar, and Peter Waterman, eds., *World Social Forum: Challenging Empires*, 111–121. New Delhi, The Viveka Foundation.

Wiarda, Howard J. 2007. "Has the 'End of History' Arrived?" In Howard J. Wiarda, ed.. *Globalization: Universal Trends, Regional Implications*, 52–77. Boston: Northeastern University Press.

Winter, Jay. 2006. *Dreams of Peace and Freedom: Utopian Moments in the 20th Century*. New Haven, CT: Yale University Press.

Wintrebert, Raphaël. 2007. *Attac, la politique autrement? Enquête sur l'histoire et la crise d'une organization militante*. Paris: Éditions La Découverte.

World Social Forum (WSF). 2002. "Charter of Principles." Available at: www.forumsocialmundial.org.br/main.php?id_menu=4&cd_language=2

Worsley, Peter. *The Trumpet Shall Sound: A Study of "Cargo" Cults in Melanesia.* London: MacGibbon & Kee, 1968.

Yeats, William Butler. 1994. *The Collected Poems of W. B. Yeats.* Originally published 1920. London: Wordsworth Editions.

Young, Zoe. 1999. "NGOs and the Global Environmental Facility: Friendly Foes?" *Environmental Politics*, 8 (1), 243–267.

Zago, Angela. 1992. *La Rebelión de los Angeles.* Caracas: Fuentes Editores.

Zapatistas. 1998. In Greg Ruggiero and Stuart Sahulka, eds., *Zapatista Encuentro: Documents from the 1996 Encounter for Humanity and against Neoliberalism.* New York: Seven Stories Press.

Zelmanov, Elaine. 2003 (May 5). "Preaching a Slow Approach." *Mother Jones.* Available at: www.motherjones.com/news/featurex/2003/05/we_406_01.html

Žižek, Slavoj. 2008. *In Defense of Lost Causes.* New York: Verso.

Zolberg, Aristide R. 1972. "Frantz Fanon." In Maurice Cranston, ed., *Prophetic Politics: Critical Interpretations of the Revolutionary Impulse.* New York: A Touchstone Book, 119–136.

Zúquete, José Pedro. 2007. *Missionary Politics in Contemporary Europe.* Syracuse, NY: Syracuse University Press.

Zúquete, José Pedro. 2008. "The Missionary Politics of Hugo Chávez," *Latin American Politics and Society*, 50, 1 (Spring), 91–121.

INDEX

Abreu e Lima, José Ignacio Ribeiro, 33
Abu-Jandal, 150
Adorno, Theodor, 10
Afghanistan, 122, 125, 126, 133
ALBA. *See* Bolivarian Alternative for Latin America and the Caribbean
Algeria, 133
Ali, 124
Alter-globalization, 2, 84, 88, 97, 101, 170
Amaru, Túpac, 40–41
Amin, Samir, 160
Andrews, Cecile, 111
Anticolonialism, 4
Apocalyptic sects, 7
ARCI, 103
Arcigola, 104
Arendt, Hannah, 5
Aron, Raymond, 5
Assassins, 125
ATTAC, 84–87, 160, 166, 169
Aum Shinrikyo, 7
Aurora movements: commonalities among, 8–10, 153–56; and communication, 157–58; critique of, 167–72; defined, 2; and direct democracy, 162–63; emergence of, 8–10; future of, 172–75; goals of, 3, 8–9, 164–67; identity in, 160–61; ideology of, 3; intellectual dimension of, 163; interrelations of, 158–59; left vs. right in, 168–69; and myths of origins/rebirth, 165; organization of, 157–64; totalitarian dangers of, 170–71; and transformation of humanity, 153–55, 164–67, 170; as

vanguards, 162; varieties of, 10, 152–53; and violence, 171
Authenticity, 16
Aymara Indians, 38, 43
Azzam, Abdullah, 123, 130, 132, 136, 145, 150, 205*n*7

Babeuf, Gracchus, 4
Bakr, Abu, 124
Bakri Muhammad, Omar, 207*n*52
Banna, Hasan al-, 135
Barber, Benjamin, 8
Battle of Seattle, 2, 85–86
Bauman, Zygmunt, 8
BeGood network, 110
Belafonte, Harry, 183*n*129
Bell, Daniel, 5, 178*n*29
Bello, Walden, 160
Berlin, Isaiah, 6
Bernanos, Georges, 49
Betto, Frei, 90
Bey, Hakim (alias Peter L. Wilson), 116–17, 121
Bin Laden, Osama, 123, 125–27, 130, 132–42, 145–46, 148–51, 158, 159, 163, 205*n*7
Black Bloc, 87
B'nai B'rith, 72
BNP. *See* British National Party
Bockelson, Jan, 3–4
Bolívar, Simón, 22, 24, 28, 31, 33, 35
Bolivarian Alternative for Latin America and the Caribbean (ALBA), 31–32, 46
Bolivarian Revolution, 22–38, 157, 170

EuroNat, 81
Europe, 49–82; ENR concept of, 55, 65–66;
New Right, 49–68; populist nationalisms,
68–82. *See also* European Union (EU)
European National Front (ENF), 81
European New Right (ENR), 49–68; and com-
munication, 157; criticisms of modernity
by, 51–59; future of, 173; and geopolitics,
63–68; goal of, 50, 164–65, 170; as intel-
lectual movement, 163; leaders of, 160;
on modernity's corrupting influence,
51–63; overview of, 49–51; and rebirth,
52–53
European Patriotic Party, 82
European Society for the Deceleration
of Time, 110
European Union (EU), 73–74, 80
Eurosiberia, 67
Evola, Julius, 57
Evo Pueblo (film), 41–42
EZLN. *See* Ejército Zapatista de Liberación
Nacional

Fanon, Frantz, 4–5
Faraj, Abdus al-Salaam, 129, 132, 206*n*33
Faye, Guillaume, 49, 53–55, 58, 62–63
Festivals. *See* Carnival; Rituals and the sacred
Fisher, William F., 98
Food. *See* Slow Food
Foundation for Biodiversity, 105
Frankfurt School, 57
Frederick I Barbarossa, 77
Free and Praiseworthy Association of
the Friends of Barolo, 103
Freedom, 142–43
Freemasonry, 71–73
Free Trade of the Americas (FTAA), 31, 46
French New Right, 56–57
French Revolution, 4
Frente Francisco de Miranda, 36
FTAA. *See* Free Trade of the Americas
Fukuyama, Francis, 7, 124, 153
Furet, Francois, 8

Gaia, 117–19
Galeano, Eduardo, 11
García Linera, Álvaro, 41
Gehlen, Arnold, 61, 191*n*100
Genoa Social Forum, 86
Geopolitics, 63–68
George, Susan, 89
Ghost Dance, 5
Giussano, Alberto da, 78

Global Day of Action, 86
Globalization: ENR criticism of, 59–60;
impact of, 1–2, 12; opposition to, 2–3,
8–10, 14, 84–86; populist nationalisms vs.,
68–69, 72, 79–82; Zapatista movement
vs., 11–21. *See also* Alter-globalization;
Capitalism; Neoliberalism
Global movements, 83–121; background
of, 83–87; goals pursued by, 98–100;
institutions opposed by, 88–92; politics
of, 101–2; raves, 112–21; Slow Food,
103–12; variety within, 97–98; WSF
controversies, 92–98
Goa, India, 120
Gramsci, Antonio, 50
Grateful Dead, 112
GRECE. *See* Groupement de Recherche et
d'Études pour la Civilisation Européenne
Greenpeace, 86
Griffin, Nick, 69, 82
Griffin, Roger, 68
Grounded Utopian Movements, 5
Groupement de Recherche et d'Études pour
la Civilisation Européenne (GRECE), 49,
51, 58, 65
Guaicaipuro, 27
Guénon, René, 56
Guevara, Ernesto "Che," 33, 35, 46
Gulf War, first, 65, 73, 131–32

Hardt, Michael, 9, 98
Hardy, Thomas, 1
Heidegger, Martin, 54, 60
Hello President (radio program), 30, 34
Herder, Johann, 61
History: Bolivia and, 40–42; populist national-
isms and, 77–79; raves and, 118; Slow
Food and, 108–9; Venezuela and, 23–27.
See also Local culture
Hobsbawm, Eric, 7
Hoffer, Eric, 163, 210*n*12
Hoffman, Abbie, 86
Hölderlin, Friedrich, 55
Honoré, Carl, 111–12
Humanity: commonality of, 8–10, 14; con-
sumerist corruption of, 40, 56–58, 75;
globalization as attack on, 13–14; and
individualism, 55–56; local identity vs.,
70–71; modernity's impact on, 51–52,
56–57, 59–60; nature and, 40, 64. *See also*
Transformation of humanity
Human rights, 56, 136
Hume, David, 173